N17286

D0322838

DRAWN

Skills *in*
GESTALT
Counselling & Psychotherapy

Series Editor
Francesca Inskipp

Skills in Counselling & Psychotherapy is a series of practical guides for trainees and practitioners. Each book takes one of the main approaches to therapeutic work and describes the core skills and techniques used within that approach.

Topics covered include

♦ how to establish and develop the therapeutic relationship
♦ how to help the client change
♦ how to assess the suitability of the approach for the client.

This is the first series of books to look at skills specific to the different theoretical approaches, making it ideal for use on a range of courses which prepare the trainees to work directly with clients.

Books in the series:

Skills in Transactional Analysis Counselling & Psychotherapy
Christine Lister-Ford

Skills in Person-Centred Counselling & Psychotherapy
Janet Tolan

Skills in Cognitive-Behavioural Counselling & Psychotherapy
Frank Wills

Skills in Rational Emotive Behaviour Counselling & Psychotherapy
Windy Dryden

Skills in Psychodynamic Counselling & Psychotherapy
Susan Howard

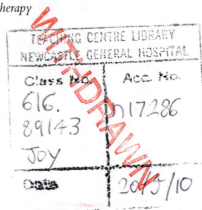

TEACHING CENTRE LIBRARY
NEWCASTLE GENERAL HOSPITAL

Class No.	Acc. No.
616. 89143 JOY	017286
Date	20/5/10

WITHDRAWN

Skills *in*
GESTALT
Counselling & Psychotherapy

Second Edition

Phil Joyce and
Charlotte Sills

Los Angeles | London | New Delhi
Singapore | Washington DC

© Phil Joyce and Charlotte Sills 2010

First edition published 2001
Reprinted 2002, 2003, 2004, 2005, 2006 (twice), 2008
This second edition published 2010

Apart from any fair dealing for the purposes of research or private
study, or criticism or review, as permitted under the Copyright,
Designs and Patents Act, 1988, this publication may be reproduced,
stored or transmitted in any form, or by any means, only with the
prior permission in writing of the publishers, or in the case of
reprographic reproduction, in accordance with the terms of licences
issued by the Copyright Licensing Agency. Enquiries concerning
reproduction outside those terms should be sent to the publishers.

SAGE Publications Ltd
1 Oliver's Yard
55 City Road
London EC1Y 1SP

SAGE Publications Inc.
2455 Teller Road
Thousand Oaks, California 91320

SAGE Publications India Pvt Ltd
B 1/I 1 Mohan Cooperative Industrial Area
Mathura Road
New Delhi 110 044

SAGE Publications Asia-Pacific Pte Ltd
33 Pekin Street #02-01
Far East Square
Singapore 048763

Library of Congress Control Number: 2009926296

British Library Cataloguing in Publication data

A catalogue record for this book is available from
the British Library

ISBN 978-1-84787-599-0
ISBN 978-1-84787-600-3 (pbk)

TEACHING COMMONS LIBRARY
NEWCASTLE GENERAL HOSPITAL

Class No.
616.
891
43
JOY

N17286

Date   2015/10

Typeset by C&M Digitals (P) Ltd, Chennai, India
Printed by MPG Books Group, Bodmin, Cornwall
Printed on paper from sustainable resources

Mixed Sources
Product group from well-managed
forests and other controlled sources
www.fsc.org Cert no. SA-COC-1565
© 1996 Forest Stewardship Council

CONTENTS

Preface: Skills in Gestalt Counselling – A Holistic Perspective   vii

Part 1: Gestalt Therapy in Practice   **1**

1   Preparing for the Journey   3

2   Phenomenology and Field Theory   17

3   Awareness   31

4   The Therapeutic Relationship   43

5   Assessment and Diagnosis   53

6   Treatment Considerations   68

7   Strengthening Support   78

8   Shame   86

9   Experimenting   94

10   Modifications to Contact: Regulating the Relationship   105

11   Unfinished Business   119

12   Transference and Counter-transference   130

13   Body Process   145

14   Working with Dreams   153

15   Using Supervision and Identifying your Personal Style   160

16 The Reflective Practitioner: Research in Gestalt   172

17 Ending the Journey   187

Part 2   Managing Challenging Encounters   **199**

18 Assessing and Managing Risk   201

19 Depression and Anxiety   212

Part 3   Gestalt Practice in Context   **227**

20 Brief Therapy   229

21 Diversity, Culture and Ethics   237

22 Spiritual Counselling   247

23 Gestalt and Coaching   254

References   267
Index   274

PREFACE

SKILLS IN GESTALT COUNSELLING —
A HOLISTIC PERSPECTIVE

In 1999, as we prepared the first edition of this book, we wrote:

> Our experience as trainers and supervisors has led us to realize how many fine
> books there are about the philosophy and theory of Gestalt and how few there
> are about actual clinical practice. Even when techniques and skills are described,
> they are scattered throughout the literature and do not provide a comprehensive
> overview for the interested practitioner. Both new and advanced students fre-
> quently express confusion or puzzlement about the different options in clinical
> situations, especially when they get stuck (as we all do). They are often unsure of
> some of the essential aspects of good general therapeutic practice such as how to
> assess risk for self-damaging or fragile clients, how to address the implications of
> cultural difference, how to problem-solve ethical dilemmas or how to structure
> a good ending to therapy. We aim to address many of these essential elements as
> well as aspects particular to Gestalt therapy, such as how to complete unfinished
> business, work with body process, 'undo' a retroflection or form a process diagnosis.
> We realize, of course, the danger in an approach that is skills-based. In the public
> and professional domain it is a frequent stereotype that Gestalt therapy is merely
> a collection of techniques, or even just two (cushion destruction and talking to an
> empty chair). We are keen therefore to emphasize our belief that Gestalt counselling
> and psychotherapy are properly based on a holistic philosophy of life and practice
> in which, secondarily, there exist certain techniques and skills.

We find that these words still hold true as we prepare the second edition.

In the last few years, there have been many developments in the wider therapy field.

- A vast quantity of neuroscientific research findings that frequently give physiological evidence for what Gestalt psychotherapists have believed and seen clinically for
  decades.
- An increasing orientation in other psychotherapies towards the importance of the
  intersubjective, the co-created nature of the therapeutic relationship – a focus that
  has been central to Gestalt for many decades.

◆ An increasing acknowledgement of the value of awareness, now incorporated or relabelled as mindfulness techniques (a mainstream element of contemporary CBT).

◆ New interest in the study of healthy living and process, the value of resilience, gratitude and optimism in what has become known as positive psychology.

◆ An increasing insistence on the need to demonstrate research evidence for therapeutic effectiveness, arising from the move to statutory or state regulation and the demands of cost-conscious agencies.

◆ An unfortunate increase in the incidence of depression and anxiety disorders, childhood trauma and mental illness generally, against a background of global issues including economic distress.

All these developments – even those that have long been at the heart of Gestalt theory and methodology – have had an impact on Gestalt practice in bringing new viewpoints and ways of thinking to bear on the therapeutic endeavour. We have tried to incorporate some of these influences in this second edition as well as address developments in thinking about ethics, supervision and coaching.

The first Part of the book follows the stages of a therapeutic journey from the initial encounter and relationship building, through the unfolding of the work to termination. We look at the skills that are essential to every stage – those which are stage-specific, and those which vary over time. We emphasize that offering a particular kind of relational contact is the heart and soul of Gestalt and the most essential 'skill' to possess. In Part Two we explore ways of assessing and managing high risk situations and also focus on working with depressed or anxious clients. In the third Part of the book, we address a variety of contexts and situations which call for particular skills and approaches.

We will assume that the reader has already read or been taught the essentials of Gestalt theory, so we do not propose to describe these in detail here. We will therefore include the minimum amount of theory – sufficient to make sense of what follows – and then suggest recommended reading at the end of each chapter. The further reading will normally be restricted to Gestalt texts, although where the topic has been usefully covered outside the Gestalt field, we have included some of these references.

A word about language. We have alternated the use of he, she and the rather awkward 'they' throughout the book, and in the examples we have normally chosen to make the counsellor and client different genders. This is solely for the purpose of clarity. We also alternate between the terms counselling/psychotherapy and counsellor/psychotherapist as we believe that the skills we describe apply across the board in therapeutic practice.

In attempting to offer you these skills and techniques, we have drawn upon years of training and guidance by many fine Gestalt practitioners, most of whom are referenced in the following chapters. In the course of our development (and true to the Gestalt tradition of assimilation following good contact) we have inevitably absorbed and incorporated many ideas and techniques. It is, therefore, quite likely that we have sometimes suggested a skill, phrase or idea that may have originated from another Gestaltist. We apologize in advance for the inevitable omission of crediting some of these influential practitioners and wish to give our sincere thanks and appreciation for all sources of Gestalt inspiration. As always, we owe a debt of gratitude to many people, in particular, the colleagues who generously gave us helpful comments and suggestions on the different chapters in this edition: Dinah Ashcroft, Maggie Davidge, Billy Desmond, Simon Cavicchia, Sally Denham Vaughan, Lawrence Hegan, Brigid Proctor, Heike Schaefer, Christine Stevens – to you all, many thanks. Also our appreciation and thanks to the teachers and colleagues who inspired us, and those who supported us through the first edition, Alice Oven and the team at Sage, Francesca Inskipp the series editor, and, of course, all our trainees, supervisees and clients who have taught us so much by their challenges and their generous sharing of themselves and their struggles.

PART ONE

GESTALT THERAPY IN PRACTICE

1

PREPARING FOR THE JOURNEY

We believe that good Gestalt practice can be described by the following five characteristics:

▶ A focus on here and now emerging experiences (through awareness, phenomenology, and the paradoxical principle of change).
▶ A commitment to a co-created, relational perspective.
▶ The therapist's offer of a dialogical relationship.
▶ A perspective of field theory and holism.
▶ A creative, experimental attitude to the therapeutic process.

Throughout the book, we will be exploring these five aspects of practice. We have assumed that the reader will have a prior understanding of theory and will therefore include the minimum to make sense of what follows (for excellent overviews of Gestalt theory we suggest Yontef and Jacobs (2007) and Woldt and Toman (2005)).

We decided to start at the beginning by addressing the issues that precede any counselling or psychotherapy commitment – the first steps that are necessary for Gestalt practice to take place. This first chapter is primarily intended for the practitioner in training and covers the following areas:

◆ Preparing your room and yourself.
◆ Seeing a client for the first time.
◆ Using an intake sheet.
◆ Explaining how Gestalt therapy works.
◆ Making a contract.
◆ Deciding who is not suitable for your practice.
◆ Keeping records of the session.

PREPARING YOUR ROOM AND YOURSELF

How you set up and arrange the room in which you work will make an important state-ment to the client. Equally, the style of your clothing and the level of its formality will influence the client's impression of you and of counselling. These details will be a major communication about yourself as a person and a therapist and also give an impression of how you intend to relate to the client. An ongoing theme of this book is that the therapeutic experience is co-constructed – this means that how you are with the client will affect how the client is with you and vice versa.

Suggestion: Imagine you are a client arriving to see you at your place of work. Visualize all the sights and sounds you would experience as you approach the door. Walk into your consulting room as if you were the client, notice what you see and the impression you receive of the room. Imagine meeting yourself as a therapist. How do you appear? What is your impact? What are your reactions as the client?

However, an equally important factor is the degree to which you are in the present moment and to which you are truly open and available to listen to the new client. Many counsellors will have the experience of arriving for a session filled with pre-occupations and worries that get in the way of being fully present for the client. While some of these reactions may clearly be relevant to the therapy, some will need to be 'bracketed' – put on one side – as probably irrelevant. It may well help, therefore, to discipline yourself to carry out a grounding exercise such as that below, before the client arrives.

Suggestion: Feel your weight on the seat, sense your feet on the ground. Become aware of your breathing, notice whether it is quick or slow, shallow or deep. Allow yourself to feel the tensions in your body and check whether your attention is freely flowing or whether you seem stuck in worrying about the past or anticipating the future. Notice whether you are mostly feeling, sensing or thinking. Acknowledge which of your concerns or worries are not relevant to the coming session and find a way of letting them go for now. Try to name what is going on inside you and then let it go. Focus on the sights and sounds of your environment, your embodied sense of yourself, living and breathing right now. Focus on the rhythmic in and out of your chest. Come fully into the present moment, this unique moment of time.
   Now, if you have seen the client before:

◆ Check your notes from last time and remind yourself of any ongoing issues.
◆ Recall anything important you need to keep in mind, for instance a forthcoming holiday, a particular characteristic of their personality that needs to be con-sidered, or the type of relationship you are in together.

◆ Remember any focus or intentions you may have for this session.
◆ Then clear your mind of all these considerations and once more come into the present moment to be available to meet your client.

SEEING A CLIENT FOR THE FIRST TIME

As a counsellor, you have a number of important tasks to perform when you first meet a client, the foremost of which is to establish connection and rapport with him. We will be exploring this core task in Chapter 4. At this point, therefore, we will simply summarize the other tasks of a first session.

Consider what expectations the client might have formed. You may have had a previous telephone conversation in which the appointment was made, and already you will both have formed some impression of each other.

We find it useful to stress to clients that the first session is a *mutual* assessment session in order for both parties to begin to decide whether therapy can be useful and whether you are the right therapist for what is needed. Ask the client for permission to take brief notes of biographical details, important historical events, and their current situation, etc. There is a contrary view that says that taking a history is antithetical to working as a Gestalt practitioner and that true Gestalt is simply an exploration of 'what the client brings' or 'what emerges'. This debate is discussed in more detail later on in the book. However, we believe that it is important for a practitioner to know how to assess a presenting problem and to consider whether the therapy they offer is going to be useful or whether some other specialist approach might be better. We believe that it is also necessary to ask certain questions to decide on the potential level of risk involved, especially as uncovering some issues in therapy or using powerful interventions can often unsettle the stability of a client and lead to possible harm (see Chapter 18). Taking a history is an essential part of making this assessment for determining the appropriateness and safety of the therapy.

USING AN INTAKE SHEET

On the next page is an example of intake sheets. Sheets 1 and 2 contain most of the important questions we suggest you will need to ask before accepting the client for ongoing therapy. They will help to guide you in your history-taking by indicating the areas in which it is important to get information. This includes the personal details, an overview of their important life events, their psychiatric history, and so on.

Remember, it is important to keep the name and address and telephone number of your clients separate from the main body of notes.

You will need to decide how much to structure the first session, making sure to leave time for the client to tell her story and make a connection with you, as well as time for you both to decide whether it will be useful to have further sessions. You will also need to explain conditions of confidentiality, your cancellation policy, etc.

CLIENT INTAKE SHEET 1

Name:

D.o.B.

Age:

Address:

Tel: (H)/mob.

    (W)

e-mail:

G.P.   Address/Tel:

Date first seen: Referred by:

[This sheet must be stored separately from case notes]

CLIENT INTAKE SHEET 2

First name or code:

Date started therapy:

Occupation: Race/Culture/Religion, etc.:

Relationship status: Children:

Parents:

Siblings:

Medical/Psychiatric history:

Drink/Drugs/Suicide attempts/Self harm history:

Current level of functioning and stress:

Significant previous experiences or events:

Previous therapy/counselling:

Presenting issues/problems:

Expectations and desired outcomes of therapy:

Contract. Frequency and duration: Fee:

Check the client has agreed to:

1) The limits of confidentiality in relation to a) supervision b) risk to client or other. 2) A period of notice before ending. 3) Cancellation and missed appointments policy. 4) Permission for recording and written material to be used for supervision and professional purposes.

For many clients, suggesting some sort of structure to the session is likely to create a sense of safety and containment while the client orientates herself to you and to the situation. Depending on your sense of the client, you might say something like:

'I would like to spend the first part of the session taking some biographical details, then I would like to hear why you have come and then perhaps we could stop ten minutes before the end to summarize and decide a plan. Is that ok?'

Alternatively, you might suggest simply hearing the story first of all. For example,

'First tell me about why you have come. Then about half-way through the session, we will discuss options for you and what further details we need to talk about before deciding what to do next'.

During the session, as well as gaining a general impression of the client, you will also be trying to assess whether Gestalt therapy will be suitable for this person. You can offer some trial interventions to see how the client will respond to this particular approach, for example:

◆ I'm noticing that your breathing is very fast/uneven/shallow. How are you feeling?
◆ How is it being here with me as you tell me this difficult story?
◆ Do you think *you* played any part in that situation?
◆ I'm feeling sad/moved as I listen to you talk about your history.

We are looking to see whether our approach will be interesting or suitable for this client. Our trial interventions enable us to gain a sense of whether the client responds to invitations to increase her awareness, accepts some responsibility for her life, reacts well to our self-disclosures or has a sense of the forming relationship. An apparently oppositional response (for example, 'What does it matter how I *feel* about the death of my mother? I want to forget about it and be happy') is often the first appearance of an impasse and leads usefully into a discussion of how you see therapy could be of help to the client.

This assessment period often takes more than one session and we suggest (especially for complex or challenging clients) that you give yourself the option of two or three sessions if need be before agreeing a contract for ongoing work or deciding to refer on. You might say:

'Thank you for telling me all this information. However, I do need to find out more/ be clearer on some aspects/discuss some implications of therapy/etc., before we can decide how therapy can best help you, so I suggest we arrange a second meeting'.

EXPLAINING HOW GESTALT THERAPY WORKS

Many clients come for therapy with unrealistic expectations and requests. Many will expect you to cure them or at least tell them what to do; some will want you to be the expert and will place themselves in your hands, expecting to adopt a passive position. It is ethical to give clients some indication of what to expect, as research has shown that a shared appreciation about the tasks is an important part of creating a working alliance. Clients are also often keen to know what Gestalt therapy actually involves. This can be quite difficult to explain briefly and you may want to prepare a short statement for yourself, which summarizes what you consider to be the fundamentals particular to your approach.

Suggestion: Imagine that your client has just asked you 'So what is Gestalt counselling – and how does it work?' What do you reply and why?

Here are some examples of statements to stimulate your thinking:

♦ Gestalt therapists believe that people potentially have all the necessary abilities to solve their problems or face their difficulties. However, sometimes they get stuck and need some assistance. I see my task as a therapist to help you see more clearly what your situation is, find out how you are part of it, and experiment with finding new solutions or ways to face the difficulty.

♦ Gestalt is a humanistic/existential therapy, which believes that people are born with the resources and ability to be in rewarding contact with other human beings, and lead a satisfying, creative life. However, often during childhood and sometimes later on, something interrupts this process and a person becomes stuck in fixed patterns and beliefs about themselves that get in the way. Gestalt aims to investigate and uncover how these patterns are still active and affecting a person's present life. I hope to support you to find new and more creative ways to resolve the problem or crisis you are facing.

♦ I practise what is sometimes called 'relational Gestalt'. This means that I believe that the patterns that emerge in our relationships – with our friends, our family, our colleagues and also ourselves, are key to who we are and how we feel. That includes our relationship here, perhaps even more so as we are discussing very deep issues and feelings. You will notice that I often pay attention to what happens between us and will invite you to do the same.

Some clients have become disillusioned and disheartened. They have effectively given up, losing awareness of their options and possibilities. For many, therapy is the first time they have been truly listened to without judgement or pressure. This can create a honeymoon period for them that can, however, be short lived! A client who is unprepared for the times of painful stuckness can become discouraged when the initial excitement of self discovery wears off. It may be important, therefore, in your initial explanation of the process of therapy, to predict that the journey will involve work on their part and commitment and, for a time perhaps, an increase of distress.

MAKING A CONTRACT

Although Gestalt therapy is ideally an exploration of 'what is' and always a journey into the unknown, clients normally seek help when they are in psychological distress and clearly want a particular sort of help, or for something to be different. What is more, psychotherapy outcome research clearly identifies the importance to successful therapy of having a shared understanding of the desired outcome of therapy. It is therefore useful to have an agreement about what would be a successful outcome for the client, especially as this will give you some baseline to judge its effectiveness. Some clients are very clear about what changes they want to make while many are simply aware of their difficulties and can only articulate their needs in a very general way. A shared focus can still be agreed with a therapy contract that is known as 'soft'; in other words it is about process or subjective experience, rather than a 'hard' contract about a particular behavioural change or outcome. For example, Jim agreed at the end of the first session that he wished to understand better why relationships with women always ended in his being rejected. It was implicit that he wanted to make better relational connections but did not need to know exactly how that would turn out (a 'soft' contract).

Of course, the direction and purpose of therapy inevitably change as new material emerges. Contracting is therefore an ongoing process (sometimes within the same session) – 'How do you want to use today's session?' or 'What is important for you right now?' Then it can and should be reviewed regularly, especially whenever the therapy seems to have shifted its focus or resolved an issue. Also, from a standpoint of competent professional practice, regular reviews are important, for example every three months, to check that the client has a sense of progress. 'It is now ten weeks since we first met. You said you wanted to understand why your relationships were unsuccessful. Do you think you any clearer now?' In Chapter 15 there are some suggestions for how to conduct a review.

The administrative contract

You will also need an administrative contract. This refers to the agreement between practitioner and client about such 'business' details as times of sessions, place, frequency, fees (if any), cancellation policy and limits to confidentiality. If you are working in an agency or on placement in any sort of counselling service, the administrative contract includes any rules or requirements the agency may have. Agreements between you and the client and the agency must be clear to all parties. Many counsellors and therapists choose to give their clients a written page describing the administrative contract in order to ensure clarity between them and to avoid the possibility of a new, anxious client not taking in the information given to her. Some agencies or training organizations will require you to have a written contract, which the client signs. This will give you permission to record the sessions, discuss the client in supervision and possibly use the material as part of accreditation requirements. An example of an administrative contract is shown below.

Information sheet

Name of Counsellor/Agency:

Address:

Contact telephone number: **Date:**

e-mail:

◆ My fee is ... for a 50-minute session. This will be reviewed annually.

◆ I need ... days' notice of a cancelled session. If you give me less notice than this, I will endeavour to find another time *within the same* week that this is convenient to both of us; however, if this is not possible, then the fee will be charged and/or you will lose the session.

◆ I keep short written notes on sessions. They are not identified by name and are stored securely.

◆ I may ask your permission to record the sessions to allow me to reflect on what we have discussed. If you agree, you may change your mind at any time and I will erase the recording.

◆ I abide by the Code of Ethics of ... (e.g. UKCP), a copy of which is available upon request.

◆ The sessions are completely confidential except under three circumstances:

a) From time to time I will discuss my work with a clinical supervisor. This is standard practice and helps me to work as well as I can with you. My supervisor is bound by the same code of ethics and confidentiality as myself.
b) If I believe you are at risk of harming yourself or others, I reserve the right to break confidentiality in order to prevent harm. However, I would only do this in extreme circumstances and would always try to discuss it with you first before taking any action.
c) If required by a court of law to give evidence (e.g. in criminal proceedings).

◆ For the purpose of further accreditation and continuing professional development I may submit written or recorded material of some sessions for evaluation. Any such written material will be disguised to protect your identity and will only be reviewed by clinicians bound by the same or a compatible Code of Ethics.

◆ Where our work extends beyond eight weeks, I recommend that we have at least three weeks' notice of ending to allow us a proper conclusion.

In some settings, for example primary care, the number of sessions is clearly prescribed. The client is offered a set contract of perhaps six, twelve or twenty sessions. Where the commitment is potentially open-ended, we have found it helpful to suggest an initial short-term contract of, say, four sessions to enable clients to have a sense of what Gestalt therapy may be like and to give them an 'taster' of whether this will be of help to them or not. We also say to the client that this will give us the chance to have a better understanding of their situation and be able to make some prediction as to how long they may need to be in therapy. Usually, Gestalt therapy happens weekly, as clients and therapists find that this provides a good balance between relational consistency and the opportunity to assimilate and integrate the work. However, sometimes there may be good reasons for varying this and it is possible for some clients to need to come more frequently and others to work with longer intervals or even irregularly. If you are thinking of agreeing a variation in contact, you should discuss it carefully with your supervisor to really check that it is not an avoidance of something.

In summary, the contract can be helpful for agreeing a direction and as a guide to ensure close collaboration between the client and the therapist. It gives you the basis and agreement to start work. It also defines your own boundaries and limits so that the client will know when you are available, what you are offering and what you are *not* offering. Finally, it provides a yardstick to which you can return for reviews.

A word about fees

If you are working in private practice or for an agency that expects the counsellor to negotiate a fee, you will be in the position of having to make a clear agreement about the fees to be paid by the client. Frequently, counsellors find this conversation difficult. They find it hard to put a monetary value on what they are offering. If you are in private practice, it may be useful to check with colleagues to find what the average fee structure is for your level of experience. It is also helpful to remember that charging a fee is an important part of the counselling relationship. It is the client's part of the bargain that *entitles* her to your interest, commitment, time and skills. Without this, the client might feel the need to adapt to you or somehow attend to your needs (as in an ordinary friendship). In fact, if you are working in an agency where no fee is charged, we believe that it is important to stress to the client what she will be 'paying' in terms of her time and commitment – even her taxes – to the process.

At the initial telephone call or interview, state your normal fee. If you decide that you want to offer a sliding scale or a certain number of low-cost places, you may say, for example, 'If that is difficult for you, I am willing to negotiate. We can discuss that when we meet.' Or, 'I have a sliding scale of fees between £ … and £ …'. Or, 'My normal fee is £ … and I have a few low-cost spaces, for which I charge £ …'. When you do meet to discuss the matter, you also need to be clear about your criteria for offering a low-cost space so that if you do so, you will not feel resentful later.

DECIDING WHO IS NOT SUITABLE FOR YOUR PRACTICE

The mark of a competent therapist is to know the limits of their ability. It is important to have a clear idea of who is out of your range of ability, experience and training. This may include people with a psychotic illness (current or in relapse), clients who are suicidal, self-damaging, or with specialized problems such as eating disorders or addiction. This is one reason for taking some biographical details early in the session. You may also prefer not to see people who have issues too close to your own. For example, if you have been recently bereaved, or are currently working through your own abuse in childhood, you may not wish to see clients who have these issues, until you have worked through them yourself.

Boundary issues are also important. You should never see a relative, friend, probably even friend of a friend, if you are to avoid a boundary clash or a conflict of role or interests (this also includes a relative or good friend of a current client). Consider if you are likely to bump into the client or any of the client's family in your ordinary life. Meeting a client or a member of the client's circle outside the therapy room may mean that you learn something about her that she has not told you. She may also feel invaded or exposed. If you decide that there is a small but manageable risk of meeting the client outside the consulting room (for instance at a supermarket, church or professional conference) you can make an agreement with your client about how you will both deal with the encounter.

Deciding not to work with a client

During the first assessment session you may well come to the conclusion that you do not want to take on the client. This is a tricky area for most counsellors. It does not easily fit our self-image to admit our lack of competence or resources to be able to help everybody all the time! However, we need, of course, to rise above our omnipotent urges and consider what is best for the client and for ourselves. It also highlights the usefulness of being tentative at the beginning of the assessment session (or on the initial phone call). You can offer a statement that the session is an opportunity for both client and therapist to decide what sort of help is needed. We recommend something like the following:

> 'I suggest that we meet for an initial consultation. This will give us both a chance to meet each other, see if we can decide together what you might need from therapy and whether I'm the right person to help you.'

Not only is it hard to admit our limitations, it is also hard for a client to hear that she is being turned away, especially as many clients already fear that they are too overwhelming, too unattractive or too disturbed. Therefore, finding the right words to turn a client down is important. We would generally start by saying something like:

'I believe I have a good grasp of the problem you are bringing and I can see how important it is. Therapy could certainly be of help, but I think that I am not the right person to offer it to you.'

We might then go on to say that we thought they needed someone who specialized in their particular issue or, less commonly, that we had a personal or boundary issue that meant we were not the right counsellor for them. (We would normally not charge for the session.)

Examples:

'The level of distress you are experiencing is such that I think that general counselling would not be helpful right now and I would recommend that you go and see your GP first and ask for his or her opinion about a referral to a specialist.'

or:

'One of the issues you have discussed is one that touches me very personally. I too lost a child (parent/partner/etc.) last year and my feelings are, of course, still close to the surface. I am pleased to have met you but it's important that you have a counsellor who will be fully there for you and not distracted by her own issues. I think it would be better if I referred you to a colleague and I will give you the name of someone who I think will be able to help you.'

In our examples we refer to finding a more suitable therapist for the client. It is almost always best to try to offer the client a referral rather than simply to turn her away. This places a responsibility upon us to be aware of what other resources are available in our area, including specialist colleagues or agencies, medical and psychiatric services, low-cost clinics and so on.

Suggestion: Part of helping the client to feel comfortable about being referred on is the counsellor feeling comfortable and confident himself. Imagine being refused by your last therapist because he did not feel competent to help you. What reactions and responses do you imagine you would have had? What might have helped you accept the decision?

KEEPING RECORDS OF THE SESSION

Records are ethically and professionally necessary, although there are no rules about what sort of notes you should take. The important thing is that they should be useful to you, not just a rule-following exercise. Some therapists rely on their written thoughts to remind them of key issues to be pursued, etc.; others prefer to work with the emergent process. At one extreme, therefore, the notes could simply be a record of the dates and times of your therapeutic meetings, and at the other extreme a detailed discussion of content and process. Be aware that your client may ask to see any notes and normally has a right to do so. It is therefore a matter of thoughtfulness and tact as well as of ethics to ensure that the respectful engagement you establish in the therapy sessions is continued in your notes. You might make a written note of the subject discussed, emerging themes, missed appointments, fee paid, etc., in fact all the details that the client will be completely aware of and could read without surprise. In the unlikely event of having to produce notes in a court of law, these can be presented as a true record of the history of the therapy.

It is perfectly acceptable to also keep a journal of your private thoughts and impressions, counter-transference reactions and so on. As long as these do not specifically identify any individual client, they are not 'notes' in any professional or legal sense and are your private property or personal diary. They may be fleeting impressions, diagnostic speculations, and questions about your life and profession that are written purely as your own experience. This journal can be used to raise questions for yourself that you may want to take to supervision. Remember, however, that a court can, if it wishes, demand to see any written material relating to the client that is in the therapist's possession, and if your diary contained names or indeed *anything* that would make the client identifiable, this material would be included.

Your formal client notes should be kept in a secure confidential place and should only be identified by a code or first name. Full name, address and telephone number should be stored in a different place. They should also be kept for a certain period of time depending on your particular professional code of ethics (six years is a common requirement) after a client has stopped working with you, both for legal reasons and in case the client should return. After that time, they can be destroyed. You should also arrange for a colleague to be your 'executor' for the unlikely possibility of illness or death interrupting your practice. This executor should be given information as to where to find your client details so that she can destroy old notes and arrange for the support and referral of current clients. It is better to choose a distant colleague for this, as your close friends will be still grieving for you. You can make a provision in your will to pay this clinical executor for her time.

RECOMMENDED READING

Bowman, C. (1998) 'Definitions of Gestalt therapy', *Gestalt Review*, 2 (2): 97–107.

Jenkins, P. (2007) *Counselling, Psychotherapy and the Law*. London: Sage.

Mackewn, J. (1997) *Developing Gestalt Counselling*. London: Sage. (**See Chapter 1**).

McMahon, G., Palmer, S. and Wilding, C. (2005) *The Essential Skills for Setting up a Counselling and Psychotherapy, Practice*. East Sussex: Routledge.

(Continued)

(Continued)

Melnick, J. (1978) 'Starting therapy – assumptions and expectations', *Gestalt Journal*, 1 (1): 74–82.

Sills, C. (2006) 'Contracts and contract making', in C. Sills (ed.), *Contracts in Counselling and Psychotherapy,* 2nd edn. London: Sage. pp. 9–26.

Woldt, A.L. and Toman, S.M. (eds) (2005) *Gestalt Therapy – History, Theory and Practice.* Thousand Oaks, CA: Sage.

Yontef. G. and Jacobs, L. (2007) 'Introduction to Gestalt therapy', in R. Corsini and D. Wedding (eds), *Current Psychotherapies.* Pacific Grove, CA: Brooks Cole. (for free downloadable PDF of this chapter go to the Pacific Gestalt Institute website: http://www.gestalttherapy.org/faculty-publications.asp)

2

PHENOMENOLOGY
AND FIELD THEORY

Scene:	In a restaurant. The authors are taking a break from their writing.
Charlotte:	Phenomenology is such an extraordinarily exciting concept, yet describing it makes it sound rather heavy and boring. How would you make it come alive?
Phil:	Well – what's going on for you now? What are you experiencing?
Charlotte:	[*looks around the room*] I'm noticing a white candle over there that is lighting up the picture behind it so it almost looks part of the picture.
Phil:	And how do you feel?
Charlotte:	Intrigued and happy.
Phil:	So you are looking round your world and getting pleasure from seeing things in harmony with each other.
Charlotte:	[*laughs*] That's me – I do like to see harmony.
Phil:	When I looked at that candle, I noticed it dripping on the table and wondered if I should do something about it. So your phenomenology right now is to see harmony around you and mine is to notice problems that I can fix. By the way, you have crumbs on your shirt.

THE PHENOMENOLOGICAL METHOD OF INQUIRY

The phenomenological approach means trying to stay as close to the client's experience as possible, to stay in the here-and-now moment and rather than *interpreting* the client's behaviour, to help him explore and become aware of how he is making sense of the world. In other words, it helps the client know 'who he is and how he is'. The phenomenological method is in fact as much an attitude as a technique. It involves approaching the client with an open mind and a genuine curiosity, where nothing matters except the discovery of his personal experience. In doing this, the awareness of the client of his own process and the choices he makes, is focused and sharpened.

The phenomenological method was first proposed by Husserl (1931) as a method of investigating the nature of existence, and later developed by existential philosophers such as Heidegger and Merleau-Ponty. A crucial phenomenological perspective is that people are always actively making meaning of their world (called intentionality) and therefore the client is always an active participant in what he is experiencing and how he is experiencing it – including his presenting problem.

Phenomenological inquiry has been adapted for the therapeutic setting so that it becomes a method for investigating the client's subjective meaning and experience of himself in the world. There are three main components. The first is *bracketing*, where the counsellor's beliefs, assumptions and judgements are temporarily suspended, or at least held lightly, in order to see the client in their situation 'as if for the first time'. The second is *description*, where the phenomenon of the client in front of you is simply described in terms of what is immediately obvious to the senses. The third is *horizontalism*, where all aspects of the client's behaviour, appearance, expressions are given potentially equal importance.

Although it is implied in the very notion of phenomenological inquiry, we believe that it is worth explicitly naming a fourth element – *active curiosity* – as this is what gives life to the other three.

The phenomenological method is an attempt to allow you a fresh experience of the client, holding your judgements and preconceptions lightly and with an open attitude. It is like the first day on holiday in a new country with a new culture, where you approach your experiences with openness to novelty and difference, only wishing to take in the newness fully and to allow understanding to emerge naturally.

There is of course no way that you can ever be free from the lens of your own subjectivity, your own particular way of making meaning of the world and of the people in it. What is more, your phenomenological inquiry – the questions you ask, what you notice, what engages your interest – will inevitably be orientated around your role as a therapist. However, we all know the difference between those times when our attitude to something is rigid, stereotyped and narrow and others when we are open and available to new meanings, new impressions and new understandings.

As we also say throughout the book, we believe that in every interaction there is always a co-construction of meaning and, in this light, your ability to be objective in any real sense is impossible: you cannot take yourself out of the relationship or stand separate from your meaning-making. The method can really only be an attempt to make you aware of your judgements and reactions to the client (and to the relationship) in order to allow a clearer perspective and understanding.

BRACKETING

This first skill in phenomenological inquiry is an attempt to identify and acknowledge the preconceptions, judgements and attitudes that the counsellor inevitably carries into the therapeutic relationship. In the moment of bracketing, the counsellor tries as far as possible to put all these to one side and be open and present to this unique client in this unique moment. Maybe you have had the experience of seeing a familiar person from a different viewpoint (maybe after a long absence) and it has felt as if you were seeing them for the first time. Often this experience is accompanied by a sense of freshness, appreciation and wonder at the unique person you had previously taken for granted. In practice, of course, it is impossible to bracket in this way for more than moments at a time and indeed it would be impossible to function without our assumptions and attitudes. Human beings are naturally drawn to make meaning and we could not live meaningfully if we did not learn from experience, draw conclusions, make judgements and form attitudes. However, human beings also tend to become rigid and stereotyping – they see what they expect to see and then lose the sense of newness and new possibility. We do not have to look far to see the consequences of stereotyped attitudes to colour, race, nationality or mental illness. Bracketing, however, is not about attempting to be *free* from preconceptions, attitudes or reactions. It is an attempt to keep us close to the newness of the here-and-now moment and avoid the danger of making hasty or premature judgements about the meaning of each client's unique experience.

Suggestion: Consider the following:

a) Jim tells you that his mother has just died from cancer.
b) Kathryn says she has been promoted to a position with more responsibility.
c) Miles tells you he has hit his seven-year-old daughter.
d) Keiko announces she is to have an arranged marriage to a man she has never met.

Imagine hearing each of these statements from a client. What is your immediate reaction, emotion or judgement on hearing each? Even on such little information you can see how quickly you form an opinion. We have often been surprised how differently the same event can be perceived by the therapist and the client: a bereavement that has meant relief or anger rather than sadness, an apparently wanted event that has meant anxiety for the client, abuse which has been justified as necessary, or a surprisingly different cultural meaning to a universal event.

It is hard to describe *how* to practise bracketing but it may help to start from a deliberate attitude that your opinions or judgements are potentially suspect or premature and that you need to wait before you reach any conclusions. At the very least, you can be aware of your preconceptions, you can hold them lightly and be prepared to change or modify them in the light of new evidence. You may find that the exercises of grounding and simple awareness described in later chapters will also help so that you listen from your heart and body rather than your head!

EXAMPLE

James:	I've just found out my partner is pregnant and she is so pleased.
[*Couns. reaction:*	*Feels an immediately positive response but hesitates.*]
Couns. response:	How is that for you? [*Brackets her own values and reaction.*]
James:	I don't know really. I'm pleased of course.
Couns. response:	You sound a little unsure.
James:	Yes I suppose I do. It's a new life. Bringing a baby into the world.
[*Couns. reaction:*	*Starts to sense some emotion other than pleasure – concern or worry perhaps?*]
Couns. response:	Is there some other feeling or concern about having a baby? [*Brackets her emerging judgement and investigates what may be unspoken.*]
James:	It's fine. But I'm worried about bringing a child up in such difficult times.

And so on ...

The initial tentativeness of the counsellor allowed a more complex meaning to arise that might have been missed if the response was more positive ('Congratulations').

The attitude of bracketing is similar in some ways to investigating a mystery. You are trying to make sense of this particular situation, ask questions, and find out: 'How do you feel about that?' or 'What does that mean for you?' 'What sense do you make of that?' 'How did that happen?' *but without an expectation of what you will find* (at least initially). You are attempting to allow the meaning of the situation to emerge and an attitude of bracketing or openness is often the best way to start.

Suggestion: Think of a client (or a friend) you have been seeing for some time. Describe him to yourself in terms of categories, for example, his occupation, gender, socio-economic group, personality style, how he sees you, what he really should do to sort himself out (!) and so on. (Do this for a minute or so.)

Now, let all that drop and imagine sitting in front of him without any prejudice or attempt to make meaning. What do you notice about him? How is he sitting? How does he hold his body? How is his hair, his skin tone, and breathing? What is the expression on his face? What images or feelings occur to you?

You can see what different impressions emerge from these two ways of knowing.

The skill of bracketing will also be crucial in the practice of creative indifference and inclusion, which we cover later in the book, as they both require a type of bracketing.

DESCRIPTION

The second skill involved in phenomenological inquiry is description. This involves staying with the awareness of what is immediately obvious and describing what you see. While the counsellor is bracketing off her assumptions and values, she confines herself to describing what she notices (sees, hears, senses, etc.), what she perceives the client to be saying or doing and what she is currently experiencing herself (without interpretation).

Typical interventions might be:

I'm noticing … (e.g. 'your breathing has speeded up').
You seem to be saying … (e.g. 'that this is very important to you').
You look … (e.g. 'distressed').
I'm aware that … (e.g. 'you've arrived ten minutes late').

The counsellor needs to stay close to the information from her contact functions and her bodily reactions. As she does this, figures of interest will emerge – the body posture of the client, the tone of voice, the rate of breathing, or a repetitive theme. She will also notice her own phenomenology, perhaps an emotional response, bodily tension or loss of interest. In this way, she describes (sometimes out loud, sometimes not) the emerging figures and themes of the client. This activity of the counsellor is also called tracking, that is, following the unfolding movement of phenomenological process over time.

EXAMPLE

Kess arrives late and sits down slowly, eyes downcast, hardly moving her body, silent. As the counsellor comments on how still her body is and the intensity of her silence, she gradually starts to look up and says she is aware of how much sadness she is holding in. The counsellor tells her he is aware of noticing small, restless movements in her clasped hands. Kess becomes more energized and starts to express her distress. Later, the counsellor notices that Kess's voice is becoming quieter and she is becoming still again. He shares this observation and Kess says she fears becoming too distressed and is reluctant to talk more.

It is amazing how powerful this technique can be for helping a client get in touch with her experience and also to uncover what gets in the way. Description offers attention, support and interest to emerging figures that may otherwise become side-tracked. The counsellor is also helping the client to bring to the surface her own interpretations, beliefs and meaning-making, as well as give her fullest attention to her feelings and experience.

A word of warning. Frequently, what the therapist notices are phenomena or reactions that are out of the client's awareness. Some clients can feel very exposed and even shamed by the experience of someone noticing their body movements, tensions, voice tone, choice of words, and so on. It is important that the therapist's comments are offered sensitively and in a way that seems relevant. The client must not be invited to feel that she has been put under a microscope. We return to this skill later in the chapter.

HORIZONTALISM

Everything that happens is potentially as important (horizontal) as anything else. This principle leads to the third skill of phenomenological inquiry. The counsellor does not assume any hierarchy of importance in what she sees or responds to. A movement of the client's body may be as meaningful as what he is talking about. This, of course, is a subtle skill. It would not be at all appropriate for the counsellor to interrupt the client's flow in a clumsy way in order to draw his attention to an irrelevancy. However, we keep in mind both Perls' reminder that Gestalt is the 'therapy of the obvious' and also the principles of field theory. Horizontalism is achieved most naturally if we are bracketing successfully and confining our interventions to descriptions of 'what is'. In this way, we trust our heightened perception to notice and name possible connections or anomalies. Of course, what is in the background, what is absent or missing, may also be of equal importance, such as in the case of a client who is talking about an imminent divorce with little emotion.

EXAMPLE

Couns: I notice that you have been looking out of the window a lot while you have been talking about your wife.
[*Counsellor gives equal weight to the looking out the window as well as the words.*]

Client: Have I? Yes, I suppose I have. I can see the top of that huge beech tree and it seems to be so far away and that's comforting somehow.

Couns: In what way is it comforting?

Client: I don't want to be talking about this – my marriage. I don't want to be telling you and it to be real and you looking at me and being sympathetic. I feel – oh I know it's silly – sort of angry at you. You're making me talk about this. You're making me see what's really going on and I don't want to.

Couns: So you feel angry with me and you go away to focus on the treetops.

Client: Exactly. It's as if you can't get to me up there, no one can make me talk about anything painful.

Couns: Does going away to keep yourself safe, feel familiar?

In this example, the counsellor gave equal weight to the phenomenon of looking out of the window and to the content of the client's words, thereby unexpectedly allowing a relational communication to emerge.

ACTIVE CURIOSITY

> One of the primary requirements of doing therapy is to be able to be fascinated with the patient. (Polster, 1985: 9)

Although not formally part of the phenomenological method, we believe that active curiosity is an essential part of the role of the counsellor in Gestalt who is attempting to understand the world of the client. You need to be interested in how situations arise, how the client makes sense of them, how *this* fits with *that* and what it means in the larger field. In doing this, you are helping the client to explore and clarify his or her own understanding. You need to be simply curious about everything that the client experiences.

Your curiosity will often lead to you asking a lot of questions. The golden rule in relation to questions is to make sure that they are part of a phenomenological *inquiry* rather than an *interrogation*. It is important to avoid making the client feel as if the Spanish inquisition has (unexpectedly) descended on him. Or as if there was a right answer towards which you are trying to manoeuvre him. Avoid closed questions that put restrictions and parameters on the answer. For example, compare these closed questions: 'Was it difficult?' 'Did you sleep well?' 'Were you sad?' with 'open' alternatives such as 'What was it like?' 'How did you sleep?' or 'How did you feel?' 'What did you experience?'

Also, beware 'why?' questions, which can close down the sort of curiosity we are suggesting. Normally a 'why?' question invites a thinking response or rationalization and often it implies criticism, for example, 'Why did you arrive late for the session …?' It is more profitable to inquire with open-ended questions, such as 'How did it happen that you were late arriving?' and 'What is it like arriving late?' – questions into the *process* of the client, rather than the content.

We also recommend two particular modes of inquiry. One is what we call a 'micro-process investigation'. Invite the client to pay minute attention to his experience over a few seconds, in order to become aware of his complex response to something. For example, if a client looks confused or reacts in an unusual way to something you said, ignore the 'why' and even the 'how' of the experience and 'What just happened *right then*?' or 'What is happening *right now*?'

EXAMPLE

Couns: What happened just then? While I was speaking, the expression on your face changed and you looked down at the floor. Then when I stopped you politely asked me to explain what I meant. I'm curious what happened in those seconds in between?

(Continued)

(Continued)

Reg:	Well you were asking me a lot of questions, and I couldn't follow them. So first of all I just felt lost.
Couns:	And then what happened?
Reg:	I began to feel stupid.
Couns:	And then?
Reg:	Then I began to feel angry with you. It felt as if you were criticizing me – telling me I was incompetent.
Couns:	And then?
Reg:	I told myself you're a trained counsellor … you must know what you are doing. So I tried to think about an answer to the questions but I felt my stomach had gone into a knot. Then I got confused and looked down.

This frame-by-frame investigation can be very useful to unpack moments when the client suddenly changes course but says 'I don't know' when you ask what happened. The suggestion to 'go back and talk me through that particular moment second by second' can often uncover important processes that happened too fast to be recognized at the time.

The second mode of inquiry is what we call 'adopting a position of clinical naïvety'. It starts by you asking a question that you may well think you know the answer to. It is particularly useful when the story you are hearing does not make sense to you or you are confused. At assessment the counsellor couldn't understand why Reg had come for counselling so asked directly,

Reg:	My problem is that I just can't cope. My doctor says I'm depressed.
Couns:	I'm not sure what you mean by 'depressed'.
Reg:	Well I feel tearful all the time.
Couns:	How long has this been going on?
Reg:	Well I haven't told anyone this, but I was made redundant last month.

The 'naïve' question can elicit what is being covered by generalizations or labels. For example, you may say, 'Can you give me an example of when you are "not coping"?' or 'I'm glad the therapy is helping you but can you tell me how?' (even if you think you can guess).

Another important caveat is that clients, unless they are well-schooled in the art of 'clienthood', cannot be expected to understand what we are doing without having it explained. Rather than simply, 'What is your foot saying?' it helps to introduce a new client to body awareness (for example), with something like, 'I have noticed that you have been tapping your foot all the time you were speaking, and I'm wondering if that indicates some restlessness or tension. If you pay attention to your foot, what do you become aware of?' This not only explains how you work and invites awareness, but it also makes sure you keep a link to what the client is talking about, so that you do not risk either getting ahead of him or falling behind.

A word on your own phenomenology

Clearly, as you practise the phenomenological method of inquiry, you are having your own responses and reactions simultaneously as you endeavour to be open to the experience of the client. As you become more familiar with the method, it becomes increasingly useful to practise it in relation to your own experience with a client, privately reflecting on your own process 'I noticed I am feeling restless/bored/anxious right now – what could this be about?'

It can be a way of paying attention to your own flow of experience, being curious, descriptive, horizontal and reflective of your reactions and judgements. This can be both a help in understanding the effect the client has on you and also sometimes a useful intervention. For example, 'As I listen to you speaking about your childhood, I have a sense of sadness in my chest that I don't understand', or 'I realize I'm feeling confused about …'

CLINICAL APPLICATION

Using the phenomenological method has several consequences. First, clients often find they are listened to without judgement, perhaps for the first time. Given the ubiquitous nature of self-criticism and blame in most clients, this can have a profoundly healing influence. Second, the method models and promotes the raising of awareness in the client. It encourages him to stay in the present, close to his experience, and be open to new possibilities of relevance. Third, it helps to uncover for you, and more importantly for the client, the particular ways he constructs the meaning of his existence and his issues. This allows the client to uncover and reassess his responsibility in how he co-creates his problems. Fourth, it models that counselling is going to be a shared investigation.

The scene: Later in the restaurant …

Charlotte: So how could we describe a movement from phenomenological inquiry into noticing patterns?

Phil: Go on further with your enquiry. What are you experiencing now?

Charlotte: OK – I am noticing the fire, and the pictures – I really like the pictures – there's an old etching of Nelson on board his ship, that lovely dog … And I'm enjoying talking to you and sipping the wine and the food and being here … and I notice I have an underlying pang of guilt that we didn't invite Jo to come with us. I hope it doesn't cause ill-feeling.

Phil: So you were enjoying what you were experiencing in the here-and-now, then you interrupted that with worrying about the past and the future. Is that a pattern for you?

Charlotte: Yes … I suppose. But my attention was called there by my underlying nagging feeling.

Phil: And suppose you stayed in the present even with that feeling?

Charlotte:	Then I guess that the feeling would mean that I am happy at this moment but what might happen next? It won't last. Something might go wrong.
Phil:	So rather than stay with whatever happens in the unpredictable existential world, you chose to worry about something you had done in the past. Is that a familiar pattern for you?
Charlotte:	All right clever-clogs. Eat your dinner.

Students often ask what aspect of the client's phenomenology they should notice or be curious about. What exactly are they meant to be following – body movements, emerging themes, beliefs or emotions? It is important to give yourself permission to experiment. To a large extent you go with what interests you, although this becomes more refined as your experience over time gives you feedback on your effectiveness. What is more, it would be naive to suggest that your attention will not, to some extent, be focused by the lens of your role as a therapist and the contract you have with the client. You will naturally be interested in what seems relevant to the presenting problem and what is missing. However, if you are applying the phenomenological method, you will favour paying attention to 'experience-near' phenomena (what is immediately obvious or experienced) rather than 'experience-far' (what the client talks 'about' or reports). You will also be checking with the client if they are noticing the same phenomenon, whether they are interested in it and their energetic response to your interest.

A relevant concept here is that of 'figure and ground'. The ground of a person's attention, their phenomenological experience, is the current or historical backdrop to their experience. It is the whole picture out of which one element emerges as 'figural'. At any moment we (and our clients) will be paying attention to a particular figure in the situation. If we practise description and horizontalism, we will be encouraging an experience of a figure that is full and vibrant and yet we will also be aware of the possible impact and implication of what is ground, as well as the significance for us of what we make figural. In our example at the start of this chapter, Charlotte was making a figure of the harmony between candle-light and picture. What was figural for Phil was the imminent problem of the dripping wax.

Suggestion: You can practise noticing what you make figural and then paying attention to other elements of the ground by tracking your own awareness. Look at what is around you now and notice how you make one thing figural and then another. You will find that you cannot give your full attention to more that one thing at a time. If you are noticing several things, there will be a subtle shifting of focus between them. Nowhere is this more evident that in the classic gestalt pictures relating to the perceptual field – for example the vase that is also two faces, or the ambiguous picture in which either the old woman or the young lady can be seen. Once you have perceived one of the images, it is impossible to see the other without letting go of your original way of perceiving.

The art of phenomenological inquiry or focusing is not only in paying attention to what is emerging moment by moment but in seeing the patterns and interruptions of gestalt formation and resolution unique to the client that underlie his therapy issues. Burley and Bloom (2008: 261) suggest that the phenomenological method allows us to identify these patterns through 'the aesthetic qualities of contacting – the felt, sensed, perceived, observed, known … qualities [that] are … the material for therapeutic insight'.

At some point, you will have accumulated enough data or information to form hypotheses about the nature of the client's particular emerging figures, the unaware ground, issues or problems and the possible interventions that might be useful. Your understanding will now be based on your immediate experience, checked out and investigated in partnership with the client, rather than on theories or speculation. Every so often it is important to make explicit the speculations that arise from your observations and responses, as a summary to the client to see how accurate it seems to them. 'I've noticed that every time you start to talk about your adoption, you look down, talk in a quiet voice and seem emotional. It looks as if this is a difficult topic to talk about – is that right?'

You might then choose to move from the phenomenological method, to making a suggestion or directive intervention in order to facilitate the process, especially if the client seems stuck.

This is a subtle and fundamental issue for the counsellor and in a sense is one of the key questions for gestalt counselling. At what point do I intervene in the unfolding process of the client? At what point do I stop following what emerges, stop forming hypotheses, tracking the process, encouraging here and now awareness in order to make a suggestion, a confrontation or offer an experiment? It is also a key issue in practitioner orientated qualitative research, which we will explore further in Chapter 16.

With higher-functioning clients, especially those who come wanting growth and exploration, the phenomenological method and general awareness-raising is often sufficient. With clients who come with a need for particular behavioural change (e.g. to overcome the behavioural effects of a trauma) or who come for a short-term contract or who are stuck in repetitive negative patterns (e.g. self-destructive behaviours), the need for active direction is often greater, especially to challenge fixed gestalts (e.g. 'I can never recover from what happened'). We cover this further in Chapter 20 on Brief Therapy and Chapter 19 on Depression.

There is no simple answer to the issue of how and when to move between inquiry and intervention other than learning from experience and experiment. However, whether your agenda is open and non-structured or tightly focused on a particular need or contract it is always useful to return regularly to the basic phenomenological method in order to explore the effects and consequences of your interventions.

FIELD THEORY

Closely allied to the notion of figure and ground is the field theoretical perspective that is central to Gestalt. In this view, a person is never fundamentally independent or isolated (although they may perceive it to be the case) but always in contact and connected with everything else in a very real sense. In the clinical setting, the client is always seen as a holistic combination of psychological and physical factors *in a particular context*. Every emerging figure of interest is, therefore, completely context-dependent for its meaning. For example, consider the different meanings and signifi-cance of the phenomenon of a ring of your front doorbell when you are (a) expecting a friend, (b) expecting a client, (c) expecting a pizza, (d) when the time is 3.00 a.m. in the morning and you are fast asleep. All these examples show how the noise of a bell is completely dependent for its meaning on the context in which it occurs.

A field theoretical perspective underpins all that has been described above and all that follows in this book. We will give a brief overview of this theory below, although the detail and complexity of it will not be covered in this book (for that, see Recommended Reading at the end of this chapter). While essential as a fundamental Gestalt perspective, it does not lend itself to a description of needed skills, and implies more a call to be aware of the further influences always present in any situation and often unnoticed or ignored.

It is also largely synonymous with a relational perspective, which recognizes that we are conceived and born in relationship and we develop always in relation with and to another. We are constantly in relationship with others, shaping and being shaped (even in their absence), and we are always under the influence of our historical relational memories.

Field theory is a fundamental pillar of Gestalt practice and theory, the basis of a holistic view of our clients that considers as potentially relevant, all aspects of body, mind and emotion, current and historical circumstances, cultural, spiritual and politi-cal influences. In fact it is a recognition of the interconnected web of influences that are always present (but often neglected or minimized) and that are influential in the understanding of a particular clinical issue.

While the term 'field' technically means *everything* – every object, situation and rela-tionship in the (known!) universe, in clinical practice it is used in a more limited way, depending on what you and the client believe to be significant field influences in each circumstance. Recent authors Robine (2001) and Wollants (2007a; 2007b) prefer to use the term 'situation' rather than 'field', 'on the grounds that it is closer to everyday experience and usage … than the more ambiguous term 'field' (Parlett in Wollants, 2007b: xv). Although we have chosen not to adopt it here, we anticipate that this term will become more widely used.

Three types of focus are used in practice. The first is the 'experiential field'. We see this as being the field of a person's awareness. It is a metaphor for the way they orga-nize their experience, their phenomenological field or 'reality', and it is unique to them. The second is the relational field between client and counsellor, the mutual influencing that takes place in the therapy session (and often in between as well). The third is the 'larger field', the larger context in which they exist, including cultural, historical, political and spiritual influences.

The field is the ground from which every experience or figure arises. Given the com-plexity and almost infinite possibilities of different influences that will be affecting every person, it is impossible to take all of it into account in the task of therapeutic understand-ing. Some influences are clearly more significant for different people at different times and many important influences will be out of the awareness of either client or counsellor.

All this has challenging implications for a counsellor. She needs to develop the habit of keeping a flexible focus on the client's situation, regularly alternating between a narrow and a broad field perspective, shuttling her attention back and forth from the client's immediate figure, to the relational field, to the client's experiential field, to the wider field – constantly remaining open to possible connections and influences.

Suggestion: Take a large piece of paper and, in the middle, write your own name (or the name of a client you are trying to understand). Then draw three or four increasingly large circles around the central figure. In the first circle, draw shapes, colours or marks to somehow represent your (or the client's) immediate family, both current and historical. Then, in the next circle, do the same for friends, colleagues and other important people, activities and interests. For the next circle, represent culture, race or religion and in the next, the country, environment or global context. Now go back and represent other influences you think are significant. Move back and look at the drawing to see what sense you make of this field of influences you have drawn. If you have chosen a client for the exercise, notice if you have drawn the picture according to what the client has emphasized about his life or what you think are important influences. This is a snapshot of some of the field conditions that you have identified as important at this moment. This picture will change over time and also, of course, does not represent the field influences that are out of awareness.

From a field theoretical perspective, the client (and also the counsellor) is always actively organizing the field, both in terms of his current needs and in terms of his earlier or historical field configurations, his fixed gestalts or unfinished business from the past. The counsellor needs to understand how he is doing this, what meanings he makes, what fixed or flexible patterns he uses to make contact, and what lies out of his awareness in the larger field of influence or possibility. In the initial stages of therapy, the work is often to bring the client's awareness to the fact that he is *always* organizing or interpreting his field and thereby effectively co-creating his experience.

RECOMMENDED READING ON PHENOMENOLOGY

Burley, T. and Bloom, D. (2008) 'Phenomenological method', in P. Brownell (ed.), *Handbook for Theory, Research and Practice in Gestalt Therapy*. Newcastle: Cambridge Scholars Publishing.

Clarkson, P. and Mackewn, J. (1993) *Key Figures in Counselling and Psychotherapy: Fritz Perls*. London: Sage. (**See pp. 92–95.**)

Crocker, S.F. (2005) 'Phenomenology, existentialism and Eastern thought in Gestalt therapy', in A.L. Woldt and S.M. Toman (eds), *Gestalt Therapy – History, Theory and Practice*. Thousand Oaks, CA: Sage.

(Continued)

(Continued)

Langer, M. (1989) *Merleau-Ponty's Phenomenology of Perception: A Guide.* London: Macmillan.
Spinelli, E. (2005) *The Interpreted World: An Introduction to Phenomenological Psychology.* London: Sage. (**See Chapter 6.**)
Van de Reit, V. (2001) 'Gestalt therapy and the phenomenological method', *Gestalt Review,* 5 (3): 184–94.
Yontef, G. (1993) *Awareness, Dialogue and Process: Essays on Gestalt Therapy.* Highland, NY: Gestalt Journal Press. (**See Chapter 6.**)

RECOMMENDED READING ON FIELD THEORY

Kepner, J. I. (2003) 'The embodied field', *British Gestalt Journal,* 12 (1): 6–14.
Meara, A. (1999) 'The butterfly effect in therapy', *Gestalt Review*, 3 (3): 205–25.
Parlett, M. (1997) 'The unified field in practice', *Gestalt Review*, 1 (1): 16–33.
Parlett, M. (2005) 'Contemporary Gestalt theory: field theory', in A.L. Woldt and S.M. Toman (eds), *Gestalt Therapy – History, Theory and Practice.* Thousand Oaks, CA: Sage.
Philippson, P. (2006) 'Field theory: mirrors and reflections', *British Gestalt Journal,* 15 (2): 59–63.
Robine, J.-M. (2003) 'I am me and my circumstance', Jean-Marie Robine interviewed by Richard Wallstein. *British Gestalt Journal,* 14 (2): 85–110.
Staemmler, F.-M. (2005) 'Cultural field conditions: a hermeneutic study of consistency', *British Gestalt Journal,* 14 (1): 34–43.
Staemmler, F.-M. (2006) 'A Babylonian confusion? On the uses and meanings of the term "field"', *British Gestalt Journal,* 15 (2): 64–83.
Wollants, G. (2007) *Gestalt Therapy: Therapy of the Situation.* Turnhout, Belgium: Faculteitvoor Mens en Samenleveing.

3

AWARENESS

The promotion and encouragement of full and free-flowing awareness is the corner-stone of Gestalt practice, as Perls et al. made explicit:

> Awareness is like the glow of a coal, which comes from its own combustion; what is given by introspection is like the light reflected from an object when a flash-light is turned on it. (Perls et al., 1989 [1951]: 75)

However, there are many different meanings attributed to 'awareness'. It is sometimes associated negatively with being 'self-conscious' (as in embarrassment) or excessively introspective (as in over-analysing oneself). These meanings miss the mark for, in Gestalt, awareness is not about thinking, reflecting or self-monitoring.

> Awareness is a form of experience which can be loosely defined as being in touch with one's own existence, with *what* is ... the person who is aware knows *what* he does, *how* he does it, that he has alternatives and that he *chooses* to be as he is. (Yontef, 1993: 144–5, emphasis in original)

At its best, awareness is a non-verbal sensing or knowing what is happening here and now. It is a fundamentally positive, essential quality of all healthy living. It is the energy for assimilation and growth at the contact boundary, for self-knowledge, choice and cre-ativity. One way to understand awareness is as a continuum. At one end is sleep; your body breathes, regulates its vital functions and is ready to awaken to danger. Here, aware-ness is minimal and automatic. At the other end of this continuum is full self-awareness (sometimes called full contact or peak experience). You feel fully alive, exquisitely aware of being in the moment, with a sense of connection, spontaneity and freedom. Passage along this continuum will vary from day to day, moment to moment – your experience at times being dull and routine, at other times new and challenging.

The young child often seems to inhabit a world of boundless awareness and whole-heartedness with an aliveness and spontaneity that is often lost in adulthood. Most of the loss of 'newness' is due to fixed gestalts (e.g. rigid or habitual beliefs or behaviours) that limit awareness, and to the interference of thoughts and memories of the past or anticipations of the future. If I am completely absorbed in a task or thought and unaware of myself, I am out of contact with the environment and myself. However, if I become aware, even if I continue my train of thought, the situation has subtly changed. I am aware *now* that I am thinking about the *then*. Awareness could be said to be consciousness of my existence, here, now, in this body. It is a Gestalt axiom that we can recapture this immediacy as adults and, in many ways, it is the first task in Gestalt counselling and therapy.

It is important to keep remembering that awareness is *both* knowing and being. If I suggest to a client that he pay attention to his breathing, I am suggesting that he both 'knows' he is breathing and that he has the moment-to-moment 'experience' of breathing. It is this ongoing experience of awareness that can be enormously healing in counselling. The task of the counsellor is then to highlight or identify the way a client interrupts, restricts or has lost awareness of vital aspects of his self-functioning. The restriction or blockage of awareness often manifests itself as lack of energy and vitality, or rigidity in responsiveness. Restoration of healthy self-process comes when the behaviour or attitude is brought to awareness and re-experienced directly.

One of the most important tasks, then, of the Gestalt therapist is that of raising the aware-ness of the client – awareness of what he feels and thinks, how he behaves, what is going on in his body and the information of his senses; awareness of how he makes contact – of his relationships with other people, of his impact on his environment and its impact on him.

Since the first edition of this book there has been a widely researched and accepted use of what is called 'mindfulness' or 'meditation' as a therapeutic tool. It is recognized as helpful in many presenting issues – anxiety, PTSD, stress disorders, substance abuse and borderline personality disorders. (e.g. Kabat-Zinn, 2003; Hayes et al., 2004). At its core it stresses the value of the client staying in the present moment and developing the ability to accept what is and what is happening without interference, following their unfolding experience in the here and now. We are pleased that what has been cen-tral to Gestalt for over fifty years is now being valued by other approaches.

EXPLORING AWARENESS

Simple though it may seem, perhaps the most obvious and natural way of raising awareness is for the client to tell his story to someone who herself listens with full awareness. When you consciously focus your awareness, you are 'paying attention' and it is this directed awareness that is the central therapeutic activity of the Gestalt coun-sellor. Attention can be directed to focus closely on a particular aspect of functioning (e.g. to breathing or a tense part of the body) or it can be directed broadly, to a larger holistic awareness (e.g. to an awareness of the way the client and you are relating). By taking our client's thoughts and feelings seriously, and with full attention, we invite him to do the same for himself. By reflecting back to the client what we are hearing, by asking him how he is feeling, by exploring his belief system with him, we invite him to listen to himself and also to bring his full awareness to bear on his experience and the way he makes sense of the world. By keeping 'horizontal' and by paying attention to the whole field we can help our client bring in all aspects of himself, including what is habitually ignored or missing.

In the most general way, the counsellor is attempting to encourage:

◆ Staying in the here-and-now.
◆ Sharpening and expanding awareness of ongoing experience.
◆ Directing or focusing awareness to what is minimized or avoided.

Consider the following counsellor interventions:

Focus your attention on your breathing ...
Can you sense what you are feeling right now ...?
Are you aware of what you are thinking ...?
What part of your body do you have no awareness of?
I notice that your body seems rigid and your breathing has become shallow.

The purpose of these interventions is for the client to become aware of what has been out of awareness. They are not meant to change the client's experience, but to restore or strengthen here-and-now awareness of living in the present moment. It is important also to realize that without *genuine* interest on the part of the counsellor, the interventions can become dry and mechanical. The counsellor also needs to maintain an embodied self awareness. At heart, as in the practice of phenomenological inquiry, intervention need to be founded on active, ongoing curiosity.

EXAMPLE

Ben: I'm not sure what to talk about this week. [*looks uneasy*]
Therapist: Take a moment to see what you are aware of as you sit here with me. [*She also brings her attention to her own sensations as she says this.*]
Ben: I'm not aware of anything.
Therapist: How do you feel right now?
Ben: Empty. [*silence*]
Therapist: Can you describe your 'empty' to me?
Ben: It's like I'm tense and I don't know what to do.
Therapist: How do you know you're tense?
Ben: I'm tight around my shoulders and I feel embarrassed.
Therapist: Embarrassed?
Ben: Yes. [*silence*]
Therapist: I'm interested in how your embarrassment feels to you.
Ben: I feel sort of shy.
Therapist: And what happens next?
Ben: I get afraid that you're criticizing me.

In this way Ben starts to focus his attention on his body process, becomes aware of his unease in relationship with the therapist and realizes that his apparent lack of interest at the start of the session was a protection of his fear of criticism.

THE ZONES OF AWARENESS

Perls (1969) identified what he called the three zones of awareness. They are the Inner Zone, the Outer Zone and the Middle Zone. The disadvantage of this conceptualization is that it risks creating the false impression of a division between internal and external experiencing. Awareness is always holistic and all zones are interconnected and dependent on each other. Subjectively, however, we can focus deliberately on each one in turn, and as a metaphor the zones can be very useful, both as an assessment tool for the therapist and also in helping the client to include in his awareness all aspects of himself. We will examine each in turn in order to explore their significance.

The inner zone

The inner zone of awareness refers to the embodied inner world of the client, often imperceptible to the counsellor. It includes such subjective phenomena as visceral sensations, muscular tension or relaxation, heartbeat and breathing, as well as that blend of sensation and feeling which is known as bodily-affective states. We also locate emotions in the inner zone (although they could arguably be part of all the zones).

The most obvious ways of heightening awareness of the inner zone are to draw the client's attention to his body and sensations. We may do this through questions – 'How do you feel now?' 'What are you experiencing now?', by commenting on what we observe, as in, 'I notice that your breathing is shallow', 'Notice the tension in your leg muscles', or by sharing an experience of our own that might mirror that of the client, 'I'm aware that my chest feels tight – I wonder if that is also your experience?'

> **Suggestion:** If a client seems to be out of touch with his inner zone, you may wish to guide him with the following exercise:
> See if you can fill your whole body with your awareness, being aware of your weight on the seat and your feeling of inhabiting yourself (*this can take at least a minute*). Notice what other sensations you experience in your body (*another minute*). What emotional tone or feeling do you notice? Where is it located? If you feel nothing or very little, stay with that awareness, let it deepen and then repeat the exploration.

The outer zone

This is the awareness of contact with the outside world. It includes all our behaviour, our speech and action. It includes how we use what are called *contact functions* (seeing, hearing, speaking, tasting, touching, smelling and moving), which are the major sensory ways that we receive or make contact with the world. If we pay attention to our contact functions, we can become skilled in present-moment awareness, in noticing colours, shapes, sounds, textures and so on. Our perception of the world around us can become more rich and vibrant in a way that vitalizes our experience.

There is another reason for focusing on our outer zone, however. In order for us to be aware of our choices and to make changes in the way we behave, perhaps to get different responses from other people, we have to become aware of what we are doing and its effect on others and ourselves. We need to become skilled at noticing what is going on around us. Again, the simplest way of heightening a client's awareness of his outer zone is to draw attention to his actions, movements or behaviour in his environment and to the stimuli of the outside world: 'Be aware of the world around you, what are you noticing?' 'What can you hear?' 'May I give you some feedback about how you are with me?' – and so on.

The middle zone

The middle zone consists of our thinking, emotions and reactions, fantasies and anticipations. It includes all the ways in which we make sense of both our internal stimuli and external stimuli. In short, it acts like a mediator or negotiator between the inner and outer zones. One of its major functions is to organize our experiences in order to come to some sort of cognitive and emotional understanding. Another is to predict, plan, imagine, create and make choices. It is the middle zone that includes beliefs and memories. It is, therefore, the main cause of our problems and distress in that inevitably it also holds our self-limiting 'core' beliefs, our fixed ways of understanding ourselves and the world, and our tendency to fill the present with thoughts about the past or the future. In our middle zone we also name or label our experiences, which inevitably determines how we feel about them.

Raising awareness of the middle zone is perhaps the most subtle. It is important not to make assumptions about what a person may be thinking or imagining. Thus, we might ask – 'What are you saying to yourself about what happened?' 'What sense did you make of that?' 'And if that were true, what would it mean to you?' 'What do you think about that (or imagine, or fantasize or hope for)?' 'What conclusion did you come to?' Or we might say, 'It sounds as if you're saying it's not OK to do that.'

Suggestion: You might now ask the client to reflect on the previous awareness exercises (or to any intervention you have previously made). What do you think about it? What did you make of being asked to listen to your environment? What other reactions or associations do you have? Now begin deliberately to shuttle backwards and forwards between the zones. Take it gently, so that the client really allows himself to be aware of what he is feeling, thinking, seeing, imagining and so on. Invite him to notice again what is going on in his body – 'What do you make of that? How do you feel? What do you think that might mean? What do you notice around you – how do you respond to that?'

In practice the healthy person shuttles back and forth between the zones throughout his daily life. When awareness becomes weighted in one particular zone, the effect is to unbalance his overall functioning, with sometimes quite problematic results.

EXAMPLES

Molly focused excessively on the outside world, and the opinions of others; she desensitized her own feelings and judgements. In therapy, she said that she never knew what to do or even what she wanted and that she relied on some-one else to make decisions for her (dominant outer zone awareness). Hari was constantly in a state of worrying and obsessing about life (dominant middle zone), while Deanna was so overwhelmingly aware of her bodily-affective states, almost to the exclusion of all else, that she frequently escalated into a wordless panic which she was incapable of managing (dominant inner zone).

RELATIONAL AWARENESS

The way a therapist and client relate to each other can also become a powerful vehicle in which all three zones of awareness can be investigated. The client's moment-by-moment response to the therapist demonstrates *how* he is aware and of what, as well as the ways in which he is not aware. The most important of the therapist's tools is herself – her responses to the client and her own awareness in the here and now. Without attempting to explain or interpret, she can use her presence and skills of observation in the service of the client. She responds with her own reactions and awarenesses, commenting on how the client is being in the room, his process, the areas that he seems to ignore or minimize, and discrepancies, for example, between what he feels and what he expresses in his body. She is open to exploring the client's reactions (and projections) to her, always with the aim of helping him become aware of his own experience.

Increasing awareness tends to create physical arousal during the process of discovery (and relaxation afterwards). It leads to expansion of body movement, changes in energy, flexibility of responses, vibrancy of attention and self-expression. The counsellor will try to be alert to these signs, so that she can sensitively follow the ebb and flow of the client's process of awareness. Of course, as counsellors, we cannot expect ourselves to be omniscient. At any time, it is always fine to *ask* the client what they are experiencing!

The practitioner also needs to become skilled at monitoring and recognizing the impact of her interventions and presence. Don't forget that you cannot exclude your own influence on the type of experience you are seeing in the client. You need to remind yourself frequently of the effect of your relationship and ask questions to check, such as:

'How is it for you that I'm asking you to focus on …?'

THE CYCLE OF EXPERIENCE

A traditional way of understanding the flow of awareness is through a metaphor called the 'cycle of experience' (also known as the cycle of awareness or the contact cycle). It is a simple and powerful way of tracking the formation, interruption or completion of emerging figures. It identifies stages from the moment of experiencing a sensation, to recognizing and naming it, to rising energy, to making sense of it and deciding how to respond, to taking action, coming into full contact, achieving satisfaction or completion before withdrawing energy ready for the next cycle.

Cycles of experience can be simple or complex. For example, a common cycle near the end of a therapy session is: a therapist becomes aware of the passing of time (sensation), realizes that the session is nearly ended (recognition), gets ready to interrupt and speak (mobilization of energy), calls the client's attention to the ending (action), they say goodbye (contact) and the client leaves; the therapist then reviews the session (completion/appraisal), disengages (withdrawal) and relaxes in preparation for her next

Figure 3.1   The cycle of experience

client (the fertile void). In a more complex cycle of experience, a social worker becomes aware of a growing interest in the field of counselling. She explores training opportunities and chooses a Gestalt course. Over several years, she completes the many demanding requirements of training and eventually achieves her MSc. Satisfied, she withdraws from studying to rest on a relaxing holiday (or maybe just throws a wild party!).

A difficulty, however, in using the cycle as a therapeutic tool, is that human experience is often more complicated than can easily be identified by the model. It does not allow for such complexities as the need to choose between competing figures that call for attention. There are often difficulties in identifying what constitutes each stage, and the many side roads that interrupt the movement around any cycle. It is also not a model that emphasizes the co-created nature of experience. On the other hand, it is excellent for tracking and heightening simple, singular experiences or figures and it can be the basis of a journey of self exploration.

It can be useful as a guide to finding out where a process of aware experiencing may be stuck or diverted, particularly for a client whose tendency is habitually to interrupt at the same stage of the cycle. Here are some possible scenarios:

◆ A client who has suffered trauma or abuse may disconnect from his inner zone of bodily-affective *sensation*. (An interruption before **sensation**.)

◆ A person who has an eating disorder may well be interrupting her natural process at the stage of *recognition* of her emotions, mis-labelling her sensations as hunger rather than emotional neediness. (An interruption between **sensation** and **recognition**.)

◆ A bereaved client knows that her husband has died and that she must grieve, but she just feels hopeless and drained. (An interruption between **recognition** and **mobilization**.)

◆ An anxious and agitated client who has *mobilized* an excess of energy but is unable to take effective *action*. (An interruption between **mobilization** and **action**.)

◆ A lonely client takes *action* by constantly starting new affairs but is unable to make real relational *contact*. (An interruption between **action** and **contact**.)

◆ A workaholic may competently make *contact* and complete difficult tasks, but is unable to achieve *satisfaction,* by going over in his mind how he could have done it better or criticizing himself for some minor fault. (An interruption between **contact** and **satisfaction**.)

◆ An over-dependent client who has felt nurtured by the therapy session tries to avoid leaving at the end. He is unable to *withdraw* and surrender to the separation. (An interruption between **satisfaction** and **withdrawal**.)

◆ A goal-orientated businesswoman finishes a successful and rewarding project and is immediately restless, thinking straight away about the next project or opportunity, unable to quietly rest, fearing the uncertainty of letting what happens next come naturally. (An interruption between **withdrawal** and the **void**.)

All our examples are instances where we believe that it would be healthy for the client to find a way to become aware of the interrupted energy and complete the cycle of experience. However, this is not always the case. Knowing what should follow next at any stage of the cycle is a combination of the client's awareness of his needs (and options) and your own hunches, but the *client* is the only one who can really know what completion means for him and how long it needs to take. Some cycles will complete in one session, some may take years. Some may be abandoned or modified by the client in favour of other directions.

Before we leave the cycle here we would like to draw your attention again to its final step – one that is often neglected in the literature – the stage that occurs between withdrawal and sensation, after one has completed a cycle and before being energized by the next emerging figure. It is known as the 'fertile void' (although Gaffney, 2009, prefers the term 'ground') and is so called in order to underline the value of simply 'being there', in full awareness of self in the world, allowing the emergence of what will be. For the counsellor, it is also the place of 'creative indifference' with a client, being alert and available without any agenda, ready to respond to the emerging figure (see below). It is a time to be undirected and acknowledge the unknown. It can be both a surrender to the primacy of organismic self-regulation and also a surrender to the emergence of some completely new unanticipated thought, feeling or desire – or even the spiritual dimension.

THE PARADOXICAL THEORY OF CHANGE

We now turn to another concept central to Gestalt therapy, which is in many ways a natural extension of all that has been said above. Although described as a theory, the paradoxical theory of change stated by Beisser (1970: 77) might be more accurately called a principle. It asserts that, 'Change occurs when one becomes what he is, not when he tries to become what he is not'. The principle proposes simply that a person fully accepts who they are. Trying to change according to some fixed picture is what gets in the way of the natural change process. In the last ten years many other therapeutic approaches have also started to orient around this principle, for example, acceptance and commitment therapy (ACT), mindfulness-based cognitive therapy (MBCT), emotional focused therapy (EFT) and dialectical behaviour therapy (DBT).

Clients often come for therapy believing that they can change according to a predetermined plan, or wanting just to get rid of particular unpleasant feelings, thoughts or attitudes. They hope to achieve an idealized picture or idea of how they want to be different (for example 'to be free from anxiety' or 'to be liked by everyone'). The paradoxical theory of change maintains that, instead of working to change himself, the client needs to enter as fully as possible into all aspects of his own experience, bringing then into full awareness. Once he has done this, trusting his organismic self-organization, change will naturally follow. The principle may be also understood when we realize that if a client can make this profound attitude of self-acceptance, then he is in fact making a radically different (and transformative) change to his normal attitude to himself. This point was made by Perls (1969) when he distinguished between self-actualization and 'self-image actualization'. This principle has significant implications for practice. As a therapist holding it in mind, you will overtly encourage the client to explore and embrace the 'isness' of himself.

This fundamental concept is paradoxical because it implies that in order to change, the client needs to give up *trying* to change. It asserts instead that there is a natural process of growth and change through ongoing awareness, contact and assimilation.

CREATIVE INDIFFERENCE

The most useful attitude the counsellor can adopt to facilitate this process is one of creative indifference. This concept, which has its roots in Eastern spirituality, is similar to the practice of equanimity or mindfulness in Buddhism. It does not mean, contrary to what its title might suggest, an attitude of non-caring (it would, perhaps, be more accurate therefore to call it 'creative impartiality' or 'creative neutrality'). It is based on the idea that the counsellor does not have a vested interest in any particular outcome. It is another way of facing the existential uncertainty of the unknown – not a simple task. It involves the counsellor in truly embracing the practice of genuine interest combined with an equally genuine lack of *investment in* any particular result. The counsellor is willing to accept whatever 'is and becomes'. This model of growth is easy to see in the physical world where a gardener provides the right conditions of light, warmth and water, clears away the weeds and protects against disease or insect attack. The flowers will then grow naturally and mature into their full 'flowerness'. The gardener is not trying to impose his will or 'make' the flower other than it naturally is. Counselling and therapy also involve 'trusting the process' of the client and not being attached to any particular outcome. It means the counsellor is free to engage wholeheartedly in whichever path the client chooses. It is also, of course, at the heart of field theory, the phenomenological method and the acceptance of the client's existential choice. It is trust in the healthiness of organismic self-regulation and in the deeper wisdom that lies within us all. Most of all, it is trust that if we as counsellors provide the proper conditions in the process of the therapy, the client will choose his own right direction.

It is clear, therefore, that there can be no particular skills or techniques associated with creative indifference. It is about the cultivation of an attitude that is at the heart of all the Gestalt skills. Being fully in the here and now, meeting with another person without preconditions, is a potentially frightening experience as well as an exciting one. We are facing the unknown and that can make us feel insecure. We can then feel a strong urge to take control by planning and predicting. As Gestalt counsellors, we should try to resist that urge and, instead, risk staying with the uncertainty.

This paradoxical view of change is in direct contrast with other therapy models which contract for behavioural outcomes, try to remove symptoms and see resistance as something to be overcome. In Gestalt counselling, symptoms and resistance are expressions of creative adjustments the client is making to a situation, usually where there is not enough support. Trying to remove or overcome resistance is like trying to lose or overpower an essential part of the person. When the problem or dilemma is accepted and awareness is restored, all the different aspects and parts of the client are available as resources for natural growth and change.

CASE EXAMPLE

[Taken from the practice notes of one of the authors.]

Jean-Luc had come for counselling following a series of failed relationships which had left him feeling miserable and fearful of new social situations. He said he wanted to feel happy again but did not want to 'look at the past', as he had previously experienced this as a waste of time in an earlier counselling experience. At the assessment session he wanted me to tell him what to do to feel better and hoped I would give him some answers. He thought that his social inadequacy (as he described it) was due to something he was doing wrong in social gatherings. As we started to make a contract for an initial six sessions, I explained my reluctance to agree with his picture of how I might help him and offered an alternative perspective on how we might first understand his story before coming to any conclusions about what was needed. Jean-Luc was unconvinced but agreed to try it as he was desperate and had felt some relief at telling me of his distress. During the next few weeks, he told me his story in great detail and asked less and less for my opinion or suggestions. During this time, I mostly worked with the phenomenological method, raising his self-awareness and offering a dialogic relationship. I gave no advice or instruction about being in social situations.

At our six-month review, Jean-Luc was puzzled at the fact that he seemed to be enjoying life more, felt more hopeful about his situation and had started a new relationship, which so far was not following its usual rocky path. He was at a loss to understand how things had got better without him or me 'trying' to make deliberate changes.

It has been a common experience of ours that the paradoxical principle of change is subtle, and clients often know that counselling has helped but cannot easily articulate any particular reason for it having done so.

Having said this, however, we wish to make the point that the human situation is often very complex and we believe that there is also a place for deliberate, thought-out or wished-for change that needs determination and courage. One example might be a decision to stop a self-defeating addictive behaviour; another might be a decision to follow a career as a therapist, and to persist through the obstacles of training courses to reach the desired outcome. There is a subtle discrimination to be made between introjected, cultural or societal pressures to be different and a real desire or aspiration freely chosen by the whole person in full awareness. We hope to demonstrate later in the book how a therapeutic journey can be made which respects the paradoxical theory of change and also allows for goals and desires deliberately chosen.

RECOMMENDED READING

Beisser, A.R. (1970) 'The paradoxical theory of change', in J. Fagan and I. Shepherd (eds), *Gestalt Therapy Now*. Palo Alto, CA: Science and Behaviour. pp. 77–80.

Fodor, I. (1998) 'Awareness and meaning-making: the dance of experience', *Gestalt Review*, 2 (1): 50–71.

Gaffney, S. (2009) 'The cycle of experience re-cycled: then, now ... next?', *Gestalt Review*, 13 (1): 7–23.

Hayes, S. (2005) *Get out of Your Mind & into Your Life*. Oakland, CA: New Harbinger Publications.

Kabat-Zinn, J. (2003) 'Mindfulness-based interventions: past, present and future', *Clinical Psychology: Science and Practice,* 10 (2): 144–56.

Nevis, E.C. (1992) *Gestalt Therapy. Perspectives and Applications*. New York: G.I.C. Press. (**See Chapter 1**.)

Perls, F.S. Hefferline, R. and Goodman, P. (1989 [1951]) *Gestalt Therapy: Excitement and Growth in the Human Personality*. London: Pelican Books. (**See Part One**.)

Philippson, P. (1990) 'Awareness: the contact boundary and field', *Gestalt Journal*, 13 (2): 73–84.

Ribeiro, W. (2005) 'The non-paradoxical theory of change', *International Gestalt Journal,* 28 (2): 19–23.

Staemmler, F-M. (1997) 'Cultivating uncertainty: an attitude for Gestalt therapists', *British Gestalt Journal*, 6 (1): 40–8.

Staemmler, F-M. (2009) *Aggression, Time, and Understanding*. New York: Routledge.

Yontef, G. (1993) *Awareness, Dialogue and Process: Essays on Gestalt Therapy*. Highland, NY: Gestalt Journal Press. (**See Chapter 8**.)

4

THE THERAPEUTIC
RELATIONSHIP

In the past fifteen years, 'Relational Gestalt Therapy' has become a commonplace term in Gestalt literature and training. In clinical practice this trend has led to a more central focus in the therapy room on the relationship *between* client and therapist and of the mutual influencing and co-creation of meanings. It stresses the importance of the therapeutic relationship as the core vehicle of change, and the dialogic process in which both client and therapist are touched and changed in the encounter.

A therapeutic relationship in Gestalt practice depends upon three elements that build upon each other:

◆ The provision of a safe container (described in Chapter 1).
◆ The establishment of a working alliance.
◆ The offer of a dialogic relationship in which there is willingness to engage in collaborative relational inquiry.

THE WORKING ALLIANCE

The working alliance starts with an offer of help, support and commitment from the therapist. This offer of counselling is met by the agreement of the client to the initial conditions (for example, regular attendance, fees, etc.) and a willingness to participate in the change process. As soon as you and your client have made the commitment to work together, you are starting to develop the working alliance (sometimes called a therapeutic alliance or working relationship). This alliance involves the development of an active partnership, a bond of trust between you and your client in which you share a mutual understanding of your work together and its goals.

It also means that you agree to co-operate with each other in the belief in the other's good intention. The client believes that your fundamental desire is to work in his best interest even when he finds you difficult or challenging. The therapist believes that the client is doing the best he can to willingly engage and be honest in his communications with you in this joint venture.

It is the working alliance that will sustain the work despite the times when the client has temporarily decided that you are a terrible therapist or you have decided that he is not even *trying* to help himself. On the therapist's side, such trust must be earned by her willingness to take seriously everything the client brings, to empathize, respect and to stay with the client even when the therapy gets difficult or stuck.

The working alliance will often take time to establish and may fluctuate at times, especially when the client feels 'missed' or criticized by the therapist. You may need to strengthen the alliance at these times by exploring what you did (or didn't do) that led to a weakening of trust and be prepared to own up to your part in this (for example, an unhelpful intervention or an unexpected absence). It is often the willingness of the therapist to be there for the client, openly struggling with her mistakes, that convinces the client you are wholeheartedly committed to the working alliance. It also models an availability to explore difficulties in a spirit of openness and inquiry rather than self-criticism or avoidance. Indeed, many psychotherapists believe that the inevitable rupture of the alliance, followed by the repair of that rupture through open inquiry and empathic understanding (see below in 'Dialogic Relating') constitutes the major healing in therapy.

One of the most important ways to encourage and strengthen the working alliance is to keep monitoring whether you are both 'pulling in the same direction'. You will therefore need to review together at regular intervals how relevant, helpful and effective the relationship is. This will involve monitoring progress of the agreed aims, asking what has been helpful or unhelpful in your interventions and readjusting your relationship or strategic thinking. The client needs to feel that he is an active and influential partner in what goes on in the sessions. The counsellor, on her part, needs to adjust her degree of support or confrontation to foster this partnership (see Chapter 15 for suggestions on conducting a review). In addition, the therapist needs to watch carefully for the effect of her interventions so that she can tell from her client's reactions whether she is in tune with him or whether she has missed him or gone too fast.

The strength and speed of formation of a solid working alliance will depend on several factors – the client's personality style, their history of relational trust, their self-responsibility, and your ability to demonstrate consistent understanding and support. In short-term contracts, the working alliance needs to be established quickly. In longer-term work, especially with issues of abuse or abandonment, building a working alliance may be a slow process and may in fact be the main focus of counselling for a long time.

To check whether you have a working alliance, ask these three questions:

◆ Does the client have a basic trust that you are trying to be helpful or constructive most of the time?
◆ Is there a clarity and agreement about what you are trying to do together, and your different responsibilities?
◆ Is there a commitment to staying engaged and in the relationship even when it gets difficult or painful?

Suggestion: Take a moment to think about these three questions in relation to your own therapy. When was the working alliance strongest and when was it most fragile? What made the difference? Did you ever doubt your therapist's good will or their commitment to you? Now think about a client you have struggled with and ask the same questions. How do you imagine your client would answer?

The working alliance is the necessary starting point for developing a healing relationship.

DIALOGIC RELATING

> The human heart yearns for contact – above all it yearns for genuine dialogue … Each of us secretly and desperately yearns to be 'met' – to be recognized in our uniqueness, our fullness and our vulnerability. (Hycner and Jacobs, 1995: 9)

Gestalt theory proposes a particular form of therapeutic relationship called *dialogic relating*. The concept was developed from the ideas of the philosopher Martin Buber (1958/1984) and can be described as:

> an attitude of genuinely feeling/sensing/experiencing the other person *as a person* (not an object or part-object), and a willingness to deeply 'hear' the other person's experience without prejudgement. Furthermore, it is the willingness to 'hear' what is not being spoken, and to 'see' what is not visible. (Hycner and Jacobs, 1995: xi, emphasis in original)

A therapist who offers a dialogic relationship needs to be fully present, understanding, validating and authentic with their client. This is, of course, a very tall order and in practice most of us can only aspire to offer it. However, it is the *intention* that is most important. It is also what has distinguished Gestalt from many other therapies, which believe that interpretations, skilful interventions or behavioural retraining are the main keys to success. Many of these therapies place less value on the 'realness' or present-centredness of the therapist and the relationship with the client that is such an essential part of Gestalt dialogue. A dialogic relationship starts with the therapist accepting a 'commitment to dialogue', to the *between* of the relationship where the therapist as well as the client is affected and changed by the meeting. It can then be described by several qualities which have been emphasized differently by different authors, but fundamentally include four elements; presence, confirmation, inclusion and willingness for open communication.

Presence

At its simplest, presence means that the counsellor is fully present to the client. She tries as far as possible to be in the here and now. She brings all of herself to the meeting and is willing to meet the client honestly and authentically. In doing so, she allows herself to be touched and moved by the impact of the client, to be *affected*. Sometimes this will mean being able to disclose her response in the service of the relationship, demonstrating the impact that has been experienced. This is such an important aspect of being a Gestalt practitioner that we will return to it again and again. For the moment, see if you can come into the present right now. There are many ways to approach this and we offer here a traditional Gestalt exercise.

Suggestion: Start to 'shuttle' between your 3 zones of awareness (explained in Chapter 3). Focus on your breathing, the weight of your body on the seat and try to sense where you are tense or relaxed. Don't necessarily try to change or move, just allow yourself to become aware of what you sense. Pay attention to any feelings or bodily sensations you may have. Do you feel warm or cold, calm or restless, happy or sad . . .? (The inner zone of body sensations and feelings.)

Now turn to your contact functions of seeing, hearing, smelling, tasting and touching. Allow yourself to experience each one in turn, to have a strong impression of the environment that surrounds you. (The outer zone of your surrounding environment.)

Lastly, notice how you are commenting on what you sense or receive, for example, 'I don't like the tension I notice in my stomach,' or 'I'm amazed at how much I can see when I really look around the room'. It is also likely that you are making connections to the past or wondering about the future. (The middle zone of thoughts and fantasies.)

Shuttle back and forth between these three zones of awareness, seeing where your energy or attention is mostly focused. Notice where you feel fluid and where you feel rigid or stuck. You are now in a better position to choose to be in the present moment. Pick an object in the room where you are sitting, and see if you can 'be present' to that object.

The counsellor, of course, has the subtle task of being present to both the client and the relationship. To practise presence, the therapist brings all her senses and awareness to bear and gives herself fully to the encounter. In a way, presence is a quality that emerges when you let go of (or bracket) all your concerns and strivings and allow yourself to 'be there'. It is the antithesis of playing a role or trying to give a certain impression. Beginning therapists sometimes ask 'How is a Gestalt therapist supposed to act?' as if there was a particular behaviour or role they should play. Presence is best approached by creating a space for it to appear. It also implies *being real*, which means not pretending you are interested if you are distracted, not pretending you are supportive if you feel irritated. It means allowing the client to see you as you are, not as you would like to be seen, perhaps letting go of the need to be the 'compassionate, wise healer'.

Confirmation

Our deepest, most profound stirrings of self-appreciation, self-love and self-knowledge surface in the presence of the person whom we experience as totally accepting. (Zinker, 1975: 60)

Being with a counsellor or therapist will be for many people their first experience of being truly listened to, attended to and understood by someone who takes their thoughts, feelings and needs seriously. This in itself can be a very powerful healing force. We could describe this as 'being fully received' by another human being. Some fortunate children have this experience from their mother, father or primary caregiver. Others of us have a taste of it from loving grandparents or relatives. Many developmental theorists, supported by the evidence of neurobiology research, see this type of relationship/experience as being the most important foundation of a secure, resilient sense of self. This is not to say that a perfect parent is endlessly loving and approving of everything the young child does. Simply there is a sense of being unconditionally accepted; however badly you behaved or difficult you were, you are still loved and valued.

> **Suggestion:** Think of a person (or even a pet) in your past or present by whom you have felt fully accepted. How did this make a difference to you in your life? How does it still? How does the absence of it affect you?

Confirmation does not mean that you agree with or condone everything that the client tells you. There are clearly times when you will disagree with his values or dislike some of the behaviour you hear about. Therapists may have, for example, strong opinions about issues such as racism, violence and abuse and sometimes feel the need to acknowledge their position to a client. We discuss self-disclosure later in the chapter.

The Gestalt counsellor attempts to accept or hold not only what is figural for the client, but also what is alienated, deflected or out of awareness. This includes the client's potential – the person that they might become. In this sense, confirmation is more inclusive than 'acceptance'. For example, a client who is only in touch with being self-critical is often out of touch with their ability for self-praise and the counsellor may need to confirm both these qualities. Like many desirable qualities, confirmation is something we aspire to rather than achieve. There are some clients, at some times, who are hard to confirm, especially when we are in the grip of a negative counter-transference. However, we have found that it can help if we keep close to an image of the client as a vulnerable human just like us, struggling to do the best they can in difficult circumstances.

Inclusion

This is the attempt of the counsellor to include the experience of the client in his realm of understanding.

> The therapist must feel the other side, the patient's side of the relationship, as a bodily touch to know how the patient feels. (Buber, 1967: 173)

Inclusion is an extension or broader form of empathy. In empathy, the counsellor tries to know the subjective world of the client, to see the world as he sees it, without judgement or opinion. Inclusion also encompasses the counsellor's awareness of her own feelings, reactions and experiences. She does not immerse herself so completely in the client's story or experience that she loses herself. On the contrary, she is always aware of her own existence and presence, but she chooses also to attune to the other and allow herself to be impacted by this. Inclusion involves a mixture of the perceived phenomena of the client – body expressions, emotions, content – and also a creative imagining on the part of the counsellor. However, it is often true that much interpersonal communication happens out of awareness in a variety of subtle ways and we encourage you to listen to images, sensations or feelings that you experience, which may also be giving you information about the world of your client.

> **Suggestion:** Remember a recent therapy session where a client was telling you about a problem. Picture the client in your mind and ask yourself the following questions:
>
> ◆ What is he communicating to you by his words, body posture, emotions, energy level, etc.?
> ◆ What are your own reactions, thoughts and feelings as you listen to the client?
> ◆ What particular significance do you think this problem will have in light of his previous history, for example, his childhood or self-concept?
> ◆ If you were to imagine being this client, how would you imagine he would be experiencing this problem?
>
> Now step back and ask yourself:
>
> ◆ If *you* had this problem, how would you be feeling and thinking?
> ◆ What sort of response would you want from a therapist right now?
>
> Now identify:
>
> ◆ The quality or sense you have of the co-created relationship.
>
> Having gone through the preceding steps, how could you best convey your understanding to the client?

Communicating inclusion

Inclusion can be conveyed without expressing it directly to the client. It is communicated through attitude, posture, tone of voice, all the non-verbal contact you make with your client. Being inclusive can have a profound healing effect, it can deepen the working alliance, promote trust and validate the experience of the client. However, communicating your understanding verbally can add a deeper, more powerful dimension to the client's understanding and acceptance of himself.

The most comprehensive practice of inclusion embraces all three areas (of thinking or imagery, feeling and body process). If you are attuned in this way it is likely that you will be matching your client's energy and naturally expressing your response. In your attempt to attune, you will inevitably make mistakes. This is a natural and useful process.

Part of the benefit of practising attunement is that the client senses you are struggling to understand and are willing to admit when you miss him. You will inevitably mis-attune, make corrections and receive feedback. It is crucial, therefore, to offer your interventions lightly ('I wonder if …' 'I'm imagining …' 'You seem to be …' 'As I listen, my own body is …') and to check their validity with the client who needs to feel free to tell you if you have missed him. Inclusion and presence are hard to maintain and you will need a solid sense of self-support, centredness and flexibility, to move between your own world and that of the client. You should not feel discouraged if you can only maintain them for a short time. It is the desire and intention to do so that are important.

Willingness for open communication

Open communication is the fourth tenet of the dialogic relationship. Your client must feel free to communicate to you anything that he experiences. It is also important that you are willing to openly communicate your responses to him in the spirit of an authentic meeting. We have already described that an important part of inclusion is communicating that empathy to the client so that his experience is validated. But what about all your other responses. Do you communicate them also or do you keep them to yourself? This is a question for which there is no easy answer. Our guiding principle is to share or communicate honestly what you believe will be useful to the client or lead to new ways of relating and to share (at times) what for you is getting in the way of your relationship or what might shed light on the current dynamic.

It is clearly not therapeutic to voice *every* reaction as it occurs. There are many arguments against this sort of intervention. It could divert the client's flow, put words in his mouth, or interrupt his process of self-discovery. Much important information could be missed by an attempt to interpret or understand too soon – without waiting for the complex meanings to bubble to the surface. Further, clients with shame or narcissistic issues could easily be shut down by premature self-disclosure. Or the counsellor's reactions and feelings might arise from her own life or unresolved issues and be imposed on the client. We think that a rule of thumb is for the therapist to be able to give a good reason (if asked to reflect afterwards) as to why she is choosing to tell the client about her own experience. The skill is knowing what, when, how and how much to disclose. It is important also to remember that we *cannot not* self-disclose. Our presence, how we dress and our gestures reveal ourselves to our clients. Every comment or intervention, other than simple empathic resonance, is a statement that we are a separate person with a separate mind.

Some guidelines for self-disclosure

When you decide to communicate what you are experiencing, make sure that your intervention simply describes your feeling, thought or image and that it is not laden with interpretations or judgements. You can phrase your intervention in the here-and-now.

'I'm aware that I'm feeling sad/angry/pleased as I listen to you', or 'I feel disturbed as I listen to how you were abused.' These have a much cleaner impact than, 'That was a bad thing to happen', or 'He shouldn't have treated you like that.' Alternatively, invite an exploration: 'I think something is going on between us. Do you have a sense of what is happening?' Remember that silence can be a powerful communication – both positive and negative.

After you have shared your response be attentive to the client's reaction to it. You are looking for interest and engagement, response or the lack of it, and need to be ready to help him express how he felt about what you said.

When you are unsure about self disclosing, consider the following points:

◆ Will withholding your comment diminish your ability to be with the client? We have found that simply saying that we have been temporarily distracted can release something and allow us to be more present. Equally, the loss of engagement at that moment may be a sign of some deeper dynamic in the relationship.
◆ If a feeling, thought or image persists for some time, especially if it persists over many sessions (and is one that has only occurred during the encounter with this client) you may assume that it has something to do with the material brought by the client and it may be appropriate to share it. It is only through dialogue that new meanings can emerge.
◆ Consider whether the client is bringing an issue or topic that you have strong reactions or opinions about. If yes, then probably keep the reaction to reflect on afterwards or to take to supervision.
◆ Check whether your wish to self-disclose is a counter-transference enactment that may need to be understood better or temporarily bracketed (see Chapter 12).

Generally speaking, we believe that it is *having the attitude* of willingness to practise open communication with your client that is most important. Whether you do or do not choose to communicate is a matter for the individual context.

The issue of self-disclosure becomes particularly relevant when the client asks the therapist personal questions about her life or history. It is useful to prepare yourself by thinking about the sorts of disclosures you would consider making, and why. Part of your answer will relate to your personal style of Gestalt therapy. Whatever you decide, it is important to remember that the timing of questions is always relevant. Even if you answer a particular question, it is useful also to inquire into the meaning for the client of both the question and your answer. A client who asks if you have ever experienced a situation like his, may be expressing a fear of being misunderstood. What is more, he may be encouraged or discouraged by your answer – be it in the affirmative or not. Broadly speaking, there is a lot of value in not disclosing the *content* of your life unless you have thought carefully about the significance of it. It is usually fine to say 'That's an interesting question,' I'd like a few moments to think about it, before I answer', or 'I'd like to come back to that question later.'

WORKING IN THE DIALOGIC RELATIONSHIP

When a therapist practises the four qualities above – presence, confirmation, inclusion and open communication – she is said to be offering an I–Thou or dialogic attitude towards the client. You are endeavouring to meet the client as a full human being without analysing or attempting to manipulate, but being open and available to who he is. As you attempt to offer this attitude, you will inevitably realize how hard it is to be consistent. Most therapists can only be fully present or inclusive for short periods in any session.

If the client (or any human being) were also to respond from an I–Thou position, this would be, in some ways, the pinnacle of human relational interaction. For Martin Buber this was the end point and highest achievement of dialogue: two human beings fully present to each other in what has been called an 'I–Thou Moment'. (This is the same territory as a moment of 'full and vibrant contact'.) Maybe you have been fortunate enough to have had some of these special moments in therapy (or in life!), usually brief, where a profound connection is made, often wordless, out of time, which seems to transcend the ordinary limits of the relationship. At its simplest it is an experience of selfless connection, of being fully met and satisfied with the fullness and vibrancy of the moment. At its more complex it has been described as 'the expression of the presence of God' (Zinker, 1977: 3).

As a therapist, you also have the responsibility to assess, plan and 'think about' how the therapy is going. When you operate from this position, it is called having an I–It relationship with the client. The I–It relationship is one which is based on previous experiences of life. We see people and things in terms of what we know already about them and the world. It is how we all spend our lives a great deal of the time, relating to our environment according to how we can make use of it or manage it. Effective I–It relating involves being able to predict how a person may behave, how we can affect them and how they might respond to us. This relating is, of course, an essential activity for negotiating a contract, making assessments, structuring time and dealing with clinical issues such as a sudden request for a longer session, or negotiating about when to end the therapy. It also involves reflecting on what has happened between you, thinking and feeling about your client's response to you and you to them, listening for meanings.

Offering a dialogic attitude is also in some ways a graded experiment, in that the therapist needs to continually monitor and potentially modify the intensity of her presence and genuine communication depending on what will best serve her client. This is especially true with clients who are very disturbed or have fragile self-process. Here, a responsible I–It attitude is essential to maintaining the structure and containment needed. An I–It relationship will probably be much more in evidence also in the initial stages of therapy, when you are reviewing progress and when you get stuck. Accepting this, you will try to keep I–It relating to a minimum, returning as often as possible to an I–Thou attitude.

A Gestalt therapist working dialogically will alternate between these two types of relationship, I–Thou and I–It, as the situation permits. Lynne Jacobs (1989) has described the dialogic relationship in Gestalt therapy as a continual interplay or moving back and forth between I–Thou and I–It modes.

Before we end, we want to add a thought about the prioritizing of relationship. Because of its ever-present influence, we have been emphasizing the essential, constant nature of therapeutic contact. However, there are times when our clients need to withdraw and pull back from an active relationship with us. Then the highest priority is for them to be oriented to themselves, the relationship being in the background.

In those times, the therapist's job is to practise presence and confirmation silently, as a patient and supportive witness to the process.

CONCLUSION

This chapter has described the formation of a therapeutic relationship as a sequence of steps: the establishment of a safe context, the agreement about the task of therapy and the development of a bond of trust between counsellor and client. The Gestalt therapist can then move towards a dialogic relationship – in which she offers presence, confirmation, inclusion and willingness for open communication. The sequence may not, of course, happen in this order; for example, a dialogic relationship may be needed for some time before trust develops or before you can agree on the direction you will take. However, the most important aspect of Gestalt practice is for the client to feel understood and accepted; that he is not being judged and that the therapist will take him seriously. In this sense, phenomenology and dialogue are the bedrock of all Gestalt counselling.

RECOMMENDED READING

Denham-Vaughan, S. and Chidiac. M.-A. (2007) 'The process of presence: energetic availability and fluid responsiveness', *British Gestalt Journal,* 16 (1): 9–19.

Erskine, R.G., Moursund, J. and Trautmann, R.L. (1999) *Beyond Empathy.* New York: Brunner-Mazel.

Fairfield, M. and O'Shea, L. (2008) 'Getting beyond individualism,' *British Gestalt Journal,* 17 (2): 24–37.

Gremmler-Fuhr, M. (2004) 'The dialogic relationship in Gestalt therapy,' *British Gestalt Journal,* 13 (1): 5–17.

Hycner, R.A. and Jacobs, L. (1995) *The Healing Relationship in Gestalt Therapy.* Highland, NY: Gestalt Journal Press.

Mackewn, J. (1997) *Developing Gestalt Counselling.* London: Sage. **(See Chapter 8.)**

Mayer, K. (2001) 'A relational perspective on Gestalt therapy and the phenomenological method', *Gestalt Review,* 5 (3): 205–10.

Spinelli, E. (2005) 'To disclose or to not disclose,' *International Gestalt Journal,* 28 (1): 25–41.

Staemmler, F-M. (2004) 'Dialogue and interpretation', *International Gestalt Journal,* 27 (2): 33–58.

Yontef, G. (2002) 'The relational attitude in gestalt therapy,' *International Gestalt Journal,* (1): 15–35.

Zahm, S. (1998) 'Therapist self disclosure', *Gestalt Journal,* (23) (2): 21–52.

5

ASSESSMENT AND DIAGNOSIS

The very concept of assessment creates a dilemma for many Gestaltists. The idea of deliberately attempting to adopt an objective or 'expert' stance in order to assess or diagnose a client appears to run counter to many of the fundamental principles of Gestalt practice. First, to give a diagnostic label to a client seems to imply that they are somehow fixed and static and can be reduced to a simple set of words. Second, historically and politically diagnosis has often been used as a means to depersonalize, objectify or oppress. Third, it can be used to deny the uniqueness of a client and potentially supports an expert position that claims to have a better understanding than the client has of herself. Fourth, it undermines the fundamental Gestalt principle that awareness, dialogue and full contact are of themselves all that is needed for effective psychotherapy and healing. And if that were not enough, fifth, the recognized diagnostic systems are often deeply flawed, unhelpfully reductionist and, arguably, are manipulated by politicians and the pharmaceutical industry (Verhaeghe, 2004, 2007; Leader, 2008).

However, despite all these valid arguments, we believe that there are many compelling advantages to carrying out an initial and ongoing assessment. What is more, it is professionally and ethically necessary to do so.

As we wrote this, we had a discussion about the difference between diagnosis and assessment. It seems to us that diagnosis has to do with 'identifying' an existing or enduring situation – naming it, distinguishing it from others. Assessment is a more evaluative description of the issues or situation and can be more fluid to allow for moment-by-moment change. In our opinion, a formal diagnosis in the psychotherapeutic world has a couple of limited yet important benefits which we discuss below. Otherwise, we will be using a looser definition of diagnosis, one that is more akin to assessment and is compatible with Gestalt philosophy and principles.

ASSESSMENT IS PART OF RELATING

We cannot *not* assess. As we described in Chapter 2, human beings are meaning-making creatures. Our way of making sense of the world can be said to be an ongoing form of assessment or diagnosis. We observe, encounter and try to understand all the time. For example, in the way we recognize, react to, and form impressions of people. It is almost impossible to meet a person for the first time and not form some opinion, some like or dislike. Often, these processes are barely conscious but are nevertheless a part of an ongoing relational assessment. Without this happening you would not be able to meet an old friend and say 'I recognize you, I like you, I want to be with you.'

The same process happens in the consulting room. From the moment of meeting the client, the counsellor is paying attention, in and out of awareness, to a myriad of details and impressions, the age of the person, how he walks, the expression on his face, what clothes he is wearing, his emotional tone, his style of relationship. Surfacing these reactions is the start of gathering important information and an unavoidable part of the counsellor's natural assessment.

Suggestion: Remember the last time you carried out a first assessment with a client (or the first meeting of a new social relationship). What was your first impression, what opinions, judgements and emotions did you have before you knew the person better? You may have described this as 'I had an intuition that …,' 'I somehow knew that I could trust him/not trust him …', 'I just had a feeling about him', without any obvious evidence. How much did this impression turn out to be accurate in the long run?

It is surprising how accurate first impressions can be (and also sometimes how inaccurate). (For an interesting expansion of this see Gladwell, 2006.)

Of course, accepting the reality of this 'out of awareness assessment' presents a tension or paradox that arises in many areas of Gestalt practice. On the one hand, we seek to honour and respect the uniqueness of each client, in his unique situation, in his unique relationships. We also seek to honour his unfolding dynamic process of living in relationship. On the other hand, we automatically form impressions and make judgements, like it or not. It is also true, in our experience, that many clinical phenomena and behaviours do fall into recognizable repeating patterns that have predictable consequences and treatment implications. In order to effectively help our clients, we need to be open to see and name the repeating patterns, fixed gestalts and habitual styles of contact in order to understand how their way of making contact with the world is contributing to their difficulties.

For example, clients with borderline process often need stronger therapeutic boundaries. Narcissistic clients need more attunement. Depressed clients are at greater risk of suicide, and sexually abused clients usually have great sensitivity or fragility around their body boundaries. Generalizations like these – if held *lightly* as possible guides – can sometimes help the counsellor be more effective and safer in her work.

> **Suggestion:** Take a moment to see if there are any fixed or repeating patterns of behaviour in your own life. For example, would you describe yourself as shy or outgoing, are you a 'thinking type' or a 'feeling type', do you find relationships easy or problematic, do you have any self-critical or self-limiting beliefs? Make a brief sentence of the answers – 'I am ...' Notice what it feels like to have labelled yourself. Do you find this description of yourself demeaning or is it just a 'description'. What label would you not like to have applied to you and why?

INITIAL ASSESSMENT IS VITAL FOR A COMPETENT PROFESSIONAL RESPONSE

In an 'ideal' therapeutic situation, our client would be a person who knows and embraces Gestalt principles. He would come into counselling with unlimited funds and with the sole desire of getting to know himself, become aware of and change some unhelpful patterns, fulfil his potential and see where his creativity leads him! In such a case, an initial diagnosis would not be important and the practitioner would be free to take each moment and each session as they came. From time to time she would review the work with her client, to make sure that he was getting what he wanted. Otherwise, their time would be a genuine journey of exploration.

However, it is rare that clients seek therapists with such an open agenda. Normally, clients want help with some form of psychological distress. Life 'isn't working' for them. Either they are suffering from depression, anxiety or some other inner turmoil, or they are having problems in their daily functioning – difficulties in their relationships, with their job or with some other aspect of the existential challenge of living. They come with a reasonable expectation that the therapist has the expertise to help with the problem in as short a time as possible (and are often only funded for short-term contracts). We believe it would be unprofessional, therefore, if a therapist and client did not address some important issues. Together they need to:

◆ Identify the presenting issue, its current significance and implications, and find out what sort of difference the client wants the therapy to make.
◆ Form an understanding of the meaning and implications of the problem.
◆ Identify any risks to self or other that need immediate attention.
◆ Identify any risks or disadvantages that therapy may provoke.
◆ Decide as far as possible whether the therapist is suitable and competent to help with this problem.
◆ Agree an outcome or at least a direction for counselling that is achievable.
◆ Have some way of evaluating whether the ongoing counselling journey is being effective.

This process will, of course, be provisional and updated frequently as the client changes and moves forward.

FORMAL DIAGNOSIS ALLOWS USEFUL COMMUNICATION WITH OTHER PROFESSIONALS

We believe that if Gestalt is to command respect and credibility in the larger therapeutic field, Gestalt counsellors need to be able to describe their clients in diagnostic terms that allow a dialogue with other psychotherapeutic approaches. This is crucial if referrals to another therapist, G.P., social worker or psychiatrist are necessary.

> **Suggestion:** Pick a client you have seen for some time and imagine his G.P. has asked for a report to enable him to be referred for specialist treatment for his problem (both you and the client agree this is a good idea). How would you describe his problem, the diagnosis, and the focus of your work without using Gestalt terminology?

You will find this much easier if you become familiar with a formal method of diagnosis such as the DSM–IV or ICD 10. These can also be useful in giving access to literature and resources from other professionals, for example the different types of depression, possible outcomes, suicide risks, relapse rates, associated conditions, etc. The translation of some of these other diagnostic systems into Gestalt has already borne much fruit (see Tobin, 1982 and Delisle, 1999, who impressively show the usefulness of DSM–IV personality disorders seen through a Gestalt lens).

At the simplest level, the use of a label as a descriptor sometimes simplifies the process of referral. You might telephone a colleague and ask 'Do you have space in your practice for a person who is suffering from PTSD following a road accident?' and the colleague can immediately have some idea of the nature of the referral and the likely nature, length of time and intensity of the required work.

A FLEXIBLE AND CO-CREATED DIAGNOSIS HELPS TO BUILD THE WORKING ALLIANCE

Quite separate from the formal psychiatric diagnosis is a process-focused Gestalt diagnosis, which is most useful if we can keep it *descriptive*, *phenomenological* and *flexible*, rather than simply defining and naming. Gestalt diagnosis is an attempt to see patterns, themes and repetitions that are unique to the client (a light-hearted example of this can be found at the start of Chapter 2). It is primarily a description of a process, of *how* the client is behaving in the present moment (in relationship with you and in their current field conditions). It is therefore a description of *activity* or 'gestalting'. For example, you would describe a 'narcissistic process' rather than a narcissistic person or disorder. Or you would say that the client is 'retroflecting' not retroflected.

One definition of Gestalt diagnosis is to say that it is a dynamic description of a fixed gestalt (or several fixed gestalts) in the life of the client – a process that has become static. The fixed gestalt is a description of a creative adjustment made, at some time, to previous life circumstances, which has become habitual and inappropriate in the present. Therapy is about loosening this fixed gestalt and helping the client to move from the static historical pattern to a flexible and responsive meeting in the present. A perfectly healthy person would live each moment creatively and would therefore have no 'diagnosis'.

We recommend to 'co-diagnose' with the client wherever possible. This should certainly happen at the end of the assessment session, and also at times when you have a strong hypothesis about what is happening. You might share with a client, for example, that you think his current distress may be connected with an unresolved bereavement, or that his bodily tension may be related to a holding back of anger. This also requires the counsellor to translate Gestalt jargon into language accessible to the client. For example, 'You have a lot of held-back feeling' (retroflection), 'you have a strong belief that it is wrong to cry' (an introject or core belief), 'It seems that you never got over the death of your father' (unfinished business). He can then agree, disagree or clarify and help to co-create a more accurate diagnostic understanding. He will then also be actively involved in the understanding of his own problem. It also empowers him to make counselling a shared endeavour.

ASSESSMENT HELPS YOU TO MAKE DECISIONS ABOUT SUITABILITY

The basis of competent professional and effective clinical work is to decide if Gestalt counselling is suitable for the potential client and whether you are the most suitable counsellor (see also Chapter 1). Assessment will allow you to make this a more informed decision in the following areas:

◆ Are you competent to deal with the presenting problem? This is both a professional decision and a personal one. You may not be sufficiently trained and experienced to take on a client with a long-standing mental illness, substance abuse, a history of violence or suicidal impulses (see also Chapter 18).

◆ Are you reluctant to take on the client for personal reasons. The client may scare you, re-activate an unfinished past trauma, or have an issue for which you have no sympathy. It is probably not necessary to 'like' a prospective client but you should at least feel some resonance, interest and compassion. Clients deserve our best efforts, energy and commitment and it is much better to refer on if you cannot be sure of this.

◆ Does the client want (or need) a treatment modality or intervention other than Gestalt. For example, some clients just want to lose their symptoms, be told what to do by an expert, gain support, or have a friend because they are lonely.

◆ Can you both agree how you understand the presenting problem? We make the distinction between a life circumstance (I don't have any friends, I feel miserable all the time, I can't find a partner, etc.) and an issue that they want to understand better, make some change in themselves or accept some responsibility for (e.g. I think I'm part of the reason why I have this problem). Clients who are distressed about their life circumstance but don't see or are not interested in exploring the part they play in it will expect *you* to make it different or just want you to be a sympathetic listener. With these clients you need to spend more time agreeing a contract where it is clear what the purpose of you meeting will be (and sometimes deciding that counselling is not suitable).

METHODS OF ASSESSMENT AND DIAGNOSIS IN GESTALT

Many of the theoretical concepts of Gestalt are themselves frameworks of assessment, for example the zones of awareness, modifications to contact, the degree of support, the style of contact or relationship with the therapist, and so on. It is important for you to develop a way of assessing which is compatible with *your own* particular style and approach.

The art of diagnosis lies in describing what you see and experience, making sense of this, and understanding how this causes difficulties for the client. You are looking to see how the client functions, what his beliefs are about himself (and the world) and what processes are absent, minimal, appropriate or exaggerated. As you go through a diagnostic overview, several figures will emerge as sharp or interesting. They may or may not be relevant. Part of your skill is to be alert also to what is in the ground, not yet figural for the client but possibly more important. Yontef and Jacobs (2007: 328–67) talk of 'resistance ... to the formation of a figure (a thought, feeling or need) that threatens to emerge in a context judged to be dangerous'. Some aspects of the client therefore, are 'purposely and regularly relegated to the background' yet may be quietly influencing what figures emerge. The counsellor will therefore need to be alert (and alert to hunches or intuitions) about what is missing in the client's presentation, what polarities are absent, what is implied but not spoken about.

Where possible and appropriate, your assessment should be (sensitively) shared with the client who will then tell you whether the particular features, processes or issues you have identified are also important or relevant for him. It can then become a respectful co-diagnosis.

Caveat: Before we identify the traditional list of Gestalt diagnostic criteria we would make the point that they are sometimes viewed as if one could have an objective perspective, 'the client is retroflecting his feelings,' with the implication that this is generally true for the client. We would argue that, in many way, it is impossible to separate the process of the client from the relational field that is formed at the first point of meeting between counsellor and client. *All* you see in the assessment room is potentially a response to you the therapist.

The many ways the client makes contact with the world are all responses to different field conditions. Only as you hear the story of the client and hear him describe his historical ways of making contact can you start to identify what is unique to you and him and what is generally true of his creative adjustments in a range of different relational field conditions. This makes it all the more important to check with the client. 'Is that generally true?'

We have designed a model of assessment that identifies three areas of possible focus:

◆ The client in process.
◆ The client's relational patterns.
◆ Field conditions.

Each section contains suggested questions (there are many more) to stimulate your thinking.

THE CLIENT IN PROCESS

Embodied process

This is a description of the activity of the client in the room, his bodily sensations and movement, his energy and his contact functions.

◆ *Movement.* For instance how does your client move – stiffly or in a relaxed way? Does he make a lot of movements or remain still?
◆ *Voice.* Loud or soft, distant or present, fluid or tentative, emotional or flat? What sort of language does your client use? Is it matter of fact and concrete, or poetic? Does it contain imagery? What kind? Are there pauses in the speech? When? Does the person seem to 'own' his experience, as in 'I crashed the car', as opposed to 'the car crashed'.
◆ *Seeing.* Does he make eye contact? Is his gaze steady or darting? When does he look away, and what at?
◆ *Hearing.* Does the client hear what you say easily? Does he hear correctly or appear to mishear or misunderstand?
◆ *Feelings.* How does the client experience his inner world of feelings – and how easily can he express them. What emotions does he feel and how intensely? Does he describe himself as depressed, empty, agitated, sad, tearful or frustrated? Or does he find it difficult to access any feelings at all?
◆ *Bodily process.* How much does he seem 'embodied' or disconnected from his body. Is he in touch with bodily sensations; if so, where? Does he include bodily descriptions as he talks.

Support systems

◆ *Support for self-process.* Does the client seem to be sitting well-supported in the chair? Is his breathing relaxed and even? Does he appear to be confident and sure of himself or does he appear nervous, restless or rigid with erratic breathing.

◆ What is his relationship with his environment? Does he have close friends, strong family connections? Does he feel supported by these people or is he isolated and lonely?

◆ How does he manage stress? Does he use alcohol or drugs to desensitize, or more healthy forms of relaxation such as exercise, sport, yoga or meditation to unwind and relax?

◆ As he describes his life to you, do you get the sense of a person with enough personal and environmental resources or does he seem to be living always in scarcity or in need of something he doesn't have?

Belief systems

◆ What core beliefs does the client hold about himself, others and the world? What other fixed positions does he take? Core beliefs are central and fundamental to the client's sense of who he is. They often tend to be formed in childhood in response to repeated relational experiences and they continue into adulthood, unquestioned, sometimes barely in awareness. Examples of core beliefs are: I am unlovable; other people cannot be trusted; the world is a dangerous place (more healthy people may have more positive beliefs!). However, they may also be chosen freely by the client (for instance, a religious conviction or a moral position). They often underlie and justify his creative adjustments and modifications to contact.

◆ What introjects are influential? An introject is an opinion, an attitude or an instruction unquestioningly taken in from the environment as if it were true. Examples of introjects are 'Never depend on others', or 'You will never succeed', or 'Do it to them before they do it to you.' The person who is under the influence of an introject feels a strong pressure to conform with the introject and feels uncomfortable if he tries to go against it.

◆ What sense or meaning does the client make of the circumstances relevant to his presenting problem and of his life situation? Does he think life/the world is being unfair to him, that if only his circumstances changed all would be well or does he think it is 'all his fault', or all due to bad luck?

◆ Does he see the 'glass' as half full or half empty?

The following additional four aspects of the client in process are simply named here, as they are covered in detail elsewhere in the book.

◆ Cycle of experience (see Chapter 3).
◆ Modifications to contact (see Chapter 10).
◆ Unfinished business or fixed gestalts (see Chapter 11).
◆ Polarities (See Chapter 11).

THE CLIENT'S RELATIONAL PATTERNS

How the client describes his relational experiences with other people and how he makes relational contact with you is a crucial part of the assessment process. You can begin to form a picture of how he constructs his relationships generally, his anxieties and avoidances, his beliefs, his flexibility and his style of contact. You can also identify how he makes or breaks relational contact with you in the assessment process.

The client may be present and make good contact, or he may appear not to listen, or interrupt what you say. His way of relating may change suddenly depending on the issue or relationship that he is describing. All this gives you important information about him, and you may form an impression of a particular style of relating you think is significant or problematic. It is important, as we said above, having made some sort of assessment of your client, to gently explore with him whether this is a common pattern in his life, and *whether it is a problem to him*. Is the client aware of what he is doing or how he is being? If so, is he always like that? If only sometimes, in what circumstances – is it only with you? Does he think it's a problem? It is another way of including the client in the process of his own assessment. It is not a label imposed upon him from outside, but a picture of an individual in a situation that he has helped to co-create.

EXAMPLE

The counsellor was aware of feeling more and more pleased with himself as he interviewed Beverley for the first time. It seemed that all his observations were 'spot on' for Beverley – she responded as if all his suggestions were inspired. After a while, he decided to check out a hypothesis. In a friendly and humorous way he said 'You are giving me the impression that everything I say seems to be absolutely right. That's very nice for me of course, but I wonder whether you generally have a tendency to support and agree with what other people say?' Inevitably, Beverley said,' Yes I do, how clever of you.' There was a pause as they both realized that she had done it again. Then they both laughed and she repeated in a much less adapted tone of voice, 'No really, I know I do that and I think that it may be part of the problem.' The counsellor's intervention served several purposes. It checked out the validity of his observation and hypothesis, it investigated Beverley's capacity for self-reflection, it tested out whether she could withstand a gentle confrontation and it explored how she responded to humour.

Suggestion: Imagine you are sitting next to a stranger on a long-haul flight to Australia. He or she turns out to be (astonishingly) similar in all respects to a particular current client. How do you think you would get on? What sort of relationship would start to form? What would happen next? Try this as an exercise of self-supervision about both the overt and the underlying relational dynamics.

The relationship you have with a particular client will be different from any other relationship you make. The way you create yourselves, each other and the relational field will be unique to you both.

◆ How would you describe the client's way of relating to you? Does he listen and respond appropriately or does he appear not to hear you, argue with everything you say or alternatively agree very readily as if keen to please?

◆ Do you notice any transferential responses? Is he treating you congruently or are you surprised or puzzled by his relational expectations of you? (See Chapter 12.)

Your response to the client

All the responses you have to your client are important. They might be your counter-transference (see Chapter 12), they might be based on your natural likes and dislikes, or they might be an indication of the impact she makes on other people in her life.

◆ What feelings and images do you have in response to the client?

◆ What metaphor would you use to describe him (for example, like an express train)?

◆ What reactions to you have to your client's appearance (e.g. their clothes, hair, face, skin colour)?

◆ What do has most impact on you as you listen to him – his voice tone, the cadences of his speech?

◆ What is your body resonance – for example do you feel tense or relaxed, energized or passive as you sit with him?

◆ How would you describe your way of relating to the client?

◆ How do you imagine the client sees you?

◆ Who does he remind you of?

FIELD CONDITIONS

These are the context, the situation and the influences, both local and global that form the interacting field that is the ground to every emerging figure.

Current field influences

◆ What general life circumstances are impinging on the client at the moment?

◆ What is the life stage or concern of the client (young, single, career track, family-maker, mid-life, retirement, etc.)?

Cultural factors

An awareness of the importance of race and culture in the consulting room is, of course, important throughout the counselling process, but at no time is it more important than at the assessment stage. Both counsellor and client bring as part of their ground structures, a wealth of values and assumptions – most of them not in awareness – ranging from the right way to behave in different situations to the definition of healthy living.

These considerations are true in a sense, for any relationship. Even if client and counsellor come ostensibly from the same cultural group, there will be many different assumptions and beliefs. They will both be influenced by what could be called the multi-cultural ground of their life – their family, their school, friends, associations, travels, jobs, etc., as well as the mini-culture of, say, northeast England as opposed to south. What is more, there is another level to the inter-cultural element. The therapeutic relationship is one where, however respectful and mutual the counsellor, there is a power imbalance. How could there not be when one of the two people has come to the relationship feeling distressed and having the experience of not coping well in her life? She puts herself in a vulnerable position and exposes her most private anxieties and fears to another person who, in that setting anyway, is not sharing his own vulnerabilities. Imagine the additional dynamic when the two are different genders or different ages (notice whether you had a reaction when in the example in the previous sentences, we chose to describe the client as female and the counsellor as male).

This can be particularly striking where counsellor and client come from different races. The counsellor who will be involved in any sort of inter-cultural or inter-racial counselling should familiarize herself as far as she can with the more obvious differences in norms. However, she must remember that there will be countless subtle assumptions made – particularly if one of the pair is part of the dominant culture. She must be ready to explore phenomenologically and sensitively, and she must be even slower to define or label.

CHECKLIST

What are the obvious differences between you and your client in the following areas?

Culture	Race	Nationality	Age	Physical ability
Class	Gender	Sexual orientation	Power	Personality style

What implications might this have for the client, for you, for your relationship? What difficulties might you foresee, and what might you do to address these?

The historical field

What stressful or significant events have happened in the past year? The last few years?

The presenting issue of the client is often the consequence of a creative adjustment that was made long before and has now become a fixed gestalt. Much of this will be out of the client's awareness and only understandable with knowledge of earlier field conditions or responses. Some of this will emerge naturally in the course of therapy, but some will not. In order to understand fully what the client is bringing, the counsellor may need to investigate not only the current field, but also the historical field. Taking a history is subordinate to the here-and-now situation, but it has many advantages.

EXAMPLE

Nerys had come for counselling because of relationship difficulties. The counsellor worked dialogically 'in the present' for many weeks with some success, but was puzzled that the relationship did not seem to become deeper, given Nerys's obvious need for this kind of support. It was only when the counsellor actively investigated her history that the following information emerged. Nerys had been fostered several times as a child after being abandoned by her parents and had no experience or expectations of supportive or consistent relationships. She had not thought it relevant to mention this to the counsellor and only gradually started to see the importance to her current situation.

Suggestion: Ask the client to take a large piece of paper and draw on it a line all the way across the middle (a 'lifeline'). Ask him to write his major events on this line, such as his first school experience, first girlfriend/boyfriend, first job and other major life events. This may take some time and the line may have to be re-drawn as he remembers more and more; he may start to draw the line with natural peaks and troughs. Then ask him to step back and look at the whole to see what patterns start to emerge. Is there a theme of disappointment or loss for example? Are there periods of engagement and periods of isolation? What is the most important part of the lifeline for him? This diagrammatic representation of the client's life can be very revealing. You can also ask him to chart his emotional reactions to these life events on the same piece of paper, using a different colour pen.

COLLATING THE ASSESSMENT MATERIAL

Opposite is a Client Assessment Sheet, which will help you collate the information and themes. You may wish to use it after the initial interview as a way of thinking about your client, and then add to it from time to time as other important information emerges. Be aware of what you notice, but do not try to make sense of it all within the session – you need to be in the present moment too! In fact, it is rare for a busy counsellor to have the time to consider in detail all of the elements in the sheet and, in practice, certain aspects will be more figural and will form your provisional initial diagnosis.

CLIENT ASSESSMENT SHEET

The client in process

Embodied process

Support systems

Belief systems and introjects

Polarities

Interruptions on the cycle of experience

Influential modifications to contact

Unfinished business/fixed gestalts

The client's relational patterns

Nature of the relational contact with you

Your reactions and responses

Field conditions

Significant current circumstances

Significant historical events

Historical relationships

Cultural factors and issues of difference

THE ASSESSMENT OF RISK

There are many situations where the therapist needs to anticipate potential risk or danger to her client or even to herself. Among these may be when there is risk of suicide, self-harm, violence or mental illness, or when the problems involve addictive behaviour, eating disorders or personality disorders. Other risk situations may be those involving children or criminal behaviour. The elements of risk may be obvious at the initial assessment, but may also emerge during the course of therapy. In either case, before you accept or continue to work with such clients, you need to check whether you have enough specialist knowledge and arrange appropriate supervision. We suggest you read Chapter 18 for a full discussion.

CONCLUSION

A Gestalt diagnosis is an understanding or assessment of all the ways the client makes meaning and contact with his world. We believe it to be most effective and most respectful when it is co-created with the client (and indeed therapy outcome research described by Duncan and Miller (2000) stresses the importance of a shared view about the nature of the problem, its causes and treatment). The assessment you make of your client will, of course, be a part of I–It relating rather than I–Thou. However, if it is sensitively and respectfully carried out, it can be something in which the client can be fully involved. Its completion can provide a feeling of containment and structure for the counsellor and for the client and a sense of understanding. As therapy progresses the counsellor will move between modifying or updating the assessment and a bracketing of all of this to allow a full engagement and openness to the possibility of I–Thou relating.

RECOMMENDED READING

American Psychiatric Association (1994) *DSM–IV*. Washington: APA.

Delisle, G. (1999) *Personality Disorders: A Gestalt Therapy Perspective*. Cleveland, OH: Gestalt Institute of Cleveland Press.

Fuhr, R., Srekovic, M. and Gremmler-Fuhr, M. (2000) and 'Diagnostics in Gestalt therapy', *Gestalt Review*, 4 (3): 237–52.

Gladwell, M. (2006) *Blink: The Power of Thinking Without Thinking*. London: Penguin.

Korb, M.P. (1984) 'Therapeutic steps and processes in maturation', *Gestalt Journal*, 7 (2): 43–59.

Melnick, J. and Nevis, S. (1997) 'Gestalt diagnosis and DSM–IV', *British Gestalt Journal*, 6 (2): 97–106.

Nevis, E.C. (1992) *Gestalt Therapy: Perspectives and Applications*. New York: G.I.C. Press. (**See Chapters 2 and 3.**)

Sperry, L. (2003) *Handbook of Diagnosis and Treatment of the Personality Disorders.* New york: Brunner-Mazel.

Swanson, C. and Lichtenberg, P. (1998) 'Diagnosis in Gestalt therapy: a modest beginning', *Gestalt Journal*, 11 (1): 5–18.

Yontef, G. (1993) *Awareness, Dialogue and Process: Essays on Gestalt Therapy.* Highland, NY: Gestalt Journal Press. (**See Chapters 9 and 13**.)

6

TREATMENT
CONSIDERATIONS

IS 'TREATMENT' A USEFUL CONCEPT?

As with assessment and diagnosis, we are aware that we are taking a somewhat controversial position in devoting a chapter to what we are calling treatment considerations, treatment planning or strategic thinking (we use the terms interchangeably). Although many Gestalt authors use the concept of treatment planning (for example, Shub, 1992; Kepner, 1995; Delisle, 1999; Yontef and Fuhr, 2005), there is still an understandable reluctance to see the concept as useful to a Gestalt therapist. In some therapeutic models, treatment planning, like diagnosis, can seem like a detached, alienating process where an 'expert' categorizes and labels the person in order to apply a standard treatment. This approach can be seen at its most extreme in the treatment of mental illness with psychotropic drugs in some hospitals. The totality of the person in her unique field conditions can get lost and the patient herself is almost never consulted more than superficially about her treatment. In addition to these reservations, some Gestaltists see treatment planning as incompatible with the formation of a dialogic relationship and with the natural, spontaneous emergence of new meanings that flows from healthy relational contact. While we take these objections seriously, we believe they can be minimized and often need to take second place to the pragmatic necessity for the anticipation of possible risk, an overview of potential needs, and a consideration of outcomes and pitfalls in any therapeutic journey.

A good treatment plan, therefore, will take into account the unique circumstances of the client and be sensitive to the dangers and objections identified above. It will be discussed and agreed with the client wherever possible and will be responsive to changing field conditions as therapy progresses.

A typical treatment plan would include:

◆ Anticipation of any risks or dangers (see Chapter 18).
◆ Consideration of the most useful type of relationship to offer this client (for example, the degree of presence and self disclosure, the balance of support or challenge).

◆ Incorporation of any relevant knowledge from previous clinical experience or clinical literature about the kinds of issues presented.

◆ An awareness of any particular necessary sequence in addressing a series of issues or obstacles to be negotiated (for example, in some personality disorders).

◆ An awareness of the culture of the client and the implications for the therapy. This would include the impact of any differences (or similarities) between the culture of the counsellor and that of the client.

◆ An awareness of the client's age, gender, physical ability, sexuality and the impact of these on the therapeutic relationship and in the client's life.

◆ The prioritization of types of intervention styles (for example, focusing on emotions, thinking or action).

◆ Awareness of any repetitive work that may be needed, especially around creative adjustments, modifications to contact and impasses.

◆ Some criteria for assessing the counsellor's effectiveness with the client.

By treatment planning, we mean a flexible, ongoing sense of direction that is updated frequently, both at the 'macro' level and also within one session. We mean an itinerary that takes second place to where the client's energy is at any moment, yet holds signposts or reminders of the special needs and risks which apply to this particular client. In this sense then, treatment considerations are helpful prioritizations and cautions to avoid dangers, rather than prescriptions for a 'best' course of action.

THE IMPLICATION OF THE DIAGNOSIS

In many cases the diagnosis itself will imply the course of action you will follow. You may meet a client in the first session who is frightened and unsupported. Or you may notice how a client takes little responsibility for their actions or tells a story of recent trauma that has never been fully expressed. These are all presentations that call forth an immediate therapeutic response or intention. For another client who wants to work on having better relationships with other people, the most obvious direction to explore will be the way she forms and modifies her relationship with you. In the course of this exploration you will inevitably come across particular difficulties, for example introjects or retroflections about being with other people, with which you will work as they become figural. With this example, it is easy to see how the direction of therapy would just evolve, with new issues being addressed as they arose naturally.

In some ways this can be the ideal form of Gestalt work, where the therapist has no preconceived ideas about outcome or direction. We would suggest that this will indeed be the case much of the time in good Gestalt therapy. However, more complex situations (outlined in this chapter) will need a deliberate sensitivity, a particular approach or direction. In these cases, we suggest that the counsellor will keep the treatment considerations in the background, consulting them from time to time while mostly staying in the ever-changing newness of the moment. As the situation or diagnostic priorities change, the treatment plan will need to be revised or adjusted accordingly. In many ways this parallels the rhythmic back and forth of an I–Thou and I–It dialogic relationship.

INVOLVING THE CLIENT

In the previous chapter, we described some of the different diagnostic lenses that can be used to try to understand the issues of the client. Which of these takes precedence at any particular moment is affected by many factors, the most important of which is the view of the client herself. The client will (sometimes) bring the most pressing need or figure at the initial assessment session. The counsellor will then summarize how she understands the problem, possibly offering additional perspectives on what is out of the client's awareness (or the unaware ground to the figure). She will then discuss with the client the best plan for the coming sessions. This agreement may be as simple as a decision to try to make sense of the problem, to see what options the client has, or to help the client to find support during a crisis. Even in complex situations such as remembered childhood trauma, or repeated relationship failures, it is important and useful to find a way to envision a shared direction. This might involve an agreed sequence (though not necessarily linear) of developing trust, telling their story in detail, remembering specific episodes, finding what is unfinished in their past and so on. These sorts of discussions are usually most fruitful at times of review, when the client has more of a sense of the progression and possibilities of therapy and is able to have a more informed opinion of what would be helpful in the future.

There are occasions, of course, when it is not wise to share your thinking for the future. The client may not have enough support to hear your hunches (and consequent thinking) about past abuse, idealized others or personality style. The counsellor needs to strike a delicate balance between openness and what is therapeutically useful.

EXAMPLE

Kathryn, an attractive woman in her fifties, attended her first session in a state of anxiety. She cried for most of the time and explained to the counsellor that she had frightened herself recently when she went to a dental appointment, was made to wait and then lost her temper and shouted at the receptionist. This was disturbing for her because she said she NEVER got angry. She didn't know where it came from. Since that time she had felt weepy and miserable. She was also worried about feeling estranged from her family and friends. The counsellor felt engaged and interested and both agreed they had made a good connection by the end of the session. They decided on a contract to work together for six weeks and then review where they had got to. They discussed their shared understanding of the problems (overwhelming emotions, feeling isolated) and agreed to use the sessions for exploring the situation and focusing on increasing Kathryn's support for self-process (a shared diagnosis and treatment plan). At the sixth session review, Kathryn was intrigued as she began to see a pattern in the way she related to the people in her life by suppressing her anger and then withdrawing. She was feeling much more stable (thus changing

---

part of the diagnosis) and she was keen to continue the exploration of herself. They agreed to continue the sessions on an open-ended basis (aiming at a review in six months). The focus would now be Kathryn's continuing exploration of herself and finding new ways of managing the relationships in her life (a revised treatment plan).

CONDUCTING REVIEWS

Although, in a sense, you are continually reviewing, assessing, readjusting and re-contracting with a client (sometimes all in one session), it is also useful to have formal review sessions. You may want to suggest that the client think about it during the week preceding the review. At these sessions you can:

◆ Revisit the original contract or the last review and the aspirations and needs the client came with, in the first assessment session.
◆ Check whether the client and you think the contract is still relevant or how it is progressing.
◆ Note what new issues have emerged or what has changed for the client.
◆ Ask the client how they have found being in therapy with you so far, what aspects of it they have found particularly useful, what aspects unhelpful, whether there is anything they would like you to have done differently or would have liked to have done differently themselves.
◆ Discuss any changes that need to be made in the contract or counselling relationship.
◆ Agree a further short-term contract or a continuing long-term contract (or a date for leaving).

We would suggest a review in this manner approximately every three to six months for long-term clients and about half-way through for short-term contracts. After ending with a client, it can also be very useful to offer a follow-up review in six months' or one year's time for the client to return to touch base, or to evaluate their situation since leaving therapy. Some counsellors offer this follow-up session free to enable them to research sustained effectiveness after ending.

SPECIAL CONSIDERATIONS FOR PARTICULAR DIAGNOSES

In practice, many clients present with low self-support, fragile self-process or with complex difficulties needing specialist knowledge. Failure to take account of the implications of a particular client profile can lead us, despite the best of intentions, into making damaging mistakes. For example, a new client with a deep narcissistic injury may ask you for an honest opinion about herself; a client who fits the criteria of borderline personality may plead with you to extend the session; a sexually abused client may ask you to hold her while she remembers the trauma. In all these cases, the request of the client needs to be considered in the light of accepted clinical experience about the likely effects of meeting these wishes. In planning the counselling, therefore, the first question the practitioner must answer is – does this client have any special circumstances, conditions or difficulties that require either specialist knowledge or a particular treatment approach? If so, it is useful to consult the literature and a supervisor or colleague who has specialist knowledge in that area.

We will cover in more detail in Chapter 18 considerations of risk for more disturbed clients.

UNDERSTANDING THE DYNAMIC RELATIONSHIP BETWEEN THE DIAGNOSTIC FEATURES

Many diagnostic features will be part of an interlinked system that needs to be taken into consideration. For example, how does a particular creative adjustment fit into the larger gestalt of the client's self-organization and lifestyle? A client may be desensitized or retroflected as a general style of functioning. What would happen if this modification to contact was changed or transformed? Is it protecting the client from some more serious disturbance? Many creative adjustments are ways of managing a difficult and even dangerous threat to the person's stability or survival. A retroflection may be protecting the client from murderous rage; desensitization may be shielding the client from unbearable pain. The timing of 'undoing the retroflection' may be very significant. The counsellor needs to form a general understanding of the connections and underlying dynamics of the diagnostic features before deciding on strategy. A thorough phenomenological investigation before taking action may then be part of a new treatment consideration.

DECIDING PRIORITIES

In addressing these questions, you may start to see how some treatment sequences are necessary or desirable and we would argue that it is useful and sometimes crucial to think through the priorities of your work. Having drawn up a list of diagnostic features (perhaps following the checklist in Chapter 5), you will need to decide which aspects will require immediate attention and which can wait or will follow naturally on in the progress of the work.

EXAMPLE

Jennifer came to counselling wanting help in leaving an abusive relationship with her partner. Both she and the counsellor agreed that she was retroflecting a lot of anger, had low self-esteem and a lack of support in her social environment. However, it was also clear to the counsellor that she was distrustful of the process of counselling, had little awareness of the

---

part she played in her marital relationship and blamed all her friends for being unsupportive.

Jennifer's counsellor decided that she would need to work on building a supportive working alliance, engage Jennifer in an understanding of the dynamics of her relationship with her partner and look at the reasons for her unsupportive social network. Jennifer agreed to the plan. Over the first few weeks she became increasingly trusting of the counsellor – starting to talk about how she sometimes provoked her partner and how she demanded that her friends unquestioningly take her side against him. It was only much later that the counsellor (with Jennifer's agreement) decided that she was ready to connect with her retroflected anger and effectively confront her partner and friends in a way that would not just escalate the tension.

In some cases, especially in cases of potential danger, for example suicidal risk or mental illness, the counsellor will need to decide how to prioritize the treatment sequences. This is particularly true when working with clients who have fragile self-process or who have survived sexual abuse. In these situations, the overriding initial treatment strategy is usually to provide a supportive and containing relationship before starting to work more intensively. There are several impressive examples of this kind of prioritizing in the Gestalt literature. Shub (1992) offers a useful 'longitudinal model' of Gestalt therapy consisting of initial, mid and latter phases. Melnick and Nevis (1997) offer a diagnosis and treatment system using the cycle of experience; Clemmens (2005) proposes developmental stages and tasks involved in long-term recovery from addiction; Delisle (1999) describes strategies and sequences for working with personality disorders; Kepner (1995) outlines a 'Healing Tasks Hologram' that can be employed to guide the counsellor in working with childhood abuse; Brownell (2005) describes treatment planning sequences in mental health issues.

TREATMENT PHASES

The unique nature of each person, his or her therapeutic journey and the relationship made with the therapist preclude any *general* treatment plan to be followed by *all* clients. However, we have found that most clients' therapeutic journeys seem to have common areas of focus and some universal needs or tasks in terms of growth. The following guide is intended to help you organize your thinking rather than be a commitment to linear progression. It can also be used as a guide to check any areas you may have overlooked. (We will be discussing ways of working in these areas throughout the book.) The order in which these phases and areas of focus appear and are addressed can vary greatly, although in a broad sense, the more complex tasks of the later phases build on the earlier more fundamental ones. Many of the tasks, of course, are addressed, reworked or integrated in all of the phases. We have chosen to divide the tasks into five phases. The first phase is seen from the point of view of the counsellor's tasks; the client's task at that stage is just to turn up! The other phases are described as the client's role in his own journey.

The beginning — phase one

In many ways this phase contains the essential conditions for Gestalt therapy. A Gestalt therapist uses the phenomenological method to raise awareness, offers a dialogic relationship, promotes healthy functioning and encourages the development of self and environmental support. With some clients this will be enough to reactivate healthy process and allow the resolution of the presenting issues. This may be ideal for a short-term intervention. If, however, the client has the option and chooses to continue, these conditions and the relevant skills and techniques will continue to be needed in some form or another throughout the whole of the therapy journey.

PHASE ONE

- Creating a safe container for therapeutic work.
- Developing the working alliance.
- Using phenomenological inquiry.
- Raising awareness and self responsibility.
- Offering a dialogic relationship.
- Increasing self support, especially with clients who have fragile self-process.
- Identifying and clarifying needs and emerging themes.
- Prioritizing the diagnostic features.
- Considering cultural and other issues of potential difference.
- Planning for special conditions (for example, self harm, sexual abuse, personality disorders).
- Co-creating the treatment plan.

Clearing the ground — phase two

This phase moves into more specific strategy and often more directive interventions. It assumes a good enough therapeutic relationship with enough support to allow challenge and experimentation with new perspectives and behaviours. It is more relevant for clients with complex or long-standing problems for whom the basic conditions above have not proved sufficient.

PHASE TWO

- Exploring introjects and modifications to contact.
- Addressing unfinished business.
- Supporting self-expression.
- Experimentation with new behaviour and expanding options.
- Engaging increasingly in a more mutual dialogic relationship.

The existential encounter — phase three

This is the phase where the client may have worked through many of her issues and made some useful changes but has reached a deeply stuck place or impasse. In many ways, it can be the most difficult and the most rewarding part of the journey. It is here that you will need to depend on a strong working alliance, as at times the client may feel discouraged, rejecting, and unsure if she is willing to face the heightened anxiety of the impasse. It is a time of strong and sometimes primitive emotions. The client may contact powerful, disturbing polarities and you will need to be very well supported in your own supervision and therapy. The client may potentially face what feels like a life-threatening situation or at least one that seems hopeless or full of despair. This is a time when some clients need to make a profound decision about whether to work through this or whether to be satisfied with what they have already achieved.

PHASE THREE

- Facing the void or the unknown; trusting in organismic self-organization.
- Re-owning lost or alienated parts.
- Making an existential decision to live and move on.
- Systematic and persistent work around destructuring self-limiting core beliefs, negative life themes and script beliefs.
- Choosing to live with courage in the face of uncertainty.
- Connecting with spiritual meaning.
- Experiencing a developmentally reparative relationship.

Integration — phase four

The client by this stage may have successfully negotiated the crises above and is in the territory of integration. We wish to remind the reader at this point to remember what we said at the start about the limits of this type of linear theoretical structure. Clients will ideally integrate and assimilate naturally as the work progresses. However, at other times they will need to do this consciously and deliberately. The assimilation may then reveal other issues or problems, which will have to be worked through.

PHASE FOUR

◆ Re-organizing in the light of new insights and understanding.
◆ Focusing on improving relational contact.
◆ Connecting to the larger field of community and society.
◆ Accepting the uncertainty and anxiety that can come with newness.
◆ Accepting responsibility for living choicefully.

Ending — phase five

This most important phase is covered in depth in Chapter 17. We simply list the tasks here.

PHASE FIVE

◆ Grieving in anticipation of the loss of relationship.
◆ Allowing re-cycling of issues.
◆ Celebrating what has been achieved.
◆ Accepting what has not been achieved.
◆ Anticipating and planning for future crises.
◆ Letting go and moving on.

CONCLUSION

Phase one and, to a lesser extent, phase two, are often sufficient for clients with good self-support in a temporary crisis, clients seeking self-understanding and personal development or counselling for specific life crises and brief therapy. Phase two is more relevant for relationship problems and difficult bereavement. Phase three is the territory for issues of trauma, personality structure, spiritual crises or crises of meaning. Phase four is the stage of integration, one which will ideally follow every major change.

We suggested in the section on diagnosis that it should be held lightly, and adjusted frequently with the co-operation of the client. This willingness to contain the polarities of structure and flexibility is at the heart of ethical strategy for practice.

RECOMMENDED READING

Benjamin, L. (2003) *Interpersonal Diagnosis and Treatment of Personality Disorders,* 2nd edn. London: Guilford Press.

Delisle, G. (1999) *Personality Disorders: A Gestalt Therapy Perspective.* Cleveland, OH: Gestalt Institute of Cleveland Press.

Greenberg, E. (2002) 'Love, admiration, or safety: a system of Gestalt diagnosis of borderline, narcissistic, and schizoid adaptations', *Gestalt!* 6 (3) (Winter), http://www.g-gej.org/6-3/diagnosis.html

Kepner, J.I. (1995) *Healing Tasks in Psychotherapy.* San Francisco, CA: Jossey- Bass.

Korb, M.P. (1984) 'Therapeutic steps and processes in maturation', *Gestalt Journal,* 7 (2): 43–59.

Melnick, J. and Nevis, S. (1997) 'Gestalt diagnosis and DSM–IV', *British Gestalt Journal,* 6 (2): 97–106.

Nevis, E.C. (1992) *Gestalt Therapy: Perspectives and Applications.* New York: G.I.C. Press. (**See Chapters 2 and 3.**)

Sperry, L. (2003) *Handbook of Diagnosis and Treatment of the Personality Disorders.* New York: Brunner-Mazel.

Woldt, A.L. and Toman, S.M. (eds) (2005) *Gestalt Therapy – History, Theory and Practice.* Thousand Oaks, CA: Sage. (**See Part II – Gestalt Applications with Specific Populations.**)

7

STRENGTHENING
SUPPORT

This chapter will look at the concept of 'support' both for the client and, equally importantly, for the counsellor. Support is a key Gestalt concept and the necessary basis of all healthy functioning. Part of the counsellor's job is to help identify the various aspects of support in the client's life in order to discover what is missing, underused or overused.

The act of walking is only possible if there are strong enough muscles and bones, a supply of energy, an ability to balance, the capacity to monitor and adjust the step to accommodate changing terrain, and so on. All of these functions could be said to be the necessary 'support' for walking. A dysfunction in any one of them (such as dizziness or a twisted ankle) leads to an inability to walk effectively or comfortably. A similar process is true in the psychological realm. Healthy self-process, clear energetic figures and satisfying contact are only possible with the support of both self and resources of the field. The strength of the support in any situation depends on the use and relationship between these resources. Healthy support is a position of *interdependence* where the person *is supported in his situation*. The issue is not whether the person is self-supported *or* environmentally supported, but rather, how he can co-operate with his environment or community for mutual support, balancing his own needs with consideration of the needs of others.

> **Suggestion:** Remember the last time you were in a crisis, for example in a personal relationship, ill health or stress at work. What helped you through the difficulty? What was missing? What support did you receive from others or would you have ideally wanted from others? How did you/could you have best supported yourself?

In developing the overall support of a client there are many areas of possible focus. They can cover the territory of body process, attitudes or beliefs, relational patterns, employment, self-care activities, spiritual practice, community resources and general field conditions Many of these will become apparent at assessment and can become part of an ongoing treatment plan. However we will focus here on two major categories.

SELF-PROCESS

Working with physical process

Perhaps the most fundamental area of support is the ways in which a client relates to his body process in the here and now. For instance, he can be invited to pay attention to his breathing and to notice which ways of breathing (speed and depth) are most supportive to him and which help him to feel calm and stable (see suggestions in Chapter 19). He can notice his posture – the way he stands, sits and moves – and experience the difference to his inner feelings that can be brought about by, for example, sitting straight up rather than hunched or slumped.

EXAMPLE

Alex significantly lacked support in many areas. Physically his breathing was shallow; his posture was rigid and tense. His relational support was also low; he had no real friends or confidants. After some negotiation, the counsellor decided to prioritize focusing on increasing the support of body process. She suggested that he experiment with different types of breath and body position as they talked. Alex soon found that when he allowed himself to breathe freely and sit relaxed and supported by the chair he felt much more free to express himself and felt more confident with the counsellor. She noticed that Alex's voice became quieter when he lost energy and was able to use this as a guide to alert him when he was losing touch with his energetic support.

Using the language of self-responsibility

In discussing self-responsibility, we are aware of the apparent contradiction with the notion of mutuality – the constant shaping and being shaped that is the inevitable consequence of being in the world with other people. There is a very real way in which we are indeed 'made' to feel or be the way we are. However, in our view, this relational truth should not interfere with the equally important view that the individual can take authorship of his life. He can push back the self-limiting boundaries of his potential, can become more aware of the influences upon him, and own his experience with authenticity and integrity. A valuable gauge of our subjective experience is the way we use language. So much of the time, the language we use reflects a passive attitude to life, a belief that we have no power over what happens to us, that we are not in charge of our lives. When we are very young or otherwise genuinely in the power of another person, or when we are physically hurt or coerced, our responses can be said to be caused by the 'outside'. However, we sometimes act as if we were permanently powerless over our internal world. We say things like 'You made me lose my temper . . .' instead of owning our own experience and acknowledging that we have responsibility for our responses by saying, 'I felt furious when you did that.' We also use expressions that deny our choice or power over our environment. We say 'It happened', 'The plate broke', rather than 'I broke the plate', and 'I can't' instead of 'I choose not to.' We encourage powerlessness by exaggerated (or understated) words such as 'It was an absolute disaster', 'I would die if that happened', and so on.

A counsellor can invite the client, first of all, to be aware of his use of language or his choice of words and can then suggest experiments using the language of self-responsibility and notice the difference it makes to how he feels about himself and his attitude towards the world. This is not trivial word-play. It can be extremely significant in both the definition and the resolution of a problem. When a client uses a sentence like 'I want life to be worth living' he puts all the responsibility for that outside of himself. The counsellor can invite him to think about the times when life *does* feel worth living and what he is contributing to the situation. Alternatively, some clients inappropriately take too much responsibility for a situation: 'I couldn't possibly say no to my friend, she'd be crushed', or 'I would feel so guilty asking for help, she's got so much to do.' Then the counsellor's job may be to invite the client to reflect on whether he is really responsible for the fragility of a person's feelings, or whether he is taking on too much. 'Has anyone ever been actually "crushed" by your saying no to them?' or 'What does "crushed" mean? What would really happen?' can be surprisingly powerful confrontations.

Suggestions about using different forms of language are *experiments* that invite a client to be aware of how his language both influences and contributes to his attitude to himself and his relationships in the world. They are not instructions for a superior way of speaking. Indeed, it is often quite disheartening to see Gestalt clients or trainees who have been trained to speak 'correctly' but have not changed their underlying attitudes.

Suggestion: Think of an event that has left you feeling disturbed in some way. Experiment with telling the story of the event first in passive language (for example: 'My friend turned up late again. Suddenly the thought struck me that she was making me feel powerless with her unpredictability and that it was getting me down'). Then tell the story again, this time paying attention to your language and taking responsibility for your experiences (for example: 'My friend turned up late again. Suddenly I realized that I was feeling powerless in the face of her unpredictability and I didn't like it.') Notice any difference in your sense of self-agency and self-esteem as you do so, as well as any ways in which you had been discounting your ability to feel differently.

Identifying with your own experience

Resnick (1990) proposed that identifying with your own experience is the best support for self-process. This means accepting who you are, with the experience you are having at that moment. He was highlighting how destabilizing it is if we have to put energy into denying or avoiding our experience or into hiding it from others. If we believe, for example, that we 'shouldn't' feel angry, hurt, envious, competitive, then we will often shut down our awareness of those feelings and in doing so lose awareness of other resources.

As the counsellor practises the phenomenological method and offers a dialogic relationship, she will also be modelling a focus and acceptance of present experience and will be encouraging such identifying. However, a more proactive approach is to practise *owning* with acceptance – even suggesting the client say to himself, 'I am anxious/jealous/hurt, etc. *and this is my experience right now*.' It is astonishing how often clients (and ourselves) preface feelings or experience with denying qualifiers, criticisms, minimizers and deflections. We say: 'I mustn't be anxious/angry . . .', 'I really shouldn't be scared/upset about this', 'Oh well, I expect I'll get over it', 'I know it's silly but . . .', 'I love her dearly but...'

Supportive self-dialogue

Another way of increasing essential support is to help a client to identify some of the negative messages he says to himself, and design some positive and encouraging sentences to use instead. This can be illustrated most easily in an example.

EXAMPLE

Alyssa identified that whenever she made even a small mistake she would say to herself 'Oh I'm so stupid. I can never get anything right.' She realized that this thought accompanied a feeling of anxiety and a tensing of muscles in her solar plexus. The counsellor asked her to think about the truth of the matter. Was she stupid? Most certainly not. Alyssa actually had two university degrees and worked successfully as organization consultant. Did she sometimes get things right? She did. She very often – in fact usually – achieved what she set out to do. So together Alyssa and her counsellor worked out a sentence that was truthful and soothing which would help to restore Alyssa's supportive self-process. It would not have been effective to simply choose an opposite thought like 'I'm a genius. I can do anything.' Alyssa would have known that it was not true. It needed to be a sentence that brought her back to here and now reality. Alyssa chose 'I am very intelligent. I often do well at things, and sometimes I make mistakes.'

Suggestion: Remember an interaction with someone where you ended up feeling bad. Allow yourself to relive the scene – where were you, what happened, who said what, what else was going on? At the end, when you were feeling bad, what did you say to yourself, about yourself, about the other person, or people, or about life? Is this a familiar thought? If it is, come out of the scene and think about that belief realistically. The chances are that it is a self-limiting thought that is not true – or not totally true. Work out a more affirming thought that challenges your self-limiting one. Make sure your affirming statement is realistic. For example, if you said to yourself 'I couldn't possibly confront that colleague', you might choose the statement 'It is hard to confront colleagues sometimes, but I have the ability and strength to do it if I choose to.' Invent the sentence that is right for you. In your imagination, re-enter the scene and say it to yourself.

The evoked companion

We borrow Stern's (1985) wonderful phrase to describe the strategy of imagining a supportive person at a time of stress. This imagined companion could be a friend, partner, therapist, relative, or it could be someone remembered from childhood. The person is chosen for their needed qualities – lovingness, compassion or perhaps advocacy or fighting spirit – and is summoned to offer internal support when the client feels the need. This idea can be offered and practised initially as an experiment in the session to find the most supportive image. The therapy itself can provide this sort of support and many clients carry around an 'internalized counsellor' to whom they can talk in their imagination or remember as warm and encouraging. We sometimes suggest that, during holidays or periods of great difficulty, that clients set aside some quiet time to be alone and imagine being in a session, write a letter to us (perhaps to be brought the next time we meet), take a 'transitional' object from the therapy room, or give them an encouraging phrase or affirmation to remember. This can be a valuable support in times of stress and separation.

Suggestion: Who in your life have you experienced as loving and supportive, as a model to you or even as an inspiration? Think about him or her and the qualities that you have needed or admired in them. Now return to the difficult scene you were remembering in the last exercise. Imagine your supportive companion being with you at the time. What would he or she say to you?

DEVELOPING RELATIONAL SUPPORT

At the simplest level, the counsellor can encourage the client to consider how he uses available supports such as a partner, family or friends. If his therapeutic journey stirs up difficult emotions, are there people he can call upon? Does he know what other resources there are in his community? This will be a rich source of information and will bring to the surface many of his underlying beliefs about the world and his relationship to it. It may be that he is completely unaccustomed to asking for support and this whole issue will need to be explored in the sessions. He may also have many introjects or beliefs about not deserving or allowing support (often found in male cultures).

Sometimes, a therapist can be so involved in the rich dynamics of the therapy room that he can forget to pay attention to the influence of field conditions. It is important to remember that according to Asay and Lambert (1999) a full 40 per cent of positive therapeutic outcome is due to factors outside the therapy room, such as supportive family, friends, church, community, nourishing pastimes, and so on.

> **Suggestion:** On a sheet of paper, make a map of your support networks (you can also suggest this exercise to a client). Place yourself in the middle and then write or draw in the people or things in your life that nourish you. Use post-it notes or objects for each person, group or activity and place them near or far from you in relation to the intensity of their support. Then draw a chart that maps the amount of time per week you spend alone or working and how much with these friends, family or activities. Do the proportions seem right to you? What changes could you make that would increase your use of the resources?

Therapist as supportive presence

One of the most obvious relational supports is of course the counsellor! In a way, almost everything we discuss in this book is directly or indirectly involved with increasing the support of the client. This is especially true of Chapter 1 and Chapter 4, where we discussed the support provided by therapeutic boundaries, the working alliance and the dialogic attitude of the therapist. In a sense all therapeutic interventions should be supportive.

The role of challenge

However, support is by no means always comforting. There are times when the therapist needs to support by confronting or challenging fixed gestalts. It is not uncommon for new clients to use the therapeutic environment in a way that the therapist believes to be unhelpful – for example, becoming overly dependent or excessively asking for advice. In these situations, the therapist may decide to refuse what she sees as an inappropriate demand that in effect will prevent the client from reaching support for his own self-process. The subtle therapeutic dilemma of when to offer support or help and when to confront or challenge runs throughout all Gestalt therapeutic work.

EXAMPLE

The therapist had noticed how Beverley agreed readily with everything he said or suggested. She started to tremble and fidget as they talked about the idea of exploring her presenting issue of sexual abuse. The therapist knew that it was vital that the therapy not feel like a repeat of the abuse and stopped the exploration. Gently, he invited her to say what was going on for her right now and Beverley was able to say that she had not wanted to talk about the incident but didn't like to say so. As they talked she recognized her old pattern of pleasing adaptation. The therapist set up a light-hearted experiment. First, he pointed to a picture on the wall and said he liked it. Beverley agreed. Then he asked Beverley to name something in the room that she did not like. Beverley chose a lumpy chair. The therapist said he liked it – and Beverley immediately looked uncomfortable. The therapist asked Beverley to experiment with disagreeing and saying she disliked all the things the therapist indicated. They went round the room, the therapist indicating a picture, an ornament or a piece of furniture and expressing increasing levels of enthusiasm for them. Beverley – tentative at first – soon began to enjoy the game and began to articulate a variety of ways of disagreeing and expressing dislike: 'I couldn't disagree more . . . I feel completely different . . . No, I don't like that . . . No, I wouldn't want to sit there.' She began to laugh, she sat up straight and her voice took on a strength that was wholly new. At last she said: 'I take the point. I will stick up for myself in future.' There was a pause and she added wonderingly to the therapist, 'Do you know, I think that's the first time I've ever said some of those things.'

MAINTAINING COUNSELLOR SUPPORT

If you are to be an effective and competent counsellor, you need to pay attention to your own working conditions, satisfaction levels and supportive activities. We suggest the following:

◆ Have regular supervision.
◆ Know when to go for personal therapy.
◆ Have regular contact with professional colleagues through peer support groups, etc.
◆ Maintain ongoing professional development, for example attending conferences, workshops and discussion groups (reading excellent Gestalt skills books!).
◆ Maintain a balanced case-load with clients of sufficient difficulty to keep you at your growing edge without the danger of burn-out.
◆ Keep case notes and carry out reviews of each case on a regular basis to monitor your own effectiveness and satisfaction.
◆ Seek supportive activities and interests outside of the therapy world.

In addition to the above you may need to consider how to support yourself after a particularly difficult or distressing session, especially if it falls in the middle of a busy day. For one counsellor, this may be phoning a colleague or supervisor, taking a brief walk, practising a grounding or meditative exercise or remembering the good work she has done in the past. For another counsellor, it might be lighting incense or a candle, opening the window to change the atmosphere or performing a cleansing ritual. In any event your responsibility to your own support is also, in effect, your responsibility to be ready and available for the next client you will see. We suggest you also look at the helpful article on therapist self-care around trauma by Smethurst (2008) in the recommended reading.

RECOMMENDED READING

Jacobs, L. (2006) 'That which enables – support as complex and contextually emergent,' *British Gestalt Journal,* 15 (2): 10–19.

Korb, M.P., Gorrell, J. and Van De Riet, V. (1995) *Gestalt Therapy: Practice and Theory,* 2nd edn. (**See Chapter 3.**) New York: Pergamon Press.

Mackewn, J. (1997) *Developing Gestalt Counselling.* London: Sage. (**See Chapters 25 and 27.**)

Perls, L.P. (1992) *Living at the Boundary.* Highland, NY: Gestalt Journal Press.

Smethurst, P. (2008) 'The impact of trauma – primary and secondary: how do we look after ourselves?' *British Journal of Psychotherapy Integration,* 5 (1): 39–47.

8

SHAME

Shame is experienced as a feeling of being fundamentally unacceptable, unworthy or defective, which leads to a desperate urge to hide or disappear. Over time the sense of shame can become so embedded that it passes out of awareness and only shows up as an extreme reaction to criticism or judgement (and also sometimes to praise or admiration). When it is triggered in the session, the therapist often has a sense of the person shrinking from contact or having a disproportionately strong negative response to an intervention.

It is important to distinguish the difference between shame and guilt reactions: guilt is about *what you have done*, it is conditional (and restitution is possible), whereas shame at worst is about *who you are*, is unconditional (and feels unchangeable).

The dynamic of shame is about reception and acceptability, our basic connectedness in any particular situation. It is a relational process where the shame is a co-creation (rather than a deficiency or lack of resilience in the individual). This is a significant theoretical reorientation in Gestalt, which historically prioritized personal autonomy and located shame as a problem or weakness in the individual. Wheeler and others (e.g. Lee and Wheeler, 1996) led a reorientation to seeing shame and support as interrelated aspects within the relational field; both are ways of regulating contact, moving towards what is needed or retreating from being rejected. Although support is usually seen as good and shame as bad, in certain field conditions too much support can be disabling and too little shame can be unhelpful. Support in the field, for example, allows people to accept and be accepted, live authentically and risk change. Shame allows people to avoid or protect against situations that provide insufficient support and could be dangerous. It is thus a regulator or modification to contact and is always relative to particular field conditions.

THE ORIGINS OF SHAME

Shame is normally learned early in childhood. It arises when we have a desire, reach out energetically and then are ignored, rejected, criticized or told we are bad for doing or wanting whatever it is; our impulse has caused the loved parent to withdraw, abandon or seem hurt or injured. This rejection, if consistent enough, is experienced as a deeply painful feeling of shame. And yet, the child exists in a social world where it is necessary to learn and conform to the rules of social interaction in order to be an accepted part of the community (at least until he is old enough to realistically rebel).

The early process of socialization is partly through parental education. We are told the rules of social engagement – and we also feel the impact of disapproving responses to our actions (e.g. the disappointment of our parents – see Lee, 2007). Therefore, an appreciation of when an action or need will be inappropriate, or disapproved of, is a crucial necessity in social relations. In this case, the feeling of shame is a signal of a boundary. The crucial characteristic of this 'healthy shame' is that it is short-lived, associated with *appropriate* 'disapproval' and is followed by forgiveness and re-connection.

This socialization process is also carried out at the community and societal level. The amount of disapproval and the social punishment for transgression is different in different societies (so-called cultural shame). For example, in traditionally 'polite societies' (such as England and Japan), there is high disapproval for breaking social norms and sometimes severe penalties (in Japan, for example, 'loss of face' can still be so humiliating that suicide is an option). The early learning process about social acceptability leads to the phenomenon of shyness, embarrassment or shame as a necessary regulator of social relations (and therefore a modification to contact).

However, the socialization process can become so rigid and toxic that it becomes a crippling fixed gestalt. Many child-rearing, educational and religious systems actively encourage shame and label it as a realistic assessment of the individual. 'You should be ashamed of yourself' (rather than 'You have behaved inappropriately'). It implies that the child should believe that she is somehow bad or fundamentally flawed.

SHAME-BINDS

For some clients, shame seems to be so fundamentally embedded that it emerges regularly in the therapeutic relationship. This is caused by what Lee and Wheeler (1996) call 'shame-binds' that were created in a person's earliest relationships. When the young child energetically expressed a need or reached out excitedly to the environment, his caretakers responded dismissively, scornfully or even aggressively, and subsequently offered no relational reconnection, understanding or forgiveness. Repeated responses like these led him to believe that 'my crying makes people angry', or 'my excitement is too much', or 'my anger leads to being abandoned', or simply to 'I am too much.' These aspects of his self-expression or need were incorporated into a core belief that they were unacceptable in all circumstances. The feeling of shame then became inextricably linked with the original felt need. As Mackewn says:

> A permanent linkage is made between shame and the unacceptable need, with consequent loss of access to the need. The need loses its voice. The shame-linked need does not disappear. Any time it emerges unawares, the person experiences shame, both in order to continue to experience the need as 'not-me' and in order to continue to live in harmony with an environment perceived as not supporting the need. (1997: 247)

In toxic families or cultures, these regulatory mechanisms become so fixed and rigid that the person has an almost continual sense of shame about their impulses. This is what Kaufman (1989) originally called 'internalized shame' and what Lee (2007) calls 'ground shame' – the relational ground to every emerging relational figure.

So what is essentially a necessary and useful process for regulating social interactions and abiding by the rules of social contact, at best takes the form of tentativeness, embarrassment or transitory shame. But when it becomes a toxic fixed gestalt it leads to shame as an unhealthy unconditional expectation of non-acceptance and disapproval. The person can now have an automatic shame reaction to the merest stirring of his own desires or relational needs.

SHAME AS AN EMBODIED EXPERIENCE

Infant observation now clearly shows (e.g. Schore, 2003) that shame originates in the interactional field of infancy largely through non-verbal interpersonal exchanges. We also know from research into mirror neurons that there can be a direct neurological resonance that echoes the feeling of another (see Staemmler, 2007). The infant can and does vicariously experience, for example, the mother's disappointment or disapproval and the abused child the (usually disowned) shame of her abuser.

In the young child's life, the majority of relational interactions are non-verbal and somatic. If the primary care-giver is sufficiently rejecting, hostile or neglectful, the child often forms a non-verbal sense that they are not worthy of care, are deficient or even disgusting. Shame can then be triggered by a look or gesture or a bodily movement from the therapist that was typical of the rejecting care-taker. Such somatic triggers can then be missed (and cause confusion to the therapist) especially in therapeutic interactions which appear to be mainly verbal or cognitive.

> **Suggestion:** Remember a time you felt shame, describe to yourself the circumstances, the relationships and what triggered it. See if you can identify your bodily response, the tension patterns, the shape your body is moving towards. Now see if you can hear the messages you are telling yourself ('I should disappear'). Get a feel of your response to the other people and your projection of what they are thinking or feeling. Is your desire to vanish or to attack? Ask yourself what is at stake here for you? When you have completed this exploration, return to the present and make sure to support yourself in some way.

WORKING WITH SHAME IN THE THERAPEUTIC RELATIONSHIP

Jacobs (1996) outlines the particular dangers of shame in the relational field of the counsellor and client. The unequal power relationship, the transferential possibilities, the relative vulnerability of the client and the unaware defences of the therapist against her own shame, all conspire to make shame a strong possibility. The experience of shame is normally accompanied by a sense of isolation and abandonment in the client – even abandonment by himself. The overall task is to re-establish both internal and environmental relational support that has been lost. We suggest below several important ways of working.

Identify the relational trigger

Shame is always co-created, and when it becomes evident in the therapy, it can be seen as a signal of a disruption in the therapeutic relationship and a sign that you may have triggered the shame or not provided enough relational support. The first intervention is to investigate your own contribution to the shame process. This can simply be a question:

> 'What just happened between us?'
> 'Did I do or say something that disturbed you?'
> 'I could imagine you might feel shame in this/that situation.'

or a self-disclosure:

> 'I think I may have made a mistake (missed you) just then.'
> 'I remember an experience I once had where I made a mistake and felt like I wanted the earth to open up and swallow me.' (You are also then modelling not being ashamed of your own shame).

Find a way to stand next to the client

Every human being recognizes the feeling of shame. Yet the experience of it can be extremely isolating. It can be like being under the spotlight and wanting to shrink away from sight. In this situation, Gestalt interventions that highlight the counsellor's separateness – raising awareness, commenting on body posture, noticing the client discomfort – all increase the sense of being more in the gaze of a perceived shaming other. This is a time to focus on inclusion and imagine how you would feel, what you would want in the client's shoes. It is time for finding the understanding or attunement to stand alongside the client as a sensitive companion rather than an observer. Your own embodied response or resonance to the shame of the client can often give you the basis for an intervention:

> 'That's a tough place to be right now', or
> 'Does it feel like you want to curl up and disappear?' or
> 'I really feel that.'

An empathic comment that shares the experience rather than stands back from it can also be very powerful.

EXAMPLE

Wesley relived his feelings as he remembered his father's punishing, rejecting behaviour and began to shrink with shame. The counsellor's voice was full of compassion as he said, 'It's so hard to face that, isn't it?'

Attune to non-verbal cues

It is important to develop a sensitivity to the signs of the start of shame. Many shame reactions originate in a time period when the client was too young to articulate or understand the shaming process and will only be able to express it non-verbally. The client may show signs of embarrassment, a shrinking body reaction, a change in skin tone, a frozen quietness, and you sense that they have disappeared. This will enable you to react faster and lessen the chances of making it worse.

EXAMPLE

After the counsellor had commented on the way she kept pulling at her sleeve, Molly's energy dropped. She lowered her head and looked uncomfortable. The counsellor said, 'I think you didn't like what I just said. Did it feel as if I was "getting at you?"' Molly answered, 'I just feel stupid', but she looked up as if slightly surprised that he seemed to be 'blaming' himself rather than her. The counsellor invited her to say how she had understood his remark and it was clear from her answer that she felt criticized and humiliated. Then the counsellor said, 'I can really see how that sounded to you. I think I was clumsy. And I feel sad to see how much you hurt when you think you have been seen to make a mistake.'

(Note: In this way he hoped to achieve four things. First, he owned his own contribution to Molly's discomfort, thus validating it within the co-created relationship. Second, he clarified and empathized with her feeling. Third, he raised Molly's awareness to how seriously his making that mistake could affect her self-support. Fourth, he modelled accepting his mistake and staying self-supported.)

Identify the feeling for what it is

The nature of shame is such that the process is frequently out of awareness. What is often simply a situation-specific rupture in a relationship is seen and experienced as a complete invalidation of all of the person – of *who they are*; a confirmation of their complete worthlessness or badness. Part of the therapeutic task can be to help the client to identify that he is experiencing a particular feeling, sometimes called shame, and that it is only one part of who he is. This also models that it is a feeling that can be tolerated, accepted and shared with another human being. As Kepner says, these feelings 'must at least be noticed and articulated so that they become part of the spoken context rather than the unspeakable ground' (1995: 42). The healing then lies in the relational connection.

Accept the self-perception of the client as a starting point

When a client is highly critical of himself, a common temptation for the counsellor is to move into the opposite polarity and try to talk the client out of their shame-based responses – especially when it seems so obvious that they are mistaken. Trying to convince a client that they could not be 'totally to blame', were surely not 'the most stupid person in their family', or couldn't have been 'completely unlovable' can itself be re-shaming as, in effect, the counsellor becomes another person who is telling them they are wrong or mistaken.

EXAMPLE

Ro had long suffered from an eating problem she had kept secret. As she came to trust the therapist more and more, she gradually revealed her savage self-image, that she was ugly, fat and stupid. The therapist was able to remain creatively indifferent and curious, asking to hear more about the detail and degree of the attributes. Ro appeared to relax considerably as she told more and more of how she saw herself. She eventually stopped and said that it was the first time that someone had just listened without trying to persuade her she wasn't stupid, fat and ugly. She felt accepted and relieved to be understood. In subsequent sessions she reported that she still felt some relief and that she had started to think that although she still believed all those self-judgements, they didn't bother her so much any more.

Recognize the shame behind other emotions

Part of the shame reaction, in contrast to withdrawal, can be rage or fury at the counsellor. Although it is more difficult to bear for some counsellors, in some ways it is a more healthy reaction to a perceived threat, for at that moment the client is experiencing himself to be under hostile rejection or attack. Common defences against shame can be:

◆ Anger/rage at the therapist for the comment or intervention that has provoked the shame response.
◆ Contempt. An attempt to reallocate shame in the therapist.
◆ Envy. Attention is focused not on the shameful 'weakness' of the client but on envy at the perceived power or competence of the therapist (and a denigrating or undermining of that power).

The danger for the counsellor is of triggering her own shame in response to the criticism or anger. You need to support yourself, and simply hold steady. Avoid the understandable urge to react defensively or apologetically, but try to receive and bear the assault. Keep your interventions short and, where possible, empathic, demonstrating that you are surviving and not retaliating. You will then be in a better place to talk with the client in order to try to make sense of what has happened and own your part in the co-created experience. Just as important, perhaps even more so, is that you will have modelled experiencing shame, yet surviving it without withdrawing or needing to retaliate.

Being too quick to apologize or explain can deprive the client of having their experience and gaining understanding or finding a more adaptive response. In terms of a client who responds with anger or fury, it can be useful to allow them to express their feelings to a resilient, available other. 'Keep going', in response to a verbal attack, or 'I get that, what more can be done now?' or 'What do you need from me now?' (Clemmens, personal communication, 2008).

If the attack is very virulent, it is appropriate to draw a boundary, such as saying, 'I find it very hard to hear you when you are shouting like that.' Or even 'I am going to leave the room if you keep threatening me.'

Work with the body

Shame can often result in a desensitization to body awareness or a flooding of sensation. Body energy shuts down or protectively collapses and somatic self-support is lost. As we say in Chapter 13, the most useful initial support is to encourage steady breathing, bring attention back to body sensation and find a way to be mindful, letting body process be a grounding support for what is being experienced. Of course it is essential for the counsellor to come back to their own body awareness in such moments. A grounded, embodied counsellor, breathing steadily, will model and encourage self-support.

With more resilient clients, you can work on changing body postures, taking up a different position in the room, expressing a fuller assertive energetic response – or experimenting with exaggeration of the physical reactions of shrinking and expanding in the perceived shaming situation.

Experiment with contacting

A strong urge pull to hide accompanies many experiences of shame. Supporting the client to resist this and risk making contact with others, checking out his fears and fantasies, can be enormously healing. This can be especially helpful when the client experiences you as shaming and you actively encourage him to check out your side of what was happening (such as by looking at the expression on your face or by asking for your experience). The result is that the field can suddenly be experienced as much more supportive than the client imagined. However, it is important to find the right level of support. This is an occasion where too much support can be as damaging as too little. Treating the client as if he is made of glass may re-shame him by implying that he is too weak.

Encourage the expression of disgust

Philippson (2004) proposes that shame can be understood as retroflected disgust, a response to being given something that cannot be ejected (for fear of abandonment by or damage to another). The therapeutic task is to create an environment where the client can re-own his capacity for disgust and rejection. We suggest you read Philippson's paper for a detailed account of working in this way.

RECOMMENDED READING

Gillie, M. (2000) 'Shame and bulimia', *British Gestalt Journal*, 9 (2): 98–104.

Greenberg, L.S. and Paivio, S.C. (1997) 'Varieties of shame experience in psychotherapy', *Gestalt Review*, 1 (3): 205–20.

Heiberg, T. (2005) 'Shame and creative adjustment in a multi-cultural society', *British Gestalt Journal,* 14 (2): 118–27.

Kearns, A. and Daintry, P. (2000) 'Shame in the supervisory relationship', *British Gestalt Journal,* 9 (1): 28–38.

Lee, R.G. and Wheeler, G. (eds) (1996) *The Voice of Shame*. San Francisco, CA: Jossey-Bass, for the Gestalt Institute of Cleveland.

Nemirinskiy, O. (2006) 'Dialogue and shame', *International Gestalt Journal,* 29 (2): 83–9.

Philippson, P. (2004) 'The experience of shame', *International Gestalt Journal*, 27 (2): 85–96.

Wheeler, G. (1996) 'Self and shame: a new paradigm for psychotherapy', R.G. Lee and G. Wheeler (eds), *The Voice of Shame*. San Francisco: Jossey Bass.

Wheeler, G. (2002) 'Shame and belonging', *International Gestalt Journal,* 25 (2): 95–120.

Yontef, G. (1993) *Awareness, Dialogue and Process: Essays on Gestalt Therapy.* Highland, NY: Gestalt Journal Press. (**See Chapter 15.**)

9

EXPERIMENTING

She is invited to *act* or *do* something rather than simply talk about it. In that process of enactment, the 'story' about the problem becomes a present event. (Kim and Daniels, 2008: 198)

A good experiment arises naturally from the work. An unexplored theme emerges, a persistent impasse reveals itself, or the client seems to be unable to see different options to a problem. The therapist then offers her creativity, imagination and intuition to find a new possibility for exploration.

THE SEQUENCE OF THE EXPERIMENT

Experiments can be broken down into a series of overlapping stages, which can occur in any order but commonly follow the same sequence:

- Identifying the emerging figure.
- Suggesting an experiment.
- Grading the experiment for 'risk' and challenge.
- Developing the experiment.
- Completing the work.
- Assimilating and integrating the learning.

Identifying the emerging theme or figure

As the client talks you may start to see a theme or figure emerging, especially one which seems unfinished, problematic, repetitive or stuck. The theme may be something small like the way she tenses her body every time she talks about a particular subject, or a certain drop in energy whenever she remembers a particular person. Or it may be a story that always ends in the same way.

EXAMPLE

Beverley was talking about how nothing ever seemed to go right in her life. She felt despondent and hopeless, as if she had no power. As she told this story she frequently referred to situations where her husband criticized her over something she had done and took charge himself. She would intersperse these stories with 'There's nothing I can do.'

At this stage you can see a theme emerging – in this case, the unsatisfactory relationship with Beverley's husband in which a particular example or cameo exemplifies the general problem: 'It seems like your husband is always putting you down.' Alternatively, you may have a strong reaction, image or fantasy. For example, there may be an image you could share with her: 'I have this picture of you being pushed aside as if you were helpless.' In this case you have articulated for the client an emerging figure. The response of the client in terms of increased energy or interest will show you how accurate you have been in highlighting or uncovering something that has importance and meaning for her.

Suggesting the experiment

It is difficult to lay down guidelines about when it is appropriate to suggest an experiment. On the one hand, an experiment can free up an interrupted process or introduce the client to new options. On the other hand, it can be used as a deflection from the discomfort of 'what is' by going straight to action, or as a way of ignoring an issue in the relationship between therapist and client. Most Gestaltists seem to trust their intuition at this point, their sense that something else is needed, some new input of their energy. Often a simple experiment of heightening awareness (such as with the sort of intervention we described in Chapters 2 and 3) is enough to shift the client's energy so that she naturally moves into new ways of being with herself or in the world. However, sometimes the client remains stuck, despite knowing that there is something she wants to be different. Although she has new awareness or insight, she remains fixed within her old paradigm of thinking, feeling and behaving.

In order to make this shift, the client has to face the possible anxiety of new and uncertain explorations. Perls et al. (1989 [1951]) talked about therapy being a 'safe emergency', where the client has enough support and safety to face the risk of change. The first step is to negotiate whether the client is prepared to try something new. When you are offering an experiment for the first time it is useful to make an explicit verbal contract. For example:

'Your relationship with your husband seems very important and difficult for you. I have a suggestion to make about how we could understand this in a new way. It might involve me asking you to try imagining or acting out something you have not tried before. Are you interested in exploring this?'

It is vital that the client knows that she can refuse your suggestion. An experiment conducted by a client who is adapting to her counsellor is not only doomed to failure, it risks repeating and reinforcing old fixed gestalts and self-limiting patterns. The client's power to refuse should be stated explicitly, as in: 'It's fine for you to say no.' This should be combined with careful attention to body signals and other signs of adaptation, such as an over-hasty agreement. This is not to say that the client needs to be feeling *totally* committed; however, her anxiety should clearly be balanced by energy and interest (see 'Grading' below).

With more experienced clients who are familiar with experiments, we would probably only make an implicit contract by saying 'I have a suggestion – are you interested?' 'Do you want to experiment with that?' Despite this more casual approach, it is still important that the client really does understand he has a choice in refusing (even when we are very enthusiastic about our brilliant idea for an experiment!).

Grading

The next step is to find the amount of challenge that will be most productive. What is difficult for one client is easy for the next. The task is to find the level of risk that will create the safe emergency, one in which the client feels stretched but still competent. Too much risk and the client will feel retraumatized or hopeless, too little risk and the client will learn nothing. Each client will have a different sensitivity or risk threshold. Also, different activities will be challenging for different people. Some clients will find it most difficult to move physically, for example, to get out of the chair, whereas others will find it more difficult to express emotions or talk in a loud voice. It is very easy to induce shame in some clients and the therapist needs great awareness at these moments. Even the initial suggestion, 'I would like to suggest an experiment to explore this difficulty', can produce unproductive distress or shame. The reaction of the client, both verbally and bodily, to your initial suggestion, will give you some indication of the risk they may perceive.

> 'I would like to suggest that you talk to your husband about his criticism. Could you imagine him in this room with us now sitting in that chair opposite?' Beverley looked nervous at this suggestion but said, 'I think I can do that. I feel scared but I'm prepared to give it a try.'

Had Beverley found this suggestion too difficult we might have negotiated an alternative experiment with a similar process. For example, we might have asked her to remember a real episode where he criticized her and then imagine talking to him in that memory. As the experiment progresses you need to monitor the risk at all times and be prepared to grade the risk up or down, with more or less intensity depending on the changing self-support of the client.

There are several ways you can adjust the level of risk as you make the suggestion – from the least possible challenge of, say, thinking or talking about a new way of behaving, through to putting it into practice outside the consulting room. For example, the following experiments are listed in order of increasing challenge for Beverley:

- Talking *about* how she might act differently in the situation.
- Visualizing the experiment happening in her imagination.
- Telling the therapist out loud how she imagined acting differently.
- Tentatively practising the behaviour in the therapy room.
- Wholeheartedly embodying what emerges in the experiment.
- Practising the new behaviour in the real situation in between sessions.

In addition, there are several ways you can regulate the level of arousal:

- Ask her to stop for a moment and breathe.
- Suggest that she pauses and takes stock of what she is experiencing.
- Remind her that you are there as a support.
- Move closer or further away from her.
- Change the situation. For example, you might say, 'I want you to imagine that your husband cannot speak for the moment and just has to listen to what you have to say.'
- Suggest she imagines someone to support her – 'Can you imagine someone emotionally strong standing next to you?'

The overall rule of thumb is that you should convey a non-judgemental attitude to the experiment and you must avoid being invested in any particular direction. Be prepared to stop, change direction or reverse; there is no *right* outcome. It is exactly what it says – an *experiment* to see what will emerge. The client is being offered the opportunity to *play with* or *try on* a different way of being, *not* to try to reach some particular result.

Developing the experiment

An experiment starts with a simple figure, an image or theme. As the experiment develops, it will take on more form and structure. It is in this phase that the therapist is at her most creative. She responds empathically and intuitively to her client as the experiment unfolds, being ready to offer suggestions where appropriate, being willing to let go of one direction and adopt another as she tracks her client's movement. She uses skills of observation, imagination and her own counter-transference, in addition to the feedback from the client, in assessing the direction of the work and gauging the level of her own involvement.

At this point, we will expand on two of the most widely used methods of Gestalt experiment.

Amplification and moderation

An effective technique for raising awareness is to invite a client to exaggerate *how* they are behaving. The rationale behind this is that our inner experience often shows itself in our body language and behaviour. Thus, a chance gesture such as a frown or a smile, a shrug or a pointing finger, if it is attended to, exaggerated or enacted, can be a powerful indicator of what is on the edge of the client's experience. Equally, the casual use of a verbal expression or the particular tone of voice can reveal feelings that a person may be disallowing or ignoring.

Alternatively, you might find that, far from needing to amplify the energy in his communication, your client avoids his experience with the use of exaggeration or speed. Racing through the communication and using extreme language can both be ways of appearing to be quite expressive while staying out of touch with one's true feelings and thoughts. One client said that she felt so confused that 'my head was literally spinning. I simply couldn't bear it. I thought I would explode.' An experiment was offered to breathe evenly and focus on the tension in her body. As she slowed down, she began to cry. 'I was really scared,' she said, 'and I was angry.'

The empty chair

The 'empty chair' is perhaps the best known of all Gestalt techniques for experimenting. This technique is a way of amplifying what is on the edge of awareness, of exploring polarities, projections and introjections. It offers a voice to the client's experience and is a way of recognizing and re-owning alienated qualities. The empty chair is also excellent for exploring interpersonal dynamics and 'trying on' new behaviour. As this is such a well-used technique, we will explore it in detail.

The 'empty chair' experiment involves, as the name implies, the use of another chair or space in the consulting room – one that is not commonly used by either therapist or client. A very simple form of the empty chair is to invite the client to imagine someone in his current or historical life sitting on the chair. He then talks to him or her, without censoring his words. It is a good way of surfacing all aspects of a situation and bringing them into awareness. It also has the effect of making experience more immediate. The empty chair can be used to give a voice to all the different parts.

The empty chair is also the traditional way of exploring and amplifying the impasse in a 'topdog–underdog' conflict (a metaphor for the internal struggle between a controlling aspect and a subjugated aspect of a person). The 'oughts and shoulds' of the topdog are expressed from one chair and the wants and needs of the underdog are spoken from another. With the support of the therapist, the 'timid' underdog is encouraged to take his power and stand up to the bullying of the introjected topdog. A useful outcome is a mutual softening of the two positions – each one acknowledging the usefulness of the other; in this way, he can discover, own and reconcile conflicting parts of his experience.

At the beginning of therapy, when the client is unfamiliar with this sort of imaginative work, it is especially important to spend time setting the scene and engaging the client's energy and interest in the experiment. In any case, when setting up an experiment, for example a role-play involving talking to another person, allow the client to choose as much of the imagery as possible. A typical induction might be as follows:

'If you were to imagine your husband in the room, where would he be? Would he be standing or sitting? How far away from you would he be?' (Note: this helps to create a scenario that is 'realistic' – the distant and unloving husband, for example, would never be sitting in a close threesome with his wife and the therapist. He would, at best, be sitting in a far corner of the room, half turned away, reading a newspaper. It also allows the client to grade the risk straightaway with a person whom she might perceive as threatening.)

'Now close your eyes and imagine what clothes he is wearing, the look on his face, the way he is sitting or standing.' (Note: this can access the most important aspect for the client in relation to the person.) 'Slowly open your eyes and look at him. What do you feel? What do you think? What is he saying to you? Is there anything you want to say to him?' (Note: at this point you will often access the difficulty the client has in this situation. For example 'He is criticizing me', or 'I can't look him in the face.')

You may now need to re-contract and re-grade the experiment. 'Are you interested in finding a way to face your husband without collapsing … How risky would it be to tell him to stop?' The empty chair technique is easy to grade from a very simple here-and-now to a complex, active exploration of parts of self. For example, to a new client the therapist might say:

Therapist:	If he were here now, what would you like to say to him, if you didn't have to watch your words?
Beverley:	I'd tell him I'm absolutely fed up with his constant criticizing. (This might be enough, and therapist and client could continue to *talk about* the client's difficulty with her husband, exploring her feelings in the here-and-now. A slightly 'higher' grade of risk might be:)
T:	So imagine that he is here now – would you be willing to say that straight to him?
Beverley:	Er … Yes. Do you mean …?
T:	It can sometimes be useful to bring the conflicts right into the room here.
Beverley:	OK, I see.
T:	If he were in the room with us now, where do you imagine that he would be?
Beverley:	Oh that's easy – behind that desk – only it would be much bigger and his chair would be higher than mine.
T:	Keep imagining him sitting at that desk – how does he look? [*and so on*] … What do you want to say?
Beverley:	You bastard [*she shouts*], you absolute bastard. Who do you think you are? What do you think I am?
T:	Tell him who you are Beverley.
Beverley:	I'm … I'm Beverley – I'm Beverley … I'm not your … [*Beverley tails off and turns to the therapist*] I was just about to say 'I'm not your special little girl.' I've just realized something. Do you know who he reminds me of?
T:	[*disingenuously!*] Who?

In this example the empty chair was used to heighten Beverley's awareness of how she put her stepfather's face on her somewhat controlling and smothering partner. Another grade of risk might be to have the client express her most vulnerable feelings and wants to the imagined person. Yet another would be to switch chairs and talk from the other position or to involve physical expression such as cathartic release or experimenting with movement.

Caveats

When the opportunity for empty chair work arises (or indeed any experiment of this nature), the therapist has a significant choice to make. Will the client benefit most from engaging in a dialogue with parts of himself or will here-and-now contact with the counsellor in the room be more therapeutic? Clients who make contact easily with other people often benefit from exploring contact with aspects of their selves in the empathic presence of the therapist. As a client talks about a dilemma or a person with whom he is having difficulty, it is clear that the energy for that figure is growing and deepening so that it can feel suddenly as if there is a third person in the room. The shift to dialogue with that third person or part of self is a natural one. There are clients, however, for whom making real contact with another human being is paramount (for example, those who are socially isolated or who are very withdrawn). It is indeed the crux of the healing. For these individuals, a dialogue with themselves can be a further avoidance of contact with the 'real other'. Therapists will notice that the experiment quickly begins to feel empty and uninteresting. The therapist herself feels as if her presence is required simply as an audience or she may even feel irrelevant. In situations such as these, the client will be helped to be in contact with himself in a more real way by staying in contact with the therapist, telling his story, endeavouring to convey his experience to her, seeing and feeling her response, responding to that response … and so on.

There is one other caveat we wish to mention before going on to explore the many options for experiments. If your client's self-process is very fragile (for example, he has a tendency to fragmenting, borderline or dissociative process) it is a good rule of thumb to avoid two-chair dialogue with different parts of self. These clients need the stability of the therapeutic relationship to act as a boundary and container for the work. If they immerse themselves in an inner conflict, the polarities will probably be extreme and the likelihood of integration becomes less rather than more. Empty chair dialogues with these clients should be initially limited to a here-and-now exploration of an interaction with a real person in their lives, where the aim is to practise new ways of communicating or better self-management strategies.

The focus of the experiment

Ideally, as we have said, the experiment will be co-created by the counsellor and client. It will not take a predetermined form. However, we include here a list of ideas that may stimulate your own imagination. They are all vehicles for an experiment. Some clients will find it easier to experiment with visualization, others with kinaesthetic or auditory awareness, others with actions. Bear in mind (and ask) what modalities are available to the client. 'Can you visualize people easily? Can you sense the energy or emotions in your body?' And so on.

Among a wealth of possibilities, there are some general categories of experiment.

Staying at the impasse. Suggesting that the client do nothing can also be a fruitful experiment! Usually clients will try to avoid facing the difficult place by various means (for example, by deflecting or changing the subject). Suggesting that the client stays with his experience of feeling stuck or impotent can be quite profound (see Chapter 3, where we discuss the paradoxical principle of change). Remember the axiom: 'Don't just do something, sit there!'

Directing or raising awareness. Focusing on internal experience, different body positions, noticing sensations in the body or feelings, paying attention to what he is thinking, increasing awareness of tension or relaxation. All raise awareness of physical process and invite the client to notice how his thoughts and feelings are manifested in his body. Encouraging him to examine his inner experiences and name them aloud also raises awareness.

Guided visualizations. The client closes his eyes and explores (with the guidance of the counsellor) some scene from his past that he might change in his imagination or some potential future for himself. The client imagines in as much detail as possible, using all his senses.

Using art materials. The client represents his inner or outer world using crayons, paints, plasticine, etc. Normally, this is carried out on a single large sheet of paper that provides the container and boundary for the experiment.

Using other forms of expression. Use music, voice, dance, drumming, photographs, letter-writing – involve all your client's channels of self-expression.

Reversing, exaggerating or minimizing the habitual response (or inventing a new response). When the client presents a situation where they are stuck, see if you can identify a central quality or attitude such as stubbornness, guilt or perfectionism. Then imagine upon what continuum this quality might fall. For example, what would be the opposite of this quality – the other end of this polarity? Or is this quality in the middle of two possible extremes? Is the client restricting himself to just one position on this continuum? This can lead you into suggestions for widening his repertoire of response. In effect, the options are: do the opposite, do more, do less.

Enactment. There are two types of enactment or role-playing. One is when the client engages in some communication with his image of real people in his life – either historical or current. This is a particularly useful experiment because it provides direct access in the therapy room to co-created situations outside. The other is when the client embodies disowned or marginalized aspects of him or herself that are not in full awareness (see 'The empty chair' above). Here, the client is able to have a dialogue with these different qualities or parts of himself. It is often used in exploring polarities. For example, a client who is habitually kind to everybody and feels exhausted, may be asked to imagine a cruel part of himself, imagine it in the chair opposite to him, and engage it in dialogue. The client can also explore his inner dialogue, listen and give voice to different 'parts' of himself, perhaps arguments or conflicts – often moving seats in order to do so. In short, enactments are useful for completing gestalts (expressing unexpressed feelings and thoughts), clarifying core beliefs or introjects, owning disowned aspects of self and practising new behaviour.

With Beverley we might have simply suggested that she look at her husband and sense where she was tense or collapsed. We might have encouraged her to sit in a different way, look at what she was feeling, see what messages she was telling herself or see if she could get in touch with her courageous energy. We might have suggested she imagine or enact taking the opposite polarity, that she stand up for herself and deny that she had got it wrong and refuse to let him take charge. She might have experimented with telling him that she felt bullied by him or, alternatively, with exaggerating her compliant and helpless position.

Do not forget to include in your repertoire the whole area of the therapist–client relationship. Invite your client to explore the relationship with you. For example, 'Is there anything you have held back from saying to me?' 'Perhaps there is something you didn't like about what I have said or done?' or 'Could you imagine being angry with me?'

Experimentation is the territory in Gestalt therapy where the more experienced practitioner may decide to take the risk of pushing the usual safe therapeutic boundaries. There are many examples in the literature of therapists offering unusual experiments such as going for walks, visiting clients at home, meeting in cafés, teaching them swimming, meeting their mothers, playing games with them – the list is endless. While, as a basic position we err on the side of safe boundaries, we also want to support the anarchic 'rule-breaking' spirit of Gestalt practice. However, if you know that a proposed experiment might be considered very 'risky' by your colleagues, you may want first to discuss it with your supervisor.

Remember that experiments can range from the simple direction of awareness – for example, to 'pay attention to your breathing' – to a complex role-play, involving several historical figures. In the early stages, the therapist will be more active, encouraging, suggesting, and putting in her own energy. In a very real sense, any intervention the therapist makes in therapy is an experiment of some sort. It can be useful to wonder to yourself 'What is missing in this situation? What if I were to change one element? What would make a significant difference. Is there some quality the client never expresses that would make a big difference here?'

However, if the experiment is well designed, the client will gradually take over and often start to make his own adjustments to the direction of the experiment: 'No, there's something else I need to say to him,' or, 'I've just realized something I never knew before.' The therapist then sees an increase in sustained energy, as the experiment seems to take on a life of its own. Although the therapist has an idea of what might be a beneficial outcome, she has only *process* goals, for example that the client expresses appropriate emotion, experiences better support, completes unfinished business, feels satisfied, re-owns alienated parts. The therapist does not have a particular ending in mind or a particular result, she has no *content* goals. That should be entirely in the hands of the client. To emphasize what we said earlier, the therapist needs to embrace the attitude of creative indifference where anything is possible and there is no such thing as a right or wrong outcome.

Completing the work

There will be times (for example in a role-play) when the client suddenly drops out of role and appears to have stopped the experiment. You may need to verbalize at this point, 'You seem to have come out of role/interrupted the process', and check whether he wants to pause, stop, or move in a different direction. However, there will usually be a point when the experiment seems to reach a conclusion. This should generally be when the client shows signs of closure. It could be when he comes out of role, turns to you to reflect on what has happened, gains sudden insight, or when his change of energy shows he has moved to a different place. It is very easy at this point in the experiment for the therapist to be seduced by her own view of a suitable conclusion and encourage the client to continue the experiment. It sometimes takes a lot of discipline to hold to the principle of creative indifference and allow the client to reach whatever end he chooses.

In the light of this, it is impossible to say 'This is the right place to stop', only that an interesting new place has been reached. However, it is always prudent to bring the experiment to a close at least ten minutes before the end of the session, to allow time for re-establishing connection with the counsellor, debriefing, and prepare to leave the session. This can be as simple as a reminder to the client that he has to stop in a moment as the session is almost over, or it may need a more active request that the experiment is temporarily suspended (for example) until another time. The counsellor will sometimes need to be sensitive and creative in finding ways to help the client to close down the experiment and return to the present relationship.

EXAMPLE

Beverley was enacting a heated argument with her imagined husband and was trembling with emotion. The counsellor realized there were only fifteen minutes of the session left and decided to interrupt. He told Beverley that the session was coming to a close and she needed to find a way to end this confrontation for the time being. He suggested that she tell her husband she was stopping for now but was not finished with him and would return. She imagined sending him to a safe place where he would wait until she next recalled him. The counsellor then asked Beverley to focus on her breathing, pay attention to her contact functions, reorient herself to the room and the presence of the counsellor and check if she needed to do anything more to leave the experiment.

Assimilating and integrating the learning

After the experiment reaches its completion, it is important to make time for a period of assimilation and integration where often the real learning takes place. Here, the client can discuss and make sense of the meaning of what happened both cognitively and in terms of the implications for her life in general. It can also be a profound moment when she sees how much her belief system has limited her choices and possibilities. It may be necessary to plan with the client how to take this new learning into her life. This is where the interdependence between individual and environmental resources becomes key. The new insights, awareness and increased choices will probably need some time before they are integrated fully. Sometimes the client will achieve an obvious 'aha' experience, where she suddenly sees the possibility of a different way of behaving. At other times the experiment will be the first step in an exploration or completion of a larger difficulty or gestalt.

EXAMPLE

After Beverley had expressed her anger, found better self-support and was able to stand up to the image of her husband, she realized that she had always avoided conflict with her stepfather. This led to a new phase in her therapy where she began to explore the historical roots of her current difficulties. Beverley made a decision to behave in a different way outside the therapy room and confront her stepfather about a past event.

If the client interrupts the experiment in the middle, suddenly returning to the present moment, it is still important to debrief. The counsellor should verbalize that the experiment has stopped for the moment and invite the client to be aware of what precipitated the interruption, what significance that might have and what might need to happen at this point in order for her to feel sufficiently completed.

Sometimes after a powerful experiment it is appropriate to allow the work to settle during the week and discuss the learning in the next session. Be careful not to forget this vital assimilation work as it makes all the difference between a simple emotional release and a profound relearning.

RECOMMENDED READING

Brownell, P. (ed.) (2008) *Handbook for Theory, Research and Practice in Gestalt Therapy*. Newcastle: Cambridge Scholars Publishing. (**See Chapter 10 – Experimental freedom.**)

Perls, F. S. (1975) *Legacy from Fritz*. Palo Alto, CA: Science and Behavior Books. (**See Chapter 2.**)

Polster, E. and Polster, M. (1973) *Gestalt Therapy Integrated*. New York: Vintage Books. (**See Chapter 9.**)

Sills, C., Fish, S. and Lapworth, P. (1995) *Gestalt Counselling*. Oxford: Winslow Press. (**See Chapters 12 and 13.**)

Smith, E. (1986) 'Retroflection: the forms of non-enactment', *Gestalt Journal*, 9 (1): 63–4.

Spagnuolo Lobb, M. and Amendt-Lyon, N. (2003) *Creative Licence – the Art of Gestalt Therapy*. Vienna: Springer-Verlag.

Zinker, J. (1977) *The Creative Process in Gestalt Therapy*. New York: Random House.

10

MODIFICATIONS TO CONTACT: Regulating the Relationship

The Gestalt therapist believes that part of psychological health is living in a way that is creative, flexible, satisfying and growthful. This means being in relationship with the world, a process of *contacting,* and the co-created dance of the subsequent 'between'. This contacting or meeting is a continuous process but needs to be regulated or modified according to the field conditions in each unique situation.

Ideally, the process of mutual regulation is ongoing and continually revised as field conditions change. It is easy to understand this if we consider the growing child. As a baby, the natural expression of the organism in distress is to cry out and then wait (and yearn) for attention (increasing the level of demanding cry as time passes). At an older age, the creative adjustment may be to seek out a friend and ask for comfort, putting the distress into words.

Where particular needs are ongoing and repeating, the child inevitably learns ways of meeting and managing the needs, ways which are 'successful enough' and which usually become patterns of response. This is necessary and normal. However, problems arise when the habitual response is not updated for new or changed field conditions. This may be situation-specific or it may become a general style of contact across a range of situations (usually out of awareness), which can pervade all aspects of the person's way of relating in the world. The person is then not free to make new choices or adjustments and repeats the same relational response that was once useful (or at least seemed so at that time). This can be seen sometimes in an abused child who then as an adult avoids all intimate relationships, or in people who always respond to stress by overeating or drinking to excess. Many of the reasons clients seek counselling relate to creative adjustments that were once appropriate but have now become fixed gestalts.

FROM 'INTERRUPTIONS' TO 'MODIFICATIONS'
— A THEORETICAL DEVELOPMENT

In the early days of Gestalt therapy, practitioners began to notice that there were certain common patterns of energetic disruption in the process of contacting. Perls (1947) and Perls et al. (1989 [1951]) described six such patterns: *Retroflection, Confluence, Desensitization, Introjection, Projection, Egotism*. Polster and Polster in 1973 added a seventh: *Deflection*. These disturbances of contact became known as 'interruptions' and were originally seen as a hindrance to full contact and vitality. However, the under-standing of 'interruptions to contact' subsequently underwent a radical revision (e.g. Swanson, 1988; Wheeler, 1991; Mackewn, 1997). This new understanding proposed that in field theoretical terms, no 'interruption' could be considered good or bad, helpful or unhelpful, other than in reference to the meaning and needs of each unique situation. What is more, from a relational perspective, it makes little sense to use the word 'interruption'. That would imply that there is an intended way to be in relationship which could be 'interrupted'.

The term 'modifications to contact' was therefore adopted as a better way to describe a series of processes that are simply creative adjustments to the challenges of being in the world. They are all ways of attempting to manage some aspect of being human and in relationship: the management of aggressive impulses; the reception of stimuli; the regulation of attachment and separateness; the need to make sense of the world, to be authentic and respond to the demands of being in relationship with others. Each person forms useful or not so useful, regulatory or relational patterns in all these areas. A healthy person is able to vary his response depending on each new situation and the issue it evokes.

We see each of the seven commonly identified modifications as occupying one end of a potential continuum with its opposite pole and a multitude of 'shades' in between like the colours on a paint chart. There will be times when each position on the con-tinuum would be appropriate (for example, self-differentiation when there is social pressure to conform or confluence between a mother and newborn baby); and at other times the same position could be unnecessarily rigid and inappropriate depending on the need and context. We would stress, of course, that the client is the final judge of what is appropriate for him in his particular situation.

We offer our perspective of the modifications in Box 10.1. For each continuum we then suggest ways of working with polarities that have become 'hardened dichotomies' (Yontef and Jacobs, 2007). Readers who are familiar with the traditional 'interruptions' will notice that we have removed the term 'egotism' as we believe it is misleading, and replaced it with 'self-monitoring'. We have also endeavoured to use words (verbs, where possible) that reflect the modifications as active processes for reg-ulating contact, not static positions. As a consequence, we have chosen to differentiate 'introjects' as fixed beliefs from the here-and-now process of actively introjecting, for example, where the client uncritically takes in your suggestions or words (of wisdom!). We locate introjects in Chapter 11. You may prefer to identify your own dimensions, or explore the unique polarity of the particular client; the following are offered as suggestions only.

BOX 10.1

Modifications of energy and stimulus:

Retroflecting ·········· Impulsivity
Deflecting ·········· Accepting
Desensitizing ·········· Over-sensitizing

Modifications of interpersonal contact:

Confluence ·········· Differentiating
Introjecting ·········· Rejecting

Modifications of self-process:

Self-monitoring ·········· Spontaneity
Projecting ·········· Owning

GENERAL THERAPEUTIC CONSIDERATIONS

In many situations clients may have little awareness that they are regulating their contact in a particular way or that they have any other choice. Here the therapist's task is to raise the client's awareness and understanding of how they make contact. You may also need to consider what may be missing, what other positions are available on any continuum of polarities, what is 'buried' in the ground structure of the client but not in his awareness. For example, the client may not realize that he deflects from any difficult emotion by changing the subject, or that he tenses his body every time he speaks of his father. He may be unaware of other options for self-expression. You can offer a hypothesis for the client to consider or as something you have noticed and are curious about. 'I'm aware that you clench your fists every time you talk about your father – are you aware that you do this?' or, 'Have you ever considered expressing some of your anger to him?'

It may help to conceptualize the modification as a way of avoiding pain or difficult feelings. Perhaps there was a time when it kept the person safe and helped them survive. Therefore, you may need sometimes to imagine or to empathize with the pain or difficulty of the original situation in order to make sense of the client's style of self-regulating. You may also need to help the client find a new, more creative way to deal with the situation that was formerly managed by this particular fixed gestalt or relational style. This may sometimes be a major focus of therapy as the person struggles to readjust their whole way of relating.

From a relational perspective, understanding the process of a modification must always take into account the fact that it takes place in the context of a mutual influence, and is therefore to a greater or lesser extent a response to the here and now relationship. For example, the client may be deflecting, retroflecting or introjecting as a result of the type of relationship he perceives himself to be in, especially the one he has with the therapist.

We will now examine each polarity individually.

RETROFLECTING ... IMPULSIVITY

A person is said to retroflect when he holds back his impulse to take action (e.g. speech, expression of feeling, behaviour). The energetic flow is interrupted and this can have several outcomes. The withheld impulse may die naturally away. However, if the process is repeated frequently or if the impulse contains strong energy, suppressing it can lead to the energy being turned inwards toward the self. This can lead to bodily tensions, psychosomatic illnesses, impotence, depression or even self-harm.

Intervention suggestions:
◆ Explore what associated beliefs, introjects and early decisions accompany the retroflecting (or impulsivity). It is especially important to find out what the client believes will be the consequences of letting his energy move to action. A retroflection should only be 'undone' when the client and counsellor are both sure that he has enough support and understanding to manage appropriately what is released.
◆ As retroflecting is commonly held in the body, it is useful to focus on body process when working to release it. Invite the client to be aware of where in his body he feels the held energy. You may also invite him to talk from that part of him, to give it a voice. In some circumstances, you may suggest the client breathe 'into' it and practise relaxing.
◆ Enact the retroflecting in the consulting room. This is particularly useful when the client has identified the introject that is often at the heart of a retroflection ('Don't get angry', for example). The client starts to focus on his body, exaggerating the tension and repeating the introject aloud. If and when he feels ready to do so, he can release the tension and direct his energy outwards in the support of the therapy room. (See Chapter 9 on Experimenting.) Remembering that all contact is co-created, you may also invite him to tell you how you may be part of why he is retroflecting at that moment.

The other pole of this continuum is impulsiveness or unrestrained expression. This can be an inappropriate expression of feelings or of acting impulsively in a way that is dangerous to self or others, such as with self-harm or uncontrolled or violent outbursts.

Intervention suggestions:

◆ If the client recognizes that he needs to learn to control his impulsiveness, it can be very useful to help him get into the habit of consciously becoming aware of the stages of the cycle of experience. He needs to pay attention to his sensations and feelings, take an interest in them, acknowledge and recognize them. He can consider what options he has for action, then choose one. By the time he has taken himself through these steps, he will have slowed himself down and got in touch with more appropriate action. The client may find this process very difficult and it will be necessary to experience it over and over again in the consulting room. It can also be modelled for him by the therapist, who frequently invites him to be aware of his sensations, name his feelings and allow full recognition of them while they are emerging and still manageable.

◆ Grounding exercises and techniques described in earlier chapters can also be useful. Clients who are fixed in this pole often experience being taken over by their feelings. They report things like, 'I was pure anger at that moment. I felt as though I would explode.' Grounding and heightening awareness of body boundaries can be containing and calming.

DEFLECTING ... ACCEPTING

Deflecting means ignoring or turning away either an internal stimulus or one from the environment, in order to prevent full recognition or awareness. It is characterized either by blocking the stimulus itself or by turning oneself away and going off at a tangent. Clients often deflect from their feelings and impulses by endless talking, by laughing instead of taking themselves seriously, or by always focusing on the needs of the other. Deflection of the impact of others can be seen in clients who change the subject repeatedly when a particular issue is raised, who appear not to hear or see something, who misunderstand or redefine what has been said or done. Deflection is an active process of avoiding awareness, which means that the client will tend to push away your interventions also when they touch the avoided material. The process can be extraordinarily subtle, and frequently the only clue to it is when the counsellor finds that she is having a conversation about something and she has no idea how she got there!

Intervention suggestions:

◆ Model persistence in keeping to one topic and offering hypotheses as to what might be difficult. 'I guess you might find it hard to talk about being adopted – it would be easy to try to avoid even thinking about it.' At times you will need to gently but forcefully interrupt the deflective process, as, for example, 'I need to stop you for a moment ...', before sharing your observation of what they have been doing or your own reaction to the deflection. 'I am aware that every time I bring up this subject, you change the subject. Have you noticed?' Or you could say,

'I notice that you haven't answered my question and I am wondering whether that's because you are not ready to talk about this.' This, in a sense, gives permission by acknowledging the right of the client to choose not to talk about something, while at the same time raising awareness and reassuring the 'silenced part' of them that it also is important.

We have called the other pole on this continuum 'accepting'. Here, a person is available and open to experience the fullness of the world around him. This sounds like a very positive quality, but it too can create problems if used to excess. We are all bombarded by a myriad of stimuli every day, while our inner and middle zones are a continuous source of sensations, thoughts and feelings. The overly accepting person is too receptive, in contrast to the deflector, and has a tendency to pay too much attention to these stimuli. He finds it difficult to ignore them or to select what is relevant at any one time. He may be over-detailed or confused in his speech and end up being indecisive as he struggles with all the apparently significant material. At worst, this condition can be found in some people with psychotic process who are so unable to be selective about all the stimuli they receive that they lose the ability to form meaningful gestalts, and experience overwhelming confusion.

Intervention suggestions:
◆ Help the client to be more in touch with his inner and middle zones of bodily sensations, feelings and thoughts, to identify what his reactions mean and to name the actions he needs to take.
◆ Help the client to prioritize his experiences. For example, 'What is most important to you now? How do you know that? What else is important?'
◆ Practise grounding exercises that enhance the client's experience of embodiment.
◆ Explore introjects about adapting to others. Gently invite the client to explore what he imagines would happen if he ignored some things or people, missed some details, and so on.
◆ Invite the client to experiment with deliberately taking time out, being quiet, saying to you, 'I need a moment to reflect or gather myself', and, in their life, to refusing invitations or situations that would be too noisy or too stimulating.

DESENSITIZING ... OVER-SENSITIZING

Desensitizing is a process similar to that of deflecting. It is another way of avoiding contact with sensations. However, while deflection is mainly concerned with preventing a stimulus reaching the middle zone of awareness, desensitization concerns a more profound form of shutting down – at the level of the inner zone. A clue for the therapist can often be found in her own phenomenology. Therapists often find themselves feeling sleepy and heavy in the presence of a desensitized client, while the response to a deflecting client is more energized (for example, irritation, frustration or the anxious agitation that is probably the client's unacknowledged feeling).

EXAMPLE

Keiko never notices when she is hungry, or sits throughout the therapy session on the edge of her seat oblivious to her stiffening limbs; Jean-Luc's brother died and he said he felt nothing; Jennifer had been terribly abused but recounted the tale in a voice devoid of any emotion.

Intervention suggestions:
◆ Encourage attention to breathing, bodily sensations, focusing on heightening body awareness, on what they *are* aware of and where their energy is held.
◆ Ask the client to imagine how they *might* feel about the situation or how someone else might react. It might also be relevant to ask them to notice how they have acted or what they have said and then think about how a friend might be feeling if they behaved like that. This can sometimes gently bring them to themselves – certainly to engagement with a desire to find themselves.
◆ Share your own reaction to the situation about which they have desensitized, and offer possible reactions. Check to see how much resonance they have with your response.

As the client resensitizes, however, you may well find you move into unsupported territory. This is especially true when the desensitized material is particularly traumatic. Having brought the out-of-awareness material into view, you need to pay careful attention to the client's ability to support his self-process, otherwise he may then launch straight into the traumatic material without sufficient resources.

The person who experiences the other end of the polarity – over-sensitizing – is acutely aware of here-and-now stimuli, especially from his inner zone of awareness. He is attuned to himself and to the world around him and this can sometimes mean a fine level of congruence and an exquisite ability to empathize. However, at the extreme of the polarity, he can become preoccupied with his own sensations and feelings in a way that seriously disrupts contact with the other. Or, like the over-receiver, he can suffer from an overload of responsiveness and, in the helping professions, suffer from 'compassion fatigue'. On a bodily level, hypersensitivity can manifest as hypochondriasis.

Some people seem to hold both extremes of the continuum at the same time. The person who is hypochondriacal may be hyper-aware of his bodily sensations, for example, yet completely desensitized to his affective and emotional associations, thus noticing symptoms that he cannot explain.

Intervention suggestions:

◆ In many ways, the suggestions are similar to the deflecting client. It is important that the work goes very slowly, giving him time to connect with himself and what his sensations might mean. He needs to learn gradually to accept, tolerate and sometimes give names to the emerging feelings and thoughts. It can sometimes be useful if the therapist offers hypotheses about what the feelings and emotions may be, for example: 'I wonder if you are frightened about that ?' – as long as she is ready to let them go immediately if they do not resonate with the client.

◆ Where the client is hypersensitive to real or imagined criticism, it can be useful to explore what happens to him in these situations. What does he feel? What does he believe about himself and the world? Learning to do some reality testing can be very important for a client who believes that if he is not perfect he is worse than nothing. It is especially important for the therapist to be willing to explore with the client when the process happens between them.

CONFLUENCE ... DIFFERENTIATING

The healthy person can move fluently and appropriately along the continuum between merger (say in a moment of loving sexuality) and differentiation (for example, withdrawal in order to rest after a vigorous disagreement). A fixed position suggests some difficulty with either attachment or separateness. A person who fears that closeness to another person is in some way threatening (of loss, rejection, hurt or abandonment), solves the problem by either merging with the other or psychologically withdrawing.

A client who modifies contact through confluence acts as if either he is a part of the other person in a relationship or that the other person is part of him. Confluence is an inability to distinguish the interpersonal boundary. The feelings and wishes of another easily overwhelm the confluent client, who responds as if they were his own, also often becoming anxious when separation occurs or is threatened.

Intervention suggestions:

◆ Encourage the person to make 'I' statements rather than 'it' or 'we'. You can also model the process by being clear when you yourself say 'I'. For example, you might say 'I feel sad when I listen to you; how do *you* feel?' or 'I am sitting in this chair, you are sitting opposite, do you have any sense of what you want from me right now?'

◆ Look for and emphasize similarities and differences, 'It sounds as if you agreed with/felt the same as … but you also *didn't* agree with/feel the same as …'

◆ Explore and offer empathy for fears of separating, endings and loss. Often this may mean attending to important unfinished business (see Chapter 11) that may at first be out of awareness.

◆ When there is a 'clinical choice point' in the therapeutic process, share your think-ing with the client and offer options about the way forward. Which option does he feel drawn to, or does he have other suggestions? This underlines that not one but *two* people face this problem!

The client whose habitual contact style is over-differentiation is often reluctant to seek therapy. However, sometimes he will come, saying that he feels as if he does not belong in the world, he doesn't seem to get on with people as others do and thinks that he has 'something missing'. He might use a metaphor about himself, such as feeling like an alien, or being trapped in a bubble or behind an invisible wall.

Intervention suggestions:
◆ When working with this habitual style of contact, you might easily feel as if it is hard to connect with the client and nothing is happening in therapy for months on end. You may find that your attempts at inclusion and empathy seem not to 'work'. Be content to spend a long time building a working alliance and offering a gentle dialogic approach.
◆ If he is withdrawn in the session, do not pursue him to tell you 'what's going on'. It is likely to increase his withdrawal. Adopt a position of creative indifference and wait with him in silence, taking care not to fall into a withdrawn non-contact yourself. Practise inclusion (silently). Remain alert and interested. You may choose to offer an invitation occasionally – such as, 'It sounds as if it is important that you see the differences between us and I wonder what it means to you. Or 'It looks as if you need to withdraw right now and I'm fine with waiting/being with you. I just wanted to say that if you would like to talk about what is going on, I would be very interested to hear.'
◆ If your client withdraws during an exchange with you, it is possible (likely!) that it may be a response to you. You could comment that you have noticed him withdraw and wonder aloud if you said or did something from which he then wanted to move away. If he owns his withdrawal and tells you how you contributed to it, be ready to understand his experience and how he feels the need to protect himself. You might ask him what he would need to help him re-engage with you.

SELF-MONITORING ... SPONTANEITY

Healthy self-monitoring is the capacity for self-reflection and reflexivity. It could be called 'self-consciousness' in its best sense. Self-monitoring as a habitual, limiting, rela-tional style is characterized by an excessive preoccupation with one's own thoughts, feelings, behaviours and one's effect on others. This preoccupation can be positive, admiring and self-congratulatory, or alternatively critical and undermining; either way it is an avoidance of real relational contact – with self or with other. The task here is to encourage the client to move away from their self-monitoring and self-reflection into a more immediate contact with you and their environment.

EXAMPLE

Kess frequently interrupted the story of her unhappy week to look intensely out of the window. When the counsellor inquired what was happening, she said that she was thinking how stupid she was, how silly she must sound, how he must be wondering why she hadn't got her act together.

Intervention suggestions:

◆ In the therapy room, notice how the client breaks contact with you in favour of his inner dialogue and invite him back into the here-and-now *with you*. Empathize with his present experience of worrying about himself, the impression he is making or with the need to be perfectly 'right'. Over time, the development of a reliable empathic relationship will provide him with a new relational experience to counter the tendency to keep self-monitoring.

◆ Encourage grounding techniques with a focus on body process and a deliberate attention to the external environment (following the traditional Gestalt maxim to 'lose your mind and come to your senses').

At the other polarity is non-reflection or spontaneity, which, when appropriate, is the ideal state of simply being in the here-and-now, living and experiencing life without a commentary. On the other hand, it can be an absence of necessary reflection and self-monitoring. It is also the absence of the capacity to hold both self and another in mind, with awareness of mutual impact, a capacity that is intrinsic to inclusion. Ironically, non-reflection is often the cause of inappropriate counsellor behaviour, of ill-considered interventions and broken boundaries – especially associated, unfortunately, with some Gestalt practitioners in the early years.

Intervention suggestions:

◆ The habitually non-reflective client may well be using this style of self-regulation in order to avoid more painful inner experiences. It is as if he escapes from his feelings into action. Offer the space for the client to tell his story, interrupting him if he turns it into an 'exciting drama'. What sense has he made of events, what are his thoughts and opinions about them? Make sure he pauses to account for his feelings (both 'then' and those brought up by remembering).

◆ Help the client to think about what happens in those moments before feeling the urge to do something. Ask him what was happening, what he was feeling (e.g. boredom, fear, emptiness, neediness, sadness). Explore if there was a need to escape those feelings. If thinking about his experience produces agitation, focus on building self-support and appropriate environmental support.

PROJECTING ... OWNING

There is sometimes confusion about the concept of projecting. The difficulty arises as the word is used in at least three different ways. First, it is used to refer to the ability we have to imagine what is not there, to anticipate a possible future, to be creative. Artists project their vision on to the canvas, the novel and the film. In this sense it is an essential component of human functioning (and an imagination which makes us uniquely human). Second, it is used in the sense of transference, when the projected material is historical and inappropriate; for example, the client who treats the counsellor like their father or a feared teacher. Third, projection refers to how a client manages disowned or alienated parts of the self. When a client denies an aspect of his personality that is incompatible with his self-concept, he may effectively project it (out of awareness) on to another person. He then denies the quality in himself and only sees it in others: 'I'm not angry, *you* are the one who is feeling hostile'. This is the sense in which we use it here.

There are, of course, some serious questions about the relational validity of using the term 'projection' as it implies that the counsellor is a blank screen on to which the client projects. Also that it is impossible to actually 'project' aspects of yourself, and the process is, in fact, one of imagining or misattribution. It also ignores the inevitable involvement of the counsellor in all the experiencing of the client. This concept has an unfortunate history in that it was often used to deny any emotional reactiveness on the part the therapist (when commented on by the client) by saying 'That's just your projection.' In many cases we believe the client may not, in fact, be disowning a quality but that the therapist is denying his own out-of-awareness material. A relational therapist will acknowledge the co-created element of any projection, at the very least as a metaphor for a process where the client selectively notices or over-prioritizes some element of the behaviour or appearance of the counsellor – a 'hook' for the projection to catch on. It also is less problematic when the therapist has had a good enough personal therapy himself to identify his disowned parts and recognize his contributions to the relationship.

We encourage you therefore to see projecting primarily as a process of disowning an aspect of self which is then co-created as a relational experience. It can be a very rich source of information for both client and counsellor about the client's past and present inner world.

EXAMPLE

A hard-working client of ours told us of a time when he returned home after a particularly taxing day. He met his wife at the door and said to her, 'You look really tired', to which his wife perceptively replied, 'You should lie down for a couple of hours.' When he woke up, his wife said to him 'Do I look more rested now?'

Intervention suggestions:

◆ When a client sees you as critical or judgemental (when you are *sure* you are not), first explore the meaning and effect this has upon him. 'How does it feel to be with someone whom you believe is always critical of you?' Start to explore the possibility of them having the very same attribute. 'Have you ever felt critical of *me*?' Initially clients will often deny they could ever have that quality, 'No, I never feel critical of you, you are always trying your best . . .' You may need to start very gradually, for example, '*If you were to feel critical of me, what would it be?*' We have sometimes suggested that clients look around the room to find objects, colours or shapes they did not like, to practise being critical of the belongings of the therapist. This can gradually be increased in intensity until they are encouraged to say things they did not like about how the therapist talked or acted towards them (surely a rich field of possibility!).

◆ Another approach is to investigate how the client came to believe their projection. What had you done or said that led them to believe you were critical? Projection is usually co-created. Look for the 'grain of truth' in your client's view. It is very likely that you will have contributed in some way to their experience, and being willing to own that, can normalize both their experience and also the rejected attitude.

◆ After you have explored the here-and-now content of the projection, it can be useful to identify the theme as a possible link to the past. For example, 'So in your perception, I became the person who dismissed your feelings.'

The other polarity, of owning, refers to one of the corner-stones of Gestalt. It means taking responsibility for one's experience and accepting the consequences of one's actions. However, owning becomes problematic when a client takes responsibility inappropriately or paralyses himself with guilt and remorse. It can often be the main issue for survivors of childhood neglect or abuse, where a client holds himself responsible for something that was out of his control. He carries feelings of shame or self-loathing into his adult life, believing that he must in some way have deserved the way he was treated.

Intervention suggestions:

◆ An empathic inquiry into the client's feelings of responsibility and guilt can start the process of sorting out what belongs to him and what does not. Be sensitive to the possibility of triggering some much worse pain that lies beneath. Self-blame can often be the child's creative adjustment to explain and manage an intolerable situation. It is sometimes easier to take responsibility for a painful situation than to face the unbearable thought that a loved parent might be mentally ill or unsafe.

◆ Engage the client in a cognitive exploration of the situation, using his middle zone to sort out the facts. Question how he knows what things are his responsibility and what are not. This is particularly true for sexual abuse or sudden bereavement.

INTROJECTING ... REJECTING

Introjecting is a here-and-now process whereby an opinion, an attitude or an instruction is unquestioningly taken in from the environment as if it were true. Introjecting is an avoidance of considering or chewing over the validity of the offered opinion. The process of introjecting leads to held beliefs that were not accepted choicefully – called introjects.

It is likely that a client who uses introjecting as a major way of regulating contact, will actively introject what you say. He will seem to invite you to interpret his behaviour for him and never pause to reflect on your suggestions. It is easy for a counsellor not to notice this, as it is rarely unpleasant to have someone agree so wholeheartedly with one's opinions. However, it is important to monitor the process and invite the client to recognize how readily he swallows your suggestions.

Intervention suggestions.
◆ Encourage him to stop and reflect before he agrees. Invite him above all to take his time, to go inside and feel his feelings about what you have said. If he starts to feel intensely anxious at this, encourage him simply to sit with that and explore whether there may be other feelings as well (such as anger).

The opposite pole to introjecting is rejecting. It is clearly healthy to reject an attitude, a belief (or indeed an intervention from a therapist) if it does not fit with the client's values and integrity. However, sometimes a client may manifest rejection as a habitual style. For example, he may appear to disagree with or 'spit out' every intervention you make, or he may reject anything in a particular area or related to a particular issue. Sometimes, the client rejects not only the opinions of others but anything he is given, including love and attention. Rejecting can come across as mistrust, rebellion or excessive self-reliance.

Intervention suggestions:
◆ Patterns of rejecting can often be used by clients to define themselves. In the struggle to identify what is 'me' and what is 'not me', the client may find it easier to define what is 'not me' in terms of what he dislikes, disagrees with, etc., rather than identify what 'is me'. It can be useful to help him begin to find his sense of who he is by focusing on his inner zone and middle zone, recognizing the full range of his needs, feelings and sensations and putting them into words.
◆ Frequently, the rejecting attitude stems from a profound fear of being controlled or criticized. You will notice the client's tendency to avoid answering questions or following suggestions. Here, your approach will need to be accepting and open, without making demands or even asking many questions. You may 'sit alongside' the client (both figuratively and literally), inviting him to speak about whatever he likes. Support him to talk about himself and his interests rather than question him, in order to avoid the impression of trying to 'corner' him. Once a good working relationship has been established, he may easily respond well to confrontations which are more playful and humorous.

RECOMMENDED READING

Gestalt Journal (1988) 'Boundary processes', *Gestalt Journal*, special issue, 11 (2).

Mackewn, J. (1997) *Developing Gestalt Counselling*. London: Sage. **(See Chapter 12.)**

Perls, F.S. (1976 [1973]) *The Gestalt Therapy Approach, and Eyewitness to Therapy*. New York: Bantam.

Polster, E. and Polster, M. (1973) *Gestalt Therapy Integrated*. New York: Vintage Books. **(See Chapter 4.)**

Sills, C., Fish, S. and Lapworth, P. (1995) *Gestalt Counselling*. Oxford: Winslow. **(See Chapter 6.)**

Simon, L. (1996) 'The nature of the introject', *Gestalt Journal*, 19 (2): 101–30.

11

UNFINISHED BUSINESS

One of the best-known phrases in the Gestalt world is 'unfinished business'. It is a phrase we have used several times in this book. It refers to situations in the past, especially traumatic or difficult ones, which have not achieved satisfactory resolution or closure for the client.

At one end of the scale, there is simply a sense of discomfort or frustration. Clients will sometimes report a situation from the past that they keep thinking or fantasizing about. This may be about people who have died or hurt them, or situations where they felt, for example, ignored or badly treated.

At the other end, as in Post Traumatic Stress Disorder, the repetitive symptoms from previous unfinished trauma may be life-crippling and lead to a breakdown of functioning or even dissociative conditions. Severe trauma often leads to an overload phenomenon that involves fragmenting or splitting off parts of the experience (e.g. losing actual narrative memory and having only emotion or somatic symptoms). In these cases, a specialized understanding of the neurophysiological basis of trauma symptoms is necessary in order to know how to proceed best to resolve or assimilate the traumatic memory. There are also significantly new perspectives on how best to respond to survivors from natural disasters, terrorist attacks, etc. (see recommended reading on trauma at the end of this chapter).

Commonly, the energy or struggle at the heart of unfinished business moves out of awareness, the person then is only aware (if at all) of symptoms that seem unconnected or mysterious. For example, a child who was in constant fear of being hit may well have reacted at the time by consistently desensitizing his body as he resists the blow. As an adult, he may have lost all conscious memory of this, yet when it is triggered, or at a time of stress, presents with a frozen body posture, lack of sensation and unfocused anxiety. The natural process of closure has been interrupted and considerable energy is being expended to keep the unfinished situation out of awareness. This leads to a debilitating drain on his energy resources and self-support. Other examples of this phenomenon are easy to see in post-traumatic stress, where the client has flashbacks, anxiety or constant tension. In a very real sense, he is continuing to relive the trauma over and over as if it was still happening. It is as though the person is still struggling, out of awareness, to find a way to deal with the distress that overwhelmed him originally. The task in counselling is to find the support, emotional expression or closure that will allow the person to move on.

Sometimes, it is possible to identify the situation that could not be faced (but could not be left behind). The client can then start the task of completion with the counsellor. Sometimes he only needs to bring the situation into greater awareness, with enough support to enable him to move on. At other times, the client just seems to be stuck. What is unfinished or unresolved is unclear and may only show up as chronic tension or depression without an obvious cause. In this case there is a situation of conflicting forces, out of awareness, balanced in a stalemate. This is an example of what is sometimes called an impasse. One side of the impasse is an urge for growth, change and recovery. The other side, equally strong, resists the change, usually in the form of the original creative adjustment, an old and habitual pattern of response.

There are many reasons for the resisting aspect of such an impasse. Frequently, there are beliefs and fears about the consequences of change, which are deeply buried and of which the client is only dimly aware. Embedded in the impasse may be a powerful core belief or introject. What is more, old patterns are safe and familiar; they may be painful or uncomfortable but they are tried and tested ways of getting our needs met *enough,* at a time when there did not seem to be any other way of managing the difficulty. These creative adjustments were the best way that could be found at the time to cope with the events and pressures of those field conditions. It is hard for a client to abandon a practised response that may at some time have felt protective or life-saving. It is also true that starting to face or examine the impasse will inevitably reactivate the anxiety or fear, which is bound up in the creative adjustment.

The anxiety and depression that sometimes accompany major shifts in self-understanding are precisely because the client's whole existence is felt to be in jeopardy again as boundaries dissolve and re-form while a new self-organization is in the process of emerging. For the client this is a true emergence-cy. The skill of the therapist is to support the person while her boundaries expand and re-form and 'hold' her until she reaches a new stability.

In order to describe ways of working with unfinished business, premature closure and impasses, we have broken down the work into five categories. Some therapy will only require one category, some will require all. Working through could take place over one session or over several months, depending on the field conditions and the centrality of the particular issue. Where the client is a survivor of trauma, the therapist should ensure that she is supported by expert knowledge, taking the work very slowly, building up self-support before expression. This is not a time to use 'old-style' expressive Gestalt techniques which could re-traumatize the person. In the further reading section, we recommend some useful texts. See also Chapter 18 on managing risk.

EXPLORING THE GROUND

This involves exploring how the unfinished business arose, the history, beliefs and introjects that support it, 'the ground to the figure'. It is best achieved through the phenomenological method of inquiry and understanding. The following pointers may be useful:

◆ Identify the unfinished situation. This may well only emerge after much exploration and sharpening of the problem or discomfort.

EXAMPLE

Christine had lived for most of her life with a series of temporary 'stepfathers' who had found her a nuisance. She had creatively adjusted to this by withdrawing and telling herself she didn't need a father or indeed any man, and was quite self-sufficient without one. In later life, however, she came to counselling saying she had problems with intimacy. Whenever she and her boyfriend experienced challenges or difficulties in the relationship, she became uninterested and found him boring. The relationship then became stale and ended when the boyfriend left her. This had happened several times now and she was beginning to suspect she had a part to play in this rejection. The original creative adjustment had become part of her unaware ground and it took several months before she was able to see the connection. Only then could she realize how her current difficulties were linked with something unfinished from her childhood experience.

◆ Trace back with the person her clearest memory of the original situation or trauma that she feels is unfinished (or a representative example).

With the encouragement of the counsellor, Christine started to remember details of the coming and going of the 'stepfathers' in her early life. She was able to recontact her distress and pain as she was repeatedly ignored and neglected. She remembered her initial feelings of frustration and impotence that ended up with her sobbing alone in her room.

◆ We have found useful a technique from EMDR to assist clients who have difficulty in remembering, called a 'floatback' (Shapiro 2001). The client is asked to identify the most figural element of their current distress (e.g. a body sensation, a feeling or a belief about themselves). They are then asked to close their eyes and let their memory float back to the earliest time they can remember feeling or thinking that way. This can often bring surprising results, especially if the question is repeated to find the earliest distressing memory.
◆ Find where the energy is most present, for example frustrated emotional energy, body tension or rigidity or in repetitive imaginings of what could or should have happened (often including self-criticism or blame).

Christine became aware of how she tensed up and then felt lethargic when her boyfriend wanted them to move in together and how this was also her memory as a girl with new stepfathers. She also remembered that she had originally thought that there must have been something wrong with her, to be so ignored and disliked.

◆ Encourage the client to bring the feelings, thoughts, bodily sensations and beliefs into full awareness.

> Over the course of several weeks, Christine returned to the details of her child-hood memories getting more sharpness and focus, especially around her bodily reactions and emotions.

◆ Identify any interruptions or modifications to contact.

> Christine and the counsellor were able to identify several modifications to contact. She tended to retroflect her emotions, desensitize herself when intimacy was imminent and then project lack of interest on to her boyfriend.

◆ Make sure that you remember field theory principles and that both you and the client have a good understanding of the purpose, function, and interconnectedness of the particular modification to contact you are working with. Discuss the effect on the client's life, the consequences both historically and in the current situation. How would her life have been different if she had not always behaved like this? Such consideration involves carefully examining the implications of the stuck place – both those that are limiting but also those that are secondary gains (that is, they in some way meet another need which is rewarding).

> It became very clear that Christine's apparent boredom and lack of interest in moving in with her boyfriend was intimately connected with her past experi-ences and were effectively protecting her (out of awareness) from being hurt again. Christine was shocked and amazed to make these connections as she had thought that she had got over her childhood experiences.

In this phase of exploration, the opportunity to tell the story to a receptive counsellor sometimes brings closure naturally. Raising awareness in a supportive therapeutic atmosphere may be enough. This will be evident by a sense of a relief or satisfaction as if a door has closed and the client can move on.

FACING THE ISSUE OR IMPASSE

However, when this is not the case, more directive work may be necessary. It may happen that there is one particular behaviour, emotion or expression that seems to be most figural. In this situation you have a variety of options, but the basic goal is to find a way to bring to the surface that which was not expressed.

◆ Having identified the issue, the counsellor can focus the work directly on how it is maintained in the here-and-now. You can then focus on core beliefs, which sometimes these change naturally over time as the client experiences the reparative effect of the therapeutic relationship. They can also be addressed directly. One method is to work cognitively, identifying the belief, articulating it, examining it against reality and generating alternative options which are acceptable to the client as appropriate.

Christine identified that she believed 'No man will ever care about me because I am unlovable.' This was divided into two statements and carefully examined. She also focused on how she modified contact in the therapy room in a way that could reinforce her beliefs, losing interest in the (male) therapist when he came emotionally close to her and rejecting his attention so that he felt thoroughly distanced. Again, the counsellor found the work difficult at those times and was aware of occasionally feeling defensive or irritated. In supervision he discussed his own vulnerability to feeling rejected, and this enabled him to stay empathic to Christine's need to withdraw. Finally, Christine agreed to think about the possibility that 'Some men might genuinely care about me,' and 'I too am deserving of being loved.' Later in the therapy she was able to change the latter sentence to 'I am lovable.'

◆ Sometimes what needs to happen will be obvious to the client but difficult to do, at other times the client will struggle to move forward but stays at the impasse, a place where he feels profoundly stuck or paralysed. He is blocked by fear or the sense of danger as if his very life was threatened. To explore further seems unsafe or impossible. The fear can often be a nameless void or confusion, as if he was at the edge of an abyss. This is often the place of most potential change and growth. Perls et al. (1989 [1951]) describe the therapeutic task at this time as 'creating a safe emergency' for the client. The therapist makes a clinical judgement about the degree of support available and how much challenge (or emergency) the client can usefully face. From a place of creative indifference, the therapist encourages the client to stay with the discomfort and stuckness, letting energy build and trusting the process. The therapist often needs great determination to allow the painful confusion to continue without looking for an easy avoidance.

EXAMPLE

Another client, Natasha, came to therapy hoping to understand her continuing 'irrational' fear of enclosed places. As the work continued, she talked 'about' many problems with being trapped but made little progress. The therapist frequently noticed how she avoided bodily sensation in her stories of her childhood. Over time she experimented with allowing greater sensation, but started to reach a place of nameless terror where she immediately recoiled and froze. With great courage (and strong support from the therapist) she determined to

(Continued)

> *(Continued)*
>
> face this dark place gradually, and over several months moved further into the darkness, often becoming disoriented and terrified. The therapist too needed all his own support to stay with her distress but decided (after much supervision) to trust the emerging process of the client. Eventually Natasha remembered a scene of childhood abuse in a small room, a memory that she had suppressed, and was able to continue the work with her new awareness of the impasse.

A caveat: It is crucial when working with remembered trauma to avoid the possibility of encouraging the client to relive the traumatic memory without some different assimilation or closure. This can lead to an unhelpful retraumatizing and leave the client effectively worse off. It is vital that the client keeps some control and access to the here and now, with your supportive presence during such 'regressive' episodes. We suggest you also look at Chapter 7, on 'Strengthening Support' before working in this way.

WORKING WITH IMAGINATION

The previous sections have focused on exploring and facing the unfurnished business. The following ones focus on bringing imagination and creativity to experiment with the difficulty.

◆ Offer one or more experiments to try out different forms of expression. This can be done in imagination or in role-play with you in the room (see Chapter 9, 'Experimenting'). Some clients are not able to generate or imagine an appropriate response. In this case, you may have to offer them suggestions. These experiments can be as small as saying 'I miss you' to the image of a dead person, or as large as designing a ritual funeral, burial and wake for a death at which they were not present.

> Christine still felt some unresolved energy, and after retelling the story again became aware of how powerless she had felt in the face of criticism and rejection by the various men who had lived in her home. The counsellor set up a variety of experiments designed to enable a dialogue with the most figural stepfather, and with a lot of initial support Christine became angry and indignant, telling him how much she hated his intrusion. She became very energized and excited after this and felt she had found the power and assertiveness she had always sensed was missing.

◆ Sometimes the client seems to reach a place where he is not sure how much he wishes to change (for example in addiction problems). It is then sometimes useful to discuss the pros and cons of different options and the likely consequences of each one. Suggest that he allows himself to be aware of how he will end up if he does or does not change. This means that if he chooses to change, he does so in awareness of what he is relinquishing (again both the good and the bad) and what he might be gaining. He will always need to face the existential truth that if he is not making life predictable with fixed gestalts and old patterns, then he will have to face the unpredictable, unknown experience of the here and now, with all its possibilities for creative living.

◆ Catastrophic fantasies underlying reluctance to change can be explored by close questioning. 'If you keep on living your life the way you are doing now, what will happen?' Keep this up until the topic is fully explored. Do not contradict the client in any way and remain creatively indifferent. Occasionally ask a question like 'And what would be the consequence of that?' or "and how bad would that be?" The technique should not be used with a very fragile client but can be very powerful with a person who has adequate support for her self-process. For example:

Therapist:	So what are you afraid would happen if you assert yourself and make demands on your boyfriend?
Ezri:	He definitely wouldn't like it.
T:	And then what would happen?
Ezri:	He might leave me.
T:	And what would that mean?
Ezri:	Then I'd be on my own.
T:	And what would happen then?
Ezri:	[*pauses*] Well, I sort of want to say that I couldn't bear it. I couldn't live. But I suppose that's not true. I'd be terribly lonely. I'd be terribly sad. Maybe I'd go mad.
T:	And what would that look like?
Ezri:	[*pause*] Oh, I guess I probably wouldn't go mad. I'd see my friends more … [*laughs*] … Actually it's weird – I realize that the worst thing that could happen is I would hurt. That feels quite a relief.

WORKING WITH INTROJECTS

Introjects are an essential part of functioning effectively, they are the internalization of significant societal rules that allow us to fit into our communities. Clear examples can be seen in forceful instructions given to children which are absorbed often without understanding, such as 'Don't play near the railway tracks' or 'Come home before dark', 'Don't steal'. Introjects are often influential or even central to the rigidity of unfinished business. They are assumptions about the world or attributions imposed on children about themselves such as 'Never depend on others' or 'You will never succeed' or 'Do it to them before they do it to you'. The person who is under the influence of an introject feels a strong pressure to conform with the introject and feels uncomfortable if he tries to go against it. Sometimes, if he pays attention to his middle zone, the client can hear the actual instruction and, if asked, can actually say who 'gave' it to him.

> **Suggestion:** Think back to your childhood, what messages or instructions were part of your family life? Were there particular rules around eating? 'Don't put your elbows on the table', 'Don't eat with your mouth open'. What messages did you receive about your body, honesty, morality, culture? Now reflect on how many of these early instructions you still follow. Have you freely chosen all of them as an adult or are there some you just live by without question?

Many of the problems that keep the past unfinished will rest upon a belief or opinion that has been absorbed out of awareness and never questioned. It is the therapist's job to help him bring such introjects into awareness so that he can make choices about whether or not he will keep them. The therapist should not normally try to have any influence on which beliefs are useful or not. It is the prerogative of the client to decide whether he keeps or rejects them.

Intervention suggestions

◆ Identify the full implications of the introject. You can carefully explore the underlying assumptions, this brings the introject or belief into awareness:
'I notice you have a strong belief that you can never get it right'
'How did you arrive at the conclusion that expressing your emotions is a sign of weakness?'
'How did you come to believe that?'
'Is it true then that you can *never* get *anything* right?'
'Do you think that it is *always* wrong to express emotions?'
◆ Clients with enough support can be invited to exaggerate the introject in order to comprehend the extent of its limits in the present. For example, 'Tell me with all your energy and conviction that you will never let yourself become angry.' You might ask the client to say the belief out loud, or even to shout it. 'I will *never* show my anger under *any* circumstance.' This in itself sometimes brings the introject to clear awareness. It can start to show the client how rigidly he has held this belief and how unquestioningly he applies it to all situations. The client may begin to become curious at this point and even genuinely puzzled as to why he believes this so strongly.
◆ Sometimes a role-play or enactment is necessary where the client is helped to go back to face the person or the situation where he took in the introject. He can then make a new decision, reject the message, modify it, or argue with the introject giver with all of his here-and-now resources and understanding. This sort of redecision work has been called 'Transactional Analysis Gestalt' (Goulding, 1992).

Destructuring such rigid messages often allows the client to move on choicefully from the impasse.

WORKING WITH POLARITIES

Each individual is a never-ending sequence of polarities.

Whenever an individual recognizes one aspect of himself, the presence of its antithesis or polar quality is implicit. There it rests as background, giving dimension to present experience and yet powerful enough to emerge as figure in its own right if it gathers enough force. When this force is supported, integration can develop. (Polster and Polster, 1973: 61)

The rigidity at the heart of an impasse may also be due to a fixed polarity. Polarities are present in all qualities. Every aspect of a person is one side of a duality; the other side is out of awareness and forms the ground to that figure. Some are as clear as 'masculine and feminine', 'weak and strong', 'happy and sad'. Others are subtler and are unique to the individual's phenomenology. Perls was fond of identifying a polarity or split he called 'topdog' ('I should exercise more, eat a healthy diet, and read Gestalt textbooks') against its opponent called 'underdog' ('I'm too stressed today, I'll try tomorrow').

In Chapter 10 we discussed the polarities that commonly characterize modifications to contact. Other polarities are uniquely organized by each person. Healthy functioning is the ability to move flexibly along the continuum of any polarity, as the situation requires. For example, a client may have been brought up to believe that there is a polarity of only two positions, powerful or powerless, and that it is always necessary to hold the 'powerful' end of the polarity. This will mean that he will not easily allow himself to be 'powerless' as a matter of principle. This can seriously disadvantage him in relationships that call for compromise or the surrender necessary for intimacy. All parts of a continuum are potentially necessary. For example, violence is sometimes necessary for self-protection. A person cannot feel the fullness of his masculinity without an appreciation of the fullness of his femininity, and so on. Patently, this is not always true and it would be facile to insist upon it. The world does not need wanton cruelty, for example. (For some clients it is useful to think of these wholly undesirable qualities as distortions of natural attributes.) With this important caveat, however, we take the position that all positions along a polarity are natural and necessary parts of human life. The naming of one end of a polarity as bad, weak or unattractive fixes the perception of the person in a rigid position, usually leading to a belief that the judgement is somehow 'objectively' true.

> **Suggestion:** Identify an aspect or quality that you never express or that you believe to be unpleasant, something you know you possess, but try to keep hidden. It may be cruelty, criticalness, jealousy or competitiveness. Let yourself come fully in touch with that quality, accept it as truly part of you whether you like it or not. See if you can find a situation where this quality would be necessary or helpful. How would you then describe it in a positive way?

A fundamental belief in Gestalt theory is that the central unhealthy process is alienation, the splitting off of parts of yourself that seem too difficult to manage or integrate. Often, as we described in Chapter 10, this split-off part is projected on to someone else or it is pushed out of awareness. It requires energy to keep it out of awareness and also therefore reduces the availability of new energy to respond in any emerging situation. One of the main ways this happens is through a process of polarization, the client denying one end of the polarity in order to identify with the other: 'I could never tell a lie', or, 'I never let myself become angry', 'I would never be cruel to my children.' Although this process most often happens cognitively or emotionally, it can also manifest in restricted or over-expressive body energy. The therapist's task is to help the client return to flexibility and fullness of response.

◆ Start by trying to identify the opposite polarity to the quality that the client is holding rigidly. This will be unique to the client and not necessarily the most obvious; for example, the other polarity to love may be hate or it may be rejection. The client should try to imagine the opposite of the quality although you may have to assist them by making suggestions.

◆ The next step is to encourage the client to envisage the possibility of that absent polarity. Such questions as 'Could you imagine feeling . . .?' often evoke the response 'I could not possibly feel or imagine that', or, 'That seems impossible for me.' The strength of the resistance to the possibility of the other polarity can give you a clue to the energy contained in keeping it out of awareness.

◆ Two-chair work and role-play is very obviously useful here, as it is important to provide some experience of identifying with the other polarity. At first it may be 'as if'. Then, if your intervention is accurate, the client will start to inhabit and invest energy in the denied quality. You can ask the client to start a dialogue between two opposing attitudes to a problem. For example, 'I will *never* forgive that person because . . .', and 'I *will* forgive that person because . . .' Encourage the client to invest fully with as much enthusiasm and energy in each polarity in turn, taking turns to reply to the other side, keeping alert to bodily reactions, feelings and responses. It is surprising how this exercise can lead to a new integration.

◆ Explore re-framing the name of the polarity. Strong or weak can be re-framed as strong or flexible (or sensitive, or vulnerable, or open, or generous). See what makes sense to your client.

◆ It is important to remember that owning the capacity for a particular polarity does not mean the same as acting on it. Recognizing the part of oneself that can feel, for example, murderous or envious means that we recognize simply the fullness of our human possibilities.

Your intention is to re-create flexibility and range along the continuum between these two polarities so that the person can develop more resilience and more possibilities of response in dealing with both fixed gestalts and new situations. Both poles are affirmed and all positions between them are seen as potentially useful depending on the context.

INTEGRATING THE WORK

Closure of unfinished business may never be fully achieved. We believe that expecting to completely recover from all the effects of profound loss, deprivation or abuse is unrealistic. Melnick and Roos (2007) talk about the need to avoid the 'myth of closure' and accept the inevitability of many unfinished life events

The client may always have vulnerabilities in a particular area and you may have to return to the territory many times when new situations provoke a similar crisis. However, the final stage is to assimilate what has been learned, perhaps to look at the best creative adjustment to the here-and-now and then move on.

Christine decided to share her history with her current boyfriend and both agreed to discuss her fears and anxiety as they arose. Thereafter, the relationship became as much of a space for discovery and growth as the consulting room had been. Released from the binds of her unfinished business, she noticed the many ways that she had been limiting her responses to her boyfriend. She was excited by the challenges as she met new situations that called for new ways of being.

In many ways unfinished business can be seen as the chief obstacle to healthy here-and-now living, and as therapy becomes more effective you can help the person to identify newly arising potential unfinished business much more quickly.

RECOMMENDED READING

Clarkson, P. and Mackewn, J. (1993) *Key Figures in Counselling and Psychotherapy: Fritz Perls.* London: Sage. (**See pp. 68–72 and 115–20.**)

Harris, E. (2007) 'Working with forgiveness in Gestalt therapy'. *Gestalt Review*, 11 (1): 108–19.

Korb, M.P., Gorrell, J. and Van De Riet, V. (1995) *Gestalt Therapy: Practice and Theory*, 2nd edn. New York: Pergamon Press. (**See pp. 63–4 and 127–9.**)

Melnick, J. and Roos. S. (2007) 'The myth of closure,' *Gestalt Review*, 11 (1): 90–107.

Polster, E. and Polster, M. (1973) *Gestalt Therapy Integrated.* New York: Vintage Books. (**See Chapter 2.**)

USEFUL TRAUMA READING

Bauer, A. and Toman, S. (2003) 'A Gestalt perspective of crisis debriefing', *Gestalt Review*, 7 (1): 56–71.

Briere, J. and Scott, C. (2006) *Principles of Trauma Therapy. A Guide to Symptoms, Evaluation and Treatment.* London: Sage.

Brownell, P. (ed.) (2002) '9–11 Gestalt therapists, traumatic experience, and response to anxiety', *Gestalt!*, 6 (1), http://www.g-gej.org/6-1/index. html.

Hardie, S. (2004) 'Literature review of PTSD', *Gestalt!*, 8 (1) (Winter); http://www.g-gej.org/8-1/litreview.html.

Herman, J. (2001) *Trauma and Recovery.* London: Pandora.

Ogden, P., Minton, K. and Pain, C. (2006) *Trauma and the Body. A Senorimotor Approach to Psychotherapy.* New York: Norton.

Rothschild, B. (2000) *The Body Remembers.* London: Norton.

Shapiro, F. (2001) *Eye Movement Desensitising and Reprocessing.* New York: Guilford Press.

12

TRANSFERENCE AND COUNTER-TRANSFERENCE

One cannot do good therapy without dealing competently with the transference phenomena. One cannot do good therapy and ignore developmental issues either. However in Gestalt therapy we deal with both of these using the dialogic and phenomenological perspectives.
(Yontef, 1991: 18)

WHAT DO WE MEAN BY TRANSFERENCE AND COUNTER-TRANSFERENCE?

Transference is a phenomenon first described by Freud in the early 1900s in which the client was said to transfer aspects of past relationships on to the current relationship with their analyst. They would act towards the analyst *as if* he was the client's mother, father or some significant figure from the client's past. At first, Freud saw it as an interference to the analysis, but later the interpretation of transference became a major therapeutic focus. Perls (1947) was very keen to move Gestalt therapy away from this emphasis; he did not deny the reality of transference but questioned its importance. He asserted that the overriding therapeutic need is for a real relationship, and authentic contact. In their attempts to distance themselves from psychoanalytic therapy, early Gestaltists often maintained that they did not 'work with transference'. In fact, what they meant was that they did not work with it in the same way as psychoanalysts did. It is still a vital part of the therapy, as Yontef asserts in our opening quotation. Analysts tend to explore and deepen the transference, whereas Gestalt therapists attempt to understand and work with its effect in the here and now. It is still part of the 'real' relationship and is part of a mutual influencing or co-creation. This is a very important distinction from the Freudian understanding of transference as generated by the client and received by a neutral analyst. Parlett (1991: 76) quotes Hunter Beaumont's description of transference as a person 'constellating the field' according to his previous experience until, says Parlett, 'the field itself begins to determine what happens next'. In this view, the influence and effect of the therapist are crucially relevant to understanding the transference phenomena. His response to the client's presentation, in particular his transference, is called counter-transference. However, it would be more accurate in Gestalt to call this process co-transference. The following shows how a co-created transference relationship might develop.

EXAMPLE

Edith feels lonely and isolated. She expects the world to disregard her feelings and has long since lost the habit of expressing herself, so is certain that she will not be received. She talks in a desultory manner about her problems. The therapist does not feel engaged. Out of his awareness he begins to minimize the significance of what she is saying. He listens half-heartedly to her story and checks his watch. Out of her awareness Edith registers those familiar signs of uninterest. She hurries through her description of her lifeless marriage and ends up apologetically asserting that she is probably making too much of the difficulties. The session ends with them agreeing to work for four sessions, but neither of them feels very invested in the enterprise.

Fortunately, the therapist has a supervision session before he next meets Edith. In it he confesses that he has taken on a 'rather boring client' and gives a dull, uninterested account of the session. The supervisor feels the pull into a parallel process, and finds herself on the edge of believing that Edith is boring. She catches herself in time, and begins to inquire into Edith's story and the relationship she and the therapist are developing. She questions him: But, what happened then? How did Edith react to that? Where was her energy? What was her body language? The therapist realizes, to his discomfort, that he had not been curious about any of this. Gradually, he begins to realize that he and Edith had co-created a relationship of distance and lack of engagement. He explores his deeper feelings and uses two-chair work in supervision to imagine a different possible dialogue between them. At their next session, he says 'I have been thinking about you Edith, and realize that I don't know much about you and how you are feeling as you tell me about the important events in your life. Will you tell me more?' This time he stays engaged, present and inclusive. When Edith brushes over her own feelings and responses, he pauses her and asks her to focus on her body sensations. At first, this creates a sense of dis-orientation for Edith, but gradually she become more animated and the co-created field grows in vibrancy and interest as real meeting starts to take place.

The degree of transference that is co-created will be different in each situation, depending on the strength of the client's relational expectations and how much it is out of awareness for both the client and therapist. There is no doubt that the more the therapist and client can engage in an I–Thou dialogue, the less transference will occur. That said, there are times when it can be useful for the purposes of understanding, to separate out the co-transference and identify the contributions of the client and the therapist in order to help a client understand his experiences more deeply and the ways in which he constellates his world.

The process by which the client (or anyone for that matter) uses their history to understand the present, or forms relational expectations is, of course, necessary for ordinary life. It is the way that I attempt to recognize the intent of an old friend who approaches to greet me. My recognition and response (reaching out to hug her, for example) is based on my anticipation or transferring of past memories and experiences of our friendship or of similar experiences with other people. This sort of transferring is an essential and necessary function that allows us to make sense of the world based on our previous experience.

The most significant aspect of a *healthy* process is that it is constantly being updated, allowing the reality of the present to modify expectations and anticipations. However, sometimes we effectively make a decision that what *has* been true will *always* be true and we do not attempt to update our frame of reference – or more accurately we *cannot* update it: the relational patterns on which it is based are not accessible to readjustment because they form part of our out-of-awareness processing – our ground structures.

As a young child struggles to make sense of the world into which he is born, he does this by looking for patterns and finding predictable events, establishing a sense of what actions produce what results. In order to do this, he needs to establish templates or fixed gestalts of how the world is, in order to allow him to understand how to interact to get his needs met. These templates are used to understand his relationships with the important people around him, the physical world and his place in it. The earliest templates are those that stem from the relational field with his primary caregivers – usually his mother or father (but often grandparents or older sisters and brothers) – and it is these early relationships, and later school ones, that usually form the basis for his understanding of all subsequent relationships, especially his most intimate ones. The apparent insistence of transference phenomena is often due to the presence of unfinished business from past relationships, which is seeking closure.

For example, if, as a child, I had a violent, patronizing father, I would form a relational template. Each time I saw him, I might expect (or 'transfer') violent, patronizing responses. If I expected this response from every slightly arrogant man I met – even after I had grown up and left home – then this would be part of a co-created transference and a limiting way of relating.

Suggestion: Quickly complete the following six sentences using an adjective or brief description; for example, mothers are kind, caring and look after you.

Mothers are …
Fathers are …
Brothers are …
Sisters are …
Men are …
Women are …
Rabbits are …

The therapist assumes that the transferences and modifications to contact which occur in the therapy room will be reflections of the client's (and his own) relationships in the wider world. In this way, the consulting room can be a cameo of the client's relationship to his life.

HOW TO RECOGNIZE TRANSFERENCE

The hallmark of learning to identify transference phenomena is the sense of incongruity in the way the client is treating you. Transference is an *active* process, and more accurately should be called 'transferring' (although for clarity, we have chosen to continue with the more common usage). In the stronger forms of transference, you may have a sense that the client is treating you in such a strange or inappropriate way that you feel they are not seeing you at all. You will find it hard to make sense of their reaction to you, as if you are doing or saying things that only they can see. For example, some clients seem to idealize – or idolize – you after only a few sessions, telling you that you are the perfect therapist, that everything you say is deep and insightful or that only you understand them so completely. For (most) therapists this is hard to believe, especially when you have been struggling to make a good enough relationship with the client. For other clients, your holiday breaks (agreed long before) are seen by them as a deliberate desire to abandon them, to show them you don't care. On investigation, their evidence for believing this doesn't match with anything you can identify with, at least in awareness, but they seem to rigidly hold to their picture of you.

Sometimes you will only recognize transference by an incongruent reaction (countertransference) you are having to the client, such as feeling unusually tired, irritable, critical or conversely protective or loving. We will return to it later in the chapter.

Of course, accurately identifying transference (and projections) implies self-awareness and clarity in the therapist that is hard to achieve, especially as the therapist is usually playing a part in the co-created phenomenon. It is also for this reason that it is crucial for training counsellors to be in their own therapy.

> **Suggestion:** Look over the history of your own life, particularly your relationships. Are there any fixed or repeating patterns that seem to have been true throughout your life? For example, choosing partners who treated you badly, finding partners who always take care of you, finding friends who are either dominating or submissive. It is sometimes easier to see these patterns in our friends or loved ones. Do you have a friend who always seems to repeat a particular pattern in relationships and is unable to see this as clearly as you and their other friends do?

WORKING WITH TRANSFERENCE

It is clear that the therapist has an important decision to make in relation to the transference (not forgetting that it is in fact, co-transference). She needs to decide whether

her strategy is to raise awareness, to name or deconstruct the transference, respond reparatively or to allow the transference (with or without comment) for the time being. Any of these options is appropriate at different times in the therapy; for example, with very fragile or traumatized clients, a positive transference may be a useful help to forming the working alliance and therefore should not be interrupted. Also, clients who have suffered developmental deprivation may need the temporary support of a positive transferential relationship to be able to move on.

There are many ways to classify transference phenomena. We find the work of Hargaden and Sills (2002) useful. They identify three types of transferential relating, which we adapt here. They are *projective, introjective* and *transformational.*

PROJECTIVE TRANSFERENCES

These transferences are the most frequently encountered. They can be negative or positive. A negative projective transference is where the client sees or expects you to have the same negative qualities or attributes as a person from his relational past. Typically you are seen as a critical, hostile or abandoning parental figure, whom he treats as if you *were* that figure, ignoring responses or qualities that don't confirm this picture.

A positive projective transference has a similar dynamic but the client sees you in a positive way and projects that you are warm, wise and all-knowing, In its extreme form it is an 'idolizing' transference, where every thing you do or say is somehow perfectly right or confirming. Simply to be in your presence is to feel better! We use Hargaden and Sills' word 'idolizing' rather than the more commonly used 'idealizing' as we believe that 'idol' better captures the unrealistic, aggrandizing transference where the therapist is seen as 'the best there is'.

Often, what is transferred is the early relationship dynamic itself (known as the object relation). Here, it is not a particular person that is transferred into the therapy room but a dynamic relational polarity, in which – to continue the first example above – one side is critical, hostile and dismissive, the other cowed, humiliated and powerless. In this sort of dynamic, the client can take either polarity and you may find yourself taking the other.

These dynamics are a largely out-of-awareness way by which the client organizes his relational world. The relational expectations have become habitual fixed gestalts and can easily be triggered or confirmed, when the client sees an aspect of the same quality in you.

There are several circumstances where you may wish to raise awareness or name this transference as soon as you notice it. This is especially true of a negative transference where it is clear that your client is fearing or experiencing you as critical or judgemental. For example, in brief therapy settings or with more self-supported clients who have a clear change agenda that does not explicitly involve understanding their relationships, it can be useful to notice and discuss any transference phenomena that seem to be getting in the way of the task. Of course, there will always be some transference – it is a fact of life. It may develop or get stronger over a long period of time and may change or reverse (in terms of positive or negative). You have a variety of possible of responses:

Heighten awareness

◆ Allow yourself to experience the transference fully without criticism or disapproval (or appreciation!). This is a difficult task that grows easier with experience but in general you can respond to the expression of their transference with creative indifference, empathy and acceptance. Invite awareness by describing what you see,

'You seem to be distrustful every time I make a suggestion.'
'You seem reluctant to be vulnerable with me.'

◆ Explore the nature of the transference in the relationship:

'Do you have a fantasy about what I am thinking now?' or,
'You seem to be expecting me to be critical of you now.'

◆ Guess what he may be feeling and offer it, for example:

'Are you feeling irritated with me?'

It is important not to have any tone of criticism or disapproval in your voice when naming the transference, as it may well induce shame and shut down the possibility of the client exploring a powerful or difficult emotion. If you see the client do this, then stay with the emerging reaction (see Chapter 8 on shame) and return to the transference at a later time.

Understand the relational trigger

◆ As we said earlier, the transferential response of the client is almost always in response to some aspect of the counsellor, be it part of her patterns, the way an intervention is given, a gesture, an expression or a tone of voice (usually out of the counsellor's awareness). Ask about this possibility.

'You look as if you suddenly became angry just then. What happened?'
'What did I do or say that made you shut down?'

The counsellor may also offer her own experience of that remembered moment and, if it is appropriate, may choose to apologize for her part in the communication or misattunement. If a client's worst fear is that you will be angry with her, it can sometimes be enormously healing to hear the truth that you had indeed been feeling irritable, and for that to be normalized as not taking away from your commitment to them. We suggest that it is important for you to express your feelings in small doses – in other words, to talk about, for example, feeling irritated rather than furious. This is because the unequal power dynamic of any helping relationship will amplify the impact on the client.

Explore the resonance with other relationships

◆ Ask the client if his experience of you is also true of other people in his life: 'Do you find that you expect other people in your life to be critical of you?' This is a very useful way to highlight transferential processes, as the client may start to see how unlikely it is that *everyone* could be critical of him or, conversely, that if every-one feels afraid of him, there might be something that he is doing to invite that.

◆ Discuss the likely effects of co-creating the field in this way. For example, he may never ask for feedback for fear of criticism and may have effectively trained his friends and colleagues to believe he is not interested in any feedback. As a consequence, he never receives either good or bad feedback so cannot update his transferential expectations.

◆ Make the link to the original relationship. Explore the historical roots and all the different elements involved. 'Do you remember feeling like this before?' 'Who was the last person who criticized you strongly?' 'Did anyone continually ignore you when you were young?' This can lead to a valuable understanding of their relationships with early significant others.

Name or confront the transference and offer a here-and-now relationship

◆ This is, of course, the obvious option for a traditional Gestaltist and it involves naming (and challenging) the transferential expectation. You might say, 'You seem to be treating me as if I was your father, mother, teacher (etc.). I don't recognize myself in your response to me. How come you are seeing me like this?' or, 'You keep asking me to tell you what to do about this problem, as if I have all the right answers. I wonder how it is that you see me in the role of expert.'

◆ You can accept the client's reaction as valid (even though possibly transferential) and meet it authentically, self disclosing your own reactions or phenomenology. 'You are see-ing me as critical, but in fact I feel warm towards you right now', or as Perls et al. say,

> He [the therapist] meets anger with explanation of the misunderstanding, or sometimes an apology, or even with anger according to (his own) truth of the situation. (1989 [1951]: 249)

◆ With some clients it is easy for a confrontation to come across as critical, blaming or shaming, so the intervention could be given as a guess or hypothesis offered in a spirit of mutual enquiry. 'You seem to be …' or 'I wonder …'

Work through the unfinished business

◆ Transference phenomena are fixed gestalts and sometimes contain unfinished busi-ness from the past. As such, they may need to be deconstructed and worked through (see Chapter 11).

◆ If the transference is in awareness, you can usefully offer an experiment where you set up a meeting with the original source of the transference reaction. This may involve roleplay, enactments, two chair work and any other experiments that bring the historical material into the present (see Chapter 9).

Offer a confirming response

◆ At its simplest, this may be to show compassion to a transferential response of fear, or to be understanding of a transferential attack on you. For a thorough exploration of reparative therapeutic responses to relational and transferential needs see Erskine (1999).
◆ As a general rule, it is useful if the client develops a real sense that he can, and indeed should, voice all his reactions to you even if they seem irrational or difficult. Being met by a counsellor offering a supportive dialogic relationship is in itself often healing.

INTROJECTIVE TRANSFERENCES

With this second form of transference, the client 'pulls for' a relationship with you that was developmentally needed but unavailable in his past. In this case, it is the transference of the relational need for 'another' who sees, recognizes, validates, receives, attunes, soothes and supports. (It is akin to the idealizing and mirroring transferences described by Kohut, 1971, 1977.) This need to be seen and accepted continues all our lives, but is especially vital in infancy for the healthy development of the self. Clients whose early experiences were especially deprived of this sort of relationship, are likely to manifest more introjective transference. We use this word to capture the idea that the client attempts, in a sense, to introject and internalize the experience of a supportive other.

It is arguable that it is in this transferential relationship that the most important healing lies. You allow yourself to be used as the accepting, interested, responsive 'other' that was missing from the client's early life. Being available, receptive and offering a dialogic relationship may be all that is needed. We want to stress that your job is NOT to try and be the parent they did not have. It is to provide a quality of responsive presence for their here-and-now experience, including that of grieving for the parent that they did not have and can never have. Typically, you notice that your client talks a lot, describing his life in detail, while appearing not to need much input from you. However, he is highly alert to the non-verbal signs of your presence and confirmation. You may find that if you do intervene to ask a question or make a comment, the client smiles at you politely and then continues unswervingly with his account. And yet there is no sense that you are being deflected. On the contrary, you feel a consistent relational connection with him.

When there is introjective transference, it is easy to start feeling as if your years of training are irrelevant or you begin to feel slightly dream-like, or maternally protective. It is important to be open to allowing this for a period of time. This kind of relationship is likely to be foreground for a while, and then become the back-drop to what follows in the therapeutic journey. The following therapeutic considerations may be useful:

- Mirroring the client's feeling tone in one or two words allows him to feel your inclusion and understanding. This in turn helps him to listen to and empathize with himself. Long or overly cognitive comments will miss him entirely.
- Inevitably you will sometimes 'get it wrong' for your client. At those moments when the client feels disappointed or missed he is likely to feel a depth of rage or grief that can be disconcerting to both him and the therapist. It can be helpful simply to listen, gently to inquire into his experience and help him to name it with you.
- When his feelings have settled, it may be appropriate to make some links to early relationships. However, remember that in this transference the client is often repeating very old non-verbal and pre-cognitive needs. While the client is in this stage of the therapy any challenge may be experienced as unempathic rejection or a demand to be different. Keep your interventions short and simple.

TRANSFORMATIONAL TRANSFERENCES

Transformational transference is a phenomenon of a different category but in the literature has been commonly included in transference descriptions so we describe it here. It is closely related to the psychoanalytic concept of projective identification (e.g. Ogden, 1982) and Racker's (1982 [1968]) concept of concordant counter-transference, (see Staemmler (1993) and Jacobs (2002) for a Gestalt debate about this concept).

Here the therapist begins to feel strong, quite primitive emotions, which in psychoanalytic theories, are attributed to the client's repressed experience being somehow 'put into' the therapist. However, in Gestalt, we think of this phenomenon in a very different way, which distinguishes it from the idea that the client can 'put things into' the therapist. We see it as a form of deep empathic resonance, by which the therapist not only attunes to the 'experience near' feelings of the client but also to his deepest, unexplored or even disowned emotions.

The process starts when feelings that the client experiences as overwhelming and unmanageable are disowned and denied. The therapist, however, resonates with them and vicariously experiences the disowned aspects. Often they feel to her as if they are alien and unexpected intrusions. A sign that you might have picked up a rejected feeling of your client's is when you become aware of feeling something odd or alien – it could be an emotion, a sensation, an unexpected image, a bodily movement and so on. Therapists report suddenly feeling terrified, or nauseous, or dizzy, or starving hungry; one reported a sensation of burning up, another waves of murderous rage.

For the resolution of this type of transference, the therapist must be willing to own this alien feeling as her own. The client has evoked it rather than put it into her. Thus, the process of owning and integrating can be transformational for both the therapist and the client.

Possible therapeutic responses

- The therapist's role is to accept, hold and *own the feelings*, in order to do what the client could not do. As they become accepted and integrated, they can be recognized by the client, who then allows himself to re-own them in himself.

◆ Simply contain and sit with the emotion. Continue working with the client normally as far as you can, knowing that your job is complex: you need to find a way of living with that feeling and holding it alongside your dialogic presence without acting on it; you need to reflect on the feeling, explore it and assimilate it. One day you will be able to invite him to own his own fear and vulnerability, or his ravenous neediness, and so on.

With some clients you may never experience this sort of transference. If you do, we suggest that these are the times to you make good use of your supervision and your personal therapy because this is when it is easy to become disorientated and lose your relational way.

UNDERSTANDING YOUR COUNTER-TRANSFERENCE

In the original analytic tradition, *all* responses to the client were labelled as counter-transference, but as Gestaltists we believe this is unhelpfully over generalized and it is important to identify the category of your response.

◆ First, is this a realistic response to the here-and-now situation? You may feel positive towards the client – is this because the client is friendly and warm to you? Or you might feel cautious and frightened – is this because the client is difficult or aggressive? This may be an ordinary here-and-now reaction.
◆ Second, it may be *reactive* counter-transference. This is the more traditional meaning of the word where you are reacting to the transference expectations or hopes of the client (in other words, projective, introjective or transformational).
◆ Third, how much is this your own transference – that is, your own unfinished business about this sort of person (called proactive counter-transference by Clarkson, 1992)? For example, you may have a reaction of anxiety if the client reminds you of your needy mother. A good question to ask is, 'Is this a familiar feeling/thought for me?' If the answer is 'Yes', then it is best to assume that the counter-transference is, at least in large part, your own transference. You should therefore keep it for further investigation later, ideally in supervision or therapy, while, of course, bearing in mind that it will be continuing to have an influence in the co-created relationship. When you have recognized your own contribution, can you helpfully reflect on the learning about the client that comes out of your responses: how come this particular client evoked this transference in you?

Transference/counter-transference enactments

When the client is experiencing transferential feelings and thoughts, he is likely to behave in a way that invites or elicits a complementary response from the other. If the client (or any person) continually sees you and treats you as if you were cold and abandoning (e.g. like his father), it is easy to feel the pressure to conform and step into the role (especially if you have a 'cold' quality to your personality that is largely out of your awareness). You may soon start to respond 'counter-transferentially', as if you are indeed the distant, abandoning person that the client sees. You may then find you have been caught up in what is called a transference 'enactment', where you become, in effect, an active participant in the historical transference dynamics.

Suggestion: Heighten your awareness of your potential counter-transference by visualizing a particular client, pay attention to your body sensations and feelings. Now imagine that you have licence to say or do anything without fear of injury or repercussions. What would you say? What have you held back or been reluctant to admit to yourself (some shadow aspects perhaps)? How many of these reactions or impulses are familiar to you in general, how many of them are particular to this client?

Tracking your own bodily resonance as you sit with the client, your sensations and bodily responses will sometimes also allow you to pick up more subtle transferential communications before they become figural.

Having identified your counter-transference, your choices are:

◆ Use your counter-transference as information about the client's feelings or what might have happened to him that is being replayed in the present. Especially with strong feelings, you may need to carefully consider (perhaps in supervision) how to best incorporate these in the here-and-now relationship. It may be that the client is not at all ready to hear your response to him. Then your job is to 'hold' your relational response until a later time. It could be that a premature disclosure would cause shame or anxiety in the client such that he withdraws from therapy.

◆ Disclose your counter-transference. Normally, with the emphasis on the real relationship and the intersubjective field, the Gestalt counsellor aims to find a way of naming her counter-transference in order to increase the client's awareness of his influence on relationships. Temper your response with your insight and compassion, and then offer it to the client as a tentative suggestion that might help him understand some of the problems he gets into in relationships. We stress this because it is important that both client and therapist know that the intervention is being made with the intention of helping the client and not in order for the therapist to feel 'clever' or superior or to discharge her own tension. We recommend that you read the section on guidelines for self-disclosure in Chapter 4 to support your strategy on this.

EXAMPLE

Therapist: 'I've noticed something that happens between us, which might help you get a better understanding in your relationship with your boss/colleague/wife/ etc. I've noticed that when you talk, it seems to have a similar effect on me to the one that you describe in him/her. I am finding that I don't feel included in some way when you tell about your difficulty. I feel a little uninvolved. And I wonder if you would like to look at that and see if we can understand something that's happening.'

You will notice several things about the example. One is that we have deliberately used language which, while it might not be modelling the language of self responsibility ('it' is having an effect on me) uses words and phrases which will be familiar to the client. It will join his frame of reference rather than inviting him out of it. If we want to make the point that what is happening here is echoing the outside world, it is not the moment to be demonstrating new patterns of communication. The therapist also refers to the client's particular circumstances to make the intervention relevant. Another feature of the example is the therapist sounding tentative and expressing a wish to explore. This is not just manipulation or false modesty. Such an intervention (however insightful) is valueless if it does not have resonance with the client's experience and phenomenology. Thus, the therapist offers her own phenomenology for *examination* – not as truth. Finally, the therapist negotiates with the client about whether he *wants* to explore the issue. This leaves power with the client for him to take charge of the process.

> **Suggestion:** When you have a feeling as a therapist that is confusing or you think may not belong to you, try to imagine an earlier scenario in the client's life that makes sense of the feelings you are having; for example, who in the client's life might have felt how you are feeling now? When might the client have felt what you are feeling when he was younger?

We feel the need to emphasize that all therapists (rather like human beings!) make mistakes. Sometimes, you will find yourself enacting some counter-transference response, or after a session (or several sessions), as you think over what happened, you realize that your attitudes were firmly based in a co-created transferential field. It is essential to be accepting of yourself at these times. Rarely will you have done any lasting damage. In our experience, most clients are supported enough in their process to ignore what isn't helpful. Return to the next session with an openness to explore what went on, to receive and empathize with your client's reaction to you, to acknowledge and even apologize for your mistakes. Indeed, we encourage you actually to welcome these enactments, for often it is only through them that you and your client can discover a deeper layer of meaning in your relationship. All this can often provide an enormously fertile field of inquiry and encounter. Your willingness to explore and to share the task of creating a real meeting can be enriching for both of you.

EROTIC TRANSFERENCE

When a client falls in love with a therapist, it is almost always a transference phenomenon, or at least is based on the highly specialized intimacy of the counselling relationship. It can often be most problematic when the transference is erotic or sexual.

Most cultures have strong taboos on talking openly about sexuality and it is often associated with shame, insecurity or abuse. Together with the highly charged energy it carries, it is a potential minefield for the unprepared counsellor, especially as the relational nature of the encounter means that you too may be experiencing an erotic energy. However, we recommend you find a way to create an atmosphere of openness about attraction and sexuality. Clients' disclosures and questions in this area need to be given the same respect, affirmation and interest as any other subject. At these times, if you sense that there may be confusion in the client's mind about actual sexual contact, you may need to state the boundary of the relationship relating to the ethical code you subscribe to. This might be something like:

> 'I want to tell you about the limits of our relationship. The ethical code to which I subscribe, says that I am not allowed to have a relationship with you outside our sessions. That means that we will never meet as friends or have any other than a therapeutic relationship. It also means that you and I will never have any sexual contact at any time, even when we have ended counselling. This is to preserve, both for now and for the future, the nature and purpose of our therapeutic relationship.'

Having clarified this, you should be able to explore all and everything that arises in this area, although the following caveats need to be remembered.

◆ Research shows that a sexual relationship between client and therapist is almost always traumatizing and abusive in the long run, even if the relationship starts after counselling has ended.
◆ Sometimes the therapist can feel embarrassed or discomfited by a discussion about a client's love or sexual feelings towards her. It is useful to remember that if the therapist responds with anxiety or withdrawal, she risks modelling disapproval or evoking shame.
◆ If asked directly whether you find the client attractive, you need first to decide whether to answer the question or whether to explore it ('How is my opinion important to you?'). If you decide that a straight answer is appropriate, find an affirmation that is suitable. 'I think that *you are* a very attractive man/woman.' Notice the different nuance of meaning if you say instead, 'I *find you* attractive', or, 'I *am attracted to you*' (provocative and potentially boundary-threatening statements). We have found that it helps to imagine what a good parent would say to their teenage son or daughter when asked this question.
◆ Sexuality is often a misrepresented need for affection, love or affirmation. If, as a child, the client needed to be seductive in order to get attention from a parent, they may do the same to you.
◆ There is a crucial difference between adult sexuality and the sexuality of a child. Many of our clients get in contact with early issues and may, like a child, be discovering or experimenting with their sexuality and its effect on others. They will

need a boundaried (parental) response at this time, one that is warm and accepting but sets limits on what is appropriate.

◆ Clients with a history of sexual abuse may try to 'push the boundaries' as an out-of-awareness enactment of their own abusive experiences. They may ask to be touched or held or be over-interested in their attractiveness to you.

◆ Keep alert to your own sexuality or seductiveness especially as it may be out of your awareness.

◆ Erotic counter-transference feelings of the counsellor are normal and need to be discussed in supervision or therapy. They can be a rich source of understanding, although we recommend that you do not disclose them to the client. It is hard to see any therapeutic value in this; it could imply a powerful demand from the counsellor and may intimidate the client, or it could repeat a transferential dynamic.

In the practice of his art, the therapist must treat those patients who make declarations of love with tenderness and understanding. It is important to realize that the love that is shown by the patient for the therapist is just as 'genuine', even though it may not be as realistic as love occurring outside the therapeutic situation. (Storr, 1979: 78)

> **Suggestion:** Take some time to think of your own patterns in relation to sexuality. Was it talked about in your family? What messages did you receive about your own sexuality or your gender? How important is it for you to be found attractive? What support would you need in order to be able to discuss these topics with clients as they emerge?

CONCLUSION

Transference is an inevitable component of relationships and as such it invariably becomes part of most counselling relationships, whether acknowledged or not. It is the way the client organizes his relational field and is therefore a rich source of information for the counsellor. Unlike psychoanalysts, we are not interested in working with the transforming historical interpretation. We are interested in the past that is *still active* in the present, and its interaction in the relationship with the here-and-now counsellor.

We end with two last rules of thumb. The first is to know your own transference profile and vulnerability. Become familiar with your own relational expectations so that you can predict and allow for them. The second is to combine your willingness to trust the process between you with an occasional questioning of the relational dynamic. Could this relationship contain transference and counter-transference that is unacknowledged?

RECOMMENDED READING ON TRANSFERENCE

Clarkson, P. and Mackewn, J. (1993) *Key Figures in Counselling and Psychotherapy: Fritz Perls*. London: Sage. **(See pp. 132–4 and 177.)**

Erskine, R. (1999) *Beyond Empathy*. Philadelphia, PA: Brunner-Mazel. **(See Chapter 6.)**

Hargaden, H. and Sills, C. (2002) *Transactional Analysis – a Relational Perspective*. London: Routledge. **(See Chapters 4 and 5.)**

Mackewn, J. (1997) *Developing Gestalt Counselling*. London: Sage. **(See Chapter 10.)**

Melnick, J. (2003) 'Countertransference', *British Gestalt Journal,* 2 (1): 40–48.

Ogden, T. (1982) *Projective Identification and Psychotherapeutic Technique*. London: Jason Aronson.

Philippson, P. (2002) 'The Gestalt therapy approach to transference', *British Gestalt Journal,* 11 (1): 16–20.

Staemmler, F.-M. (1993) 'Projective identification in Gestalt therapy with severely impaired clients', *British Gestalt Journal*, 2 (2): 104–10.

Thomas, B.Y. (2007) 'Countertransference, dialogue and Gestalt therapy', *Gestalt Review*, 11 (1): 28–41.

RECOMMENDED READING ON THE EROTIC

Cornell, B. (2004) 'Love and intimacy – a reply to Quilter', in 'Letters to the Editor', *British Gestalt Journal,* 13 (1): 41–2.

Latner, J. (1998) 'Sex in therapy', *British Gestalt Journal,* 7 (2): 136–38.

Mann, D. (1997) *Psychotherapy: An Erotic Relationship*. London: Routledge.

Morin, J. (1996) *The Erotic Mind*. New York: Harper Perennial Library.

O'Shea, L. (2000) 'Sexuality: old struggles and new challenges', *Gestalt Review,* 4 (1): 8–25.

O'Shea, L. (2003) 'The erotic field', *British Gestalt Journal,* 12 (2): 105–10.

Quilter, S.J. (2004) 'Yes! But ... what about love?' in 'Letters to the Editor', *British Gestalt Journal,* 13 (1): 38–40.

13

BODY PROCESS

The therapist must, each hour, foster an embodied field powerful enough to support the client in holding their bodily life and experience as intrinsic to their ongoing experience.
(Kepner, 2003: 10)

How a client's body moves and expresses is the manifestation of a person's unspoken inner world. In the way she is active or holds still, in the way she reaches out or holds back, the client is physically enacting her feelings, needs, creative adjustments and beliefs. This rich vein of communication can be lost or overlooked unless the therapist is actively sensitive to her own body process and keeps alert to the unspoken messages from the body of the client.

It is also the hallmark of Gestalt as an 'embodied' therapy, one where a felt experience of your body or your aliveness is the starting point for all therapeutic work, and a continual reminder to the client to include her somatic experience in her self-awareness.

Recent neuro-scientific research has discovered an area of the brain that contains 'mirror neurons' (Rizzolatti, et al., 1996), which effectively give us an actual impression of the experiences of the other and are probably the neurological basis of the empathic response. They give us an actual felt sense of the other.

In many client presentations of anxiety, depression, physical and sexual abuse, addictions and eating disorders, the client's bodily sensations (or the lack of them) are the only available clues to what is hidden or avoided. They are the potential doorways to the underlying dynamic of the problem. For many clients bodily sensations are also the evidence of developmental issues, sometimes the only evidence of trauma history, and for some it is how they can communicate what cannot be said in words.

The bodily response of the therapist can also have the unspoken resonance, the empathic knowledge and the means of a deeper understanding of the world of the client. It is also the place where the energetic ebb and flow of the embodied relationship plays out. Gestalt is one of only a few therapies that give emphasis to body process, and actively resists the artificial splitting-off of mind and body.

> **Suggestion:** Take a moment to come to your body awareness, see what you notice about how tense you are and where, check your posture, take a snap-shot of all this: what message is your body giving you now? Now reach out both your arms in front of you as if you were holding a very large beach ball. Hold that posture for a minute; see how your feelings respond. Now change your posture, hold your arms folded against your chest and lower your head, hold this also for a minute, and see how your sense of yourself changes.

The mere changing of a body position or a simple attention to body process (e.g. feeling the sensation in your feet and limbs) can profoundly change our attitudes or feelings about our self in relation to the world.

For a Gestaltist, health is the holistic functioning of all interconnected aspects of emotion, cognition and body. For many clients, a vital step is to raise awareness of what has been avoided, or pushed out of sight, to reconnect with the energy, vitality and intelligence of body process. Restoring these natural processes can be a major factor in healing and in re-establishing 'whole person' functioning.

In many cultures, the message seems to be to disconnect, ignore, desensitize, blame or even punish the body. Every culture also has its own meanings around touch, gesture, bodily expressiveness, body boundaries and non-verbal communication. It is essential for the counsellor to be open to learn and be sensitive to the unique cultural ground of each client's body process.

We wish to make the crucial point that the starting point for any Gestalt therapy session is for the therapist to connect with an embodied sense of their own being, to continue to pay attention to their body reactions, return frequently to simple body awareness and contribute their embodied presence to the relational field. Throughout the book we have given many examples of how to 'come to your body', and we suggest you find one that you can use on a regular basis when you work with clients.

BODY PROCESS WITHOUT INVOLVING TOUCH

> Body processes can be usefully viewed as existential messages from disowned parts of self. The therapist is faced with the task of helping the client make messages from the body intelligible. (Kepner, 1987: 69)

Before we look at working with body process, we would like to make some general points. First, keep a holistic perspective; all aspects of the person are connected. Don't just 'remark' or 'notice' a body movement in a vacuum, since this can be off-putting, especially for new clients. It is better to say: 'As you have been talking about your anger at your boss, your hands have been very active – have you noticed that? Do you think they are expressing something?' Second, practise inclusion, sense how your own body is reacting or imagine how your body would feel if you were in their situation. Third, remember that as body process becomes more figural, then emotion also can become more prominent, especially that of shame.

Therapeutic suggestions

♦ **Heightening body awareness**: The first step is to sensitize yourself to the physical process of the client. Start to scan the movement, tension and activity of their body. Look for what is happening and is not happening. Is their breathing shallow or deep? Are they sitting in a particular posture? Do you have the sense of containment or of expression? Is there some repetitive motion or activity happening? As you do this, some feature or figure may arise. Invite the client to heighten her own awareness of her body. Where does she feel tension, what is her own sense of how she is holding her body?

♦ **Being aware of your own bodily reaction to the client**: You may find your body resonating or reacting in ways that will give you valuable information – for example, do you find yourself becoming tense, agitated or low in energy? Consider whether you are noticing the emergence of a counter-transference response – is your bodily response puzzling to you?

♦ **Disclosing your own somatic response**: 'My chest is feeling heavy as I listen to you.' It can also help you to gesture or touch your own body as you do so (e.g. holding your hand to your chest as you speak).

♦ **Changing 'it' language to 'I'**: In order to heighten awareness and develop a client's relationship to her body, you can suggest that the client rephrase the disowning language she uses in relation to her body. For example 'it hurts' to 'I hurt', 'My neck is tense' to 'I am tense in my neck' or 'I am tensing my neck.'

♦ **Focusing on breathing**: Perls et al. (1989 [1951]: 128–9) describe anxiety as excitement suppressed and deprived of oxygen. Breathing is central to all experience, and changing how we breathe will affect our experience of body process and emotions. Simple attention to breath can be transformative for a client.

Breathing is also an essential part of self-support. When people are frightened or startled, their breathing usually becomes rapid and shallow. You may often notice a client's breathing change as she starts to tell you about a particular situation or emotion. At these times it may be clear that her breathing is not supporting her experience. Bringing the client's attention to the change in breathing rhythm can sometimes re-establish healthy, supportive breathing. At other times, you may need to suggest that she re-focuses on her breathing to bring it into a more regular, even pattern.

If a client seems to be holding her breath either through retroflection or because of denying herself the support of the environment, she can be encouraged to breathe *out* rather than simply to breathe. This releases the tension and creates space for the in breath (the inspiration!), which will naturally follow.

♦ **Enlivening work**: Techniques for helping to increase energy are many and various. Methods we have used include suggesting to the client that she raise her voice; move around the room; visualize energy flow and direct it; use paints or other art materials.

♦ **Encouraging physical confidence**: This may be improved through exercise, massage, martial arts, yoga, walking and swimming.

♦ **Adjusting body posture**: A client can be facilitated to notice how closely linked are her inner and middle zones through experimentation with, for example, sitting erect with head straight as opposed to slumping into the chair, standing up in order to be assertive, and so on.

◆ **Grounding exercises**: Forms of meditation or awareness exercises that focus on 'I ... here ... now' we have found particularly useful. A 'shorthand' version of this is to 'be aware of your feet on the floor'.

◆ **Catharsis**: Tensions and emotions are all located in the body. Shouting, hitting cushions, screaming, singing, dancing, are all part of the cathartic repertoire. Therapists might use two-chair work, heightening and enlivening techniques and many other experiments to facilitate this sort of release. However, the counsellor needs to remain creatively indifferent to any particular outcome, remembering that each client will have a different range of expression, that every release is unique and that a premature or unsupported release can be unhelpful or even dangerous.

The other caveat is that a cathartic episode can produce a temporary sense of well-being due to the release of natural opiates. This may give rise to a potentially misleading sense of resolution. However, if the cathartic expression was simply a replay of some past pain, the effect of the piece of work will be to reinforce that fixed gestalt, despite the temporary good feelings. Catharsis is only therapeutic if the release of blocked feelings leads to a new assimilation – perhaps due to the presence of an empathic supportive counsellor; or because the experience is symbolized or understood in a new way.

◆ **Decoding messages from the body**: A well-known and effective technique here is to invite the client to 'speak from' different parts of the body. This has the effect of helping her to own and integrate the full complexity of her experience. It also demonstrates how closely our bodies manifest our thoughts, feelings and attitudes. This technique is very useful for highlighting the ways that the body can get ignored or disregarded.

If the client has some physical symptom, she can explore it from the point of view that, as Lao Tzu said, 'We choose our problems today for the gift they contain for us.' If the symptom were seen in a positive light, what function might it be serving? What secondary gain is there? For example, does the illness prevent the person from overworking? Or does it prevent her from leaving the house or attending social gatherings? Does it mean that someone has to look after her? In this way you may start to see any messages or creative adjustments the body is making to a difficult situation.

◆ **Educating**: Finally, it is important to remember that some highly intelligent and knowledgeable people are ignorant when it comes to the workings of their bodies. It can be enormously helpful and reassuring for clients to be given straightforward information about physical stress symptoms, anxiety and panic reactions, post-traumatic stress phenomena reactions, relaxation techniques, and so on.

With all these suggestions, the emphasis is always on experimenting from a place of creative indifference. You will of course have hunches, intuitions, ideas and suggestions that may lead the client in different directions, but you must remember that there is no right or wrong way for the client to relate to her body energy. There is no best way of moving, expressing or releasing physical process. Each client is unique and will have a unique degree of expression, contact and resolution.

Suggestion: The following is a focusing technique (Kelly, 1998) that you can use with clients to encourage integration of experience:

Step One: Raising awareness of bodily sensations.
Pay attention to your body self and notice what physical sensations you are aware of right now. (For example, I have butterflies in my stomach, my jaw feels tense, my legs are restless, etc.) Allow time for the client to develop a full awareness around the sensation before moving on.

Step Two: Identifying the feeling or emotion.
Stay with that sensation and see what feeling seems to belong to it. Take as long as you need. (For example, sadness, fear, anger, resentment, joy, etc.) Allow the client to stay with the feeling and its relationship to the sensation (as they are expressions of each other) before moving on.

Step Three: Identifying thoughts or images.
As you stay with your sensation and feeling, notice what thought, image or memory comes to your mind that might fit. (For example, 'I used to feel like this when I heard my parents arguing', 'I'm reminded of the time when I had to stand in front of a group of people and give a speech, etc.)
   Sometimes a client will begin with step three (memory or thought), in which case you can ask them to return to steps one and two. For example, 'As you tell me about your experience of being depressed, notice what sensations you are aware of in your body right now.' If the client reports a feeling first, again return to focusing on body sensation. For example, 'How do you know you feel sad? What sensations are you experiencing in your body? As you focus on your body, check that 'sad' is the most accurate word for your experience right now or whether you want to refine it.'

This is a useful way of working towards encouraging the integration of disowned aspects of self. It is not a formula that must always be followed. We can break out from it to work with whatever emerges and feels appropriate for the client in the moment.

A different way of experimenting is developed by Frank (2001, 2003) in a process she calls 'Developmental Body Work', a way of understanding the legacy of early psycho-physical blocks as they emerge in the here-and-now relationship with the therapist. The therapist pays attention to the non-verbal patterns of movement and response to uncover (and resolve) the unfinished business they represent.

> Observing the client, the therapist creates a task inspired from the most obvious phenomena – tilting of the client's head, holding of his or her breath, tensing of shoulders or shifting of position. The therapist knows that in staying with what is obvious – the client's most relevant existential concern – that is, the unfelt predicament – will easily emerge. (Frank, 2003: 189)

Although it is not from Gestalt theory, a recent approach by Ogden et al., (2006) call 'Sensorimotor Psychotherapy' also extends an essentially Gestalt foundation to working with the body.

ISSUES OF TOUCH

> If we believe that the body is self, then when we touch another person we are not touching a 'body', but the very self of this person with our own self. (Kepner, 1987: 75)

Touch in Gestalt therapy serves a very different function from touch in other body therapies such as massage, the Alexander technique or shiatsu. It is therefore important not to mix different forms (unless you have specialist training in integrating psychotherapy and direct body work). We believe that in order to be effective and safe in working with touch, a practitioner needs to have specialist training in the area. However, we think it is important to offer some general guidelines about touching.

◆ The increasing number of ethical complaints by clients in relation to sexuality has made many practitioners decide never to touch clients at all, as any touch can potentially be misconstrued. It is also true that in the West, touch tends to be reserved for families and intimate partners. Touch therefore carries a very high significance and may tend to be seen as maternal, paternal or sexual. In many ways, it is therefore easier to avoid any physical contact, although this would be to miss many useful possibilities. In some Latin cultures (for example), not to touch on meeting and parting is considered as strange behaviour, even between therapist and client. However, as a general guideline, it is probably best not to touch a client until the relationship is well formed and you have a sense of the significance of touch for that person, especially in the context of their early life and culture. With some clients you may wish to check before you offer even a minor physical intervention such as a hand on the shoulder: 'I have a wish to put my hand on your shoulder – how would that be for you?'

◆ You will often be able to pick up non-verbal cues from the client's body which will tell you about her fear or reluctance to be approached or touched. A common dilemma arises when the client asks for some physical contact or a hug at the end of the session. It may be best to pause and ask what that would mean for the client and how this would affect them. If you are concerned, you can be honest and say, 'I realize that I am not comfortable with that right now; can we discuss this next time we meet.' You will, of course, then need to be empathic with the feeling of rejection or irritation that the client may experience at the denial of their request.

◆ Clients' issues and difficulties around their bodies frequently tend to be pre- or non-verbal or out of awareness. The client may have been touched or handled invasively or abusively at an age where they could not articulate or understand what was going on. Sexually abused clients are also often instructed to forget or deny they were abused. It is, therefore, especially important to proceed cautiously as the client may not explicitly know that an area of their body is associated with abuse or may indeed even invite re-abuse out of awareness, thus re-creating an experience of feeling abused. If you do not have a solid, clinical reason why you would contemplate using touch, then it is best to refrain. Your impulse might be normal human compassion. It may, however, be a response to an unhelpful transferential invitation.

◆ Never touch a client anywhere unless and until you are sure of the significance and meaning of that part of the body for the client. Never, *under any circumstances*, touch the breast, buttock or genital areas of a client.

◆ If you are going to touch the client, you will also need to think about the implications of that in a relationship with an inherent power imbalance. Will you allow the client to touch you? Can she reach out to your hand in distress, touch your arm or face or give you a hug without asking permission? It is important for the therapist to be clear as to the necessary agreements about whether and how touch is offered. Also, be aware that whatever agreement is made will have implications for how the relationship is viewed.

> **Suggestion:** See if you can remember what messages were around in your family about bodies. What were the rules and regulations about touch or physical affection, nudity and the sexuality of your body? Did members of your family change in how they touched you when you became a teenager? This can also be a useful exercise to do with clients.

Having enumerated all these caveats, you might be beginning to feel thoroughly inhibited and awkward about any sort of touch. We apologize if this is the case. There are many powerful ways to use touch as an intervention into the body process – such as using light but firm pressure on the chest or lower back in order to increase breathing and catharsis. We believe that therapists should have specialized training and supervision if they wish to work in this way. However, some forms of touch can be a natural and normal extension of empathic, human relating and as such can be an important part of offering to a client a relationship in which there is a genuine meeting.

SOME GENERAL THOUGHTS ABOUT TOUCH AS A NATURAL PART OF RELATING

There are many forms of touch associated with greeting and departing, mostly ritualized, including a handshake, a kiss on the cheek, a hug. For some clients, a formalized greeting, in awareness, can be a powerful part of the containing structure of therapy and an 'anchor' of a particular sort of I–Thou meeting. On the other hand, some new clients feel under a social pressure to carry out these rituals, and while we would not of course refuse a handshake on a first meeting, it is important to invite a climate where each situation, each week, is unique and may call for different behaviour. It is easy to become complicit in a physical ritual that has never been discussed with a client. Such rituals are always usefully brought into awareness: 'I'm aware that each time we meet/end, you offer your hand, ask for a hug, pat me on the back . . . How is that for you? What does it communicate for you? Are there times when you don't want it?'

During sessions, you might offer a light touch of reassurance on the arm, a hand held in distress, a supportive arm round the shoulder, an affectionate hug at the end of a therapeutic journey, a strengthening hand on the back in an experiment to face a fear. In all these ways, a therapist can communicate directly and immediately at a profound level of contact. What is more, all of them are potentially a normal part of compassionate human relationship. Touch can be used to express affection or appreciation, to support or reassure in the face of a distressing emotion, or to communicate empathy. It can assist in an experiment or bring focus to a desensitized part of the client's body. It can communicate your presence in disconnected states, calm agitation and communicate acceptance or connection.

RECOMMENDED READING

Clance, P.R, Thompson, M.B., Simerly, D.B. and Weiss, A. (1994) 'The effects of the Gestalt approach on body image', *Gestalt Journal*, 17 (1): 95–114.

Clemmens, C. and Bursztyn, A. (2005) 'Culture and the body', in T. Levine Bar-Joseph (ed.), *The Bridge: Dialogues Across Cultures*. New Orleans: Gestalt Institute Press.

Corrigall, J. Payne, H. and Wilkinson, H. (2006) *About a Body – Working with the Embodied Mind in Psychotherapy*. London: Routledge.

Frank, R. (2001) *Body of Awareness*. Cambridge: Gestalt Press.

Frank, R. (2003) 'Embodying creativity', in M. Spagnuolo Lobb and N. Amendt-Lyon (eds), *Creative Licence – the Art of Gestalt Therapy*. Vienna: Springer-Verlag.

Hartley, L. (2009) *Contemporary Body Therapy, The Chiron Approach*. Hove: Routledge. **(See many good chapters, including Chapter 3 'Gestalt Body psychotherapy'.)**

Hunter, M. and Struve, J. (1998) *The Ethical Use of Touch in Psychotherapy*. London: Sage.

Kepner, J.I. (1987) *Body Process: A Gestalt Approach to Working with the Body in Gestalt Therapy*. New York: Gardner.

Kepner, J.I. (1995) *Healing Tasks in Psychotherapy*. San Francisco, CA: Jossey-Bass, for the Gestalt Institute of Cleveland Publications.

Kepner, J.I. (2001) 'Touch in Gestalt body process psychotherapy', *Gestalt Review*, 5 (2): 97–114.

Ogden, P., Minton, K. and Pain, C. (2006) *Trauma and the Body: A Sensorimotor Approach to Psychotherapy*. London: Norton.

Parlett, M. (2001) 'On being present at one's own life', in E. Spinelli and S. Marshall, *Embodied Theories*. London: Continuum.

Parlett, M. (ed.) (2003) 'Special focus on embodying', *British Gestalt Journal*, 12 (1): 2–55.

Smith, E., Clance, P. and Imes, S. (1998) *Touch in Psychotherapy*. New York: Guilford Press.

Staunton, T. (2002) *Body Psychotherapy*. Hove: Brunner-Routledge.

Totton, N. (2005) *New Dimensions in Body Psychotherapy*. Berkshire: Open University Press.

14

WORKING WITH DREAMS

Perls stated that dreams were the 'royal road to integration' (1969: 71). He believed that a dream is not simply unfinished business but an 'existential messenger' through which a person can understand 'one's life script, one's karma, one's destiny' (Baumgardner, 1975: 117). For him, every element of a dream was an element of the waking person, although in different degrees of awareness. All dreams, therefore, consist of projections of some aspect of the dreamer themselves. The task of the therapist is to help the client to re-own or reclaim aspects of their self that have been projected on to people or objects in the dream.

Isadore From, on the other hand, saw 'the events of a dream not as projection, but as retroflection' and actually a message about the relationship with the therapist (Muller, 1996: 72). He suggested that the work was to understand and undo the retroflection of what could not be expressed in waking life.

Sichera (2003: 96) points out that Perls et al. (1989 [1951]) actually urge the therapist not to try and understand, interpret or search for concrete meaning but to allow the dream to be like a work of art, with a hermeneutic message that needs to be received through 'careful literary and pictorial representation of it'.

We believe that all these explanations may be true at different times and that the therapist should always be open to the emergent meaning of a dream. It may be unfinished business – especially recurring dreams or nightmares which are calling to be resolved. It may also be a fractal of the dreamer's entire life story or it can indicate a current pressing issue or theme. It can represent an attempt to re-own alienated or rejected parts of ourselves. It can also be a statement about the therapeutic relationship and an opportunity for an encounter between therapist and client.

There are many ways to work with a dream in therapy and it is not necessary for the dream to be complete. It is quite possible to work with fragments of the dream or the feeling the client experienced on waking, especially as what is remembered often contains the emerging unfinished business. Perls (1969) was clear that interpretation forms no part of working with dreams in Gestalt. He stressed that the meaning of the dream was only to be found by the dreamer in exploration and experiment. He believed that dreams, especially repetitive ones, carry for the dreamer a message that can be found. The message may be a statement or description of the person's life at the moment, or the issues they are facing. For example, a repetitive dream in which you are being followed or chased clearly has a different potential message from a dream where you are alone in an empty house. Perls also believed that dreams might contain an ontological message about existence itself, such as death or embodiment.

From a Gestalt perspective, every aspect, incident, theme and process in a dream represents some aspect of the client and his life. The counsellor therefore invites the client to explore the dream from every angle. What follows is an example of one dream that a client brought to therapy and some examples of ways of working with that dream.

Jake had come to see a therapist because he was feeling miserable and stuck in his life. One day he reported the following vivid fragment of a dream which had upset him but he did not understand. As he talked, his voice was low and subdued.

'I was walking along a deserted seashore, I felt nervous and frightened, the sky was dark and overcast with waves crashing on to the shore. Then I saw someone approaching in the distance. It was my mother, much younger though. She was crying and distressed, pleading with me.'

METHODS OF EXPLORATION

Practise the phenomenological method as you listen to the dream

Go with the energy and interest of the client and notice where the energy becomes stuck or avoided. As you work with the client, also remember to keep focused on here-and-now awareness. It is important to remember that in dreams, as in life, the images, symbols and metaphors have a unique meaning for each individual. The meaning of a symbol to you may have a completely different meaning to the dreamer. The first task, therefore, is to see if there is anything immediately relevant in his life and ask the client what the objects, words, symbols, people, mean to him. What associations does he have? Associations can be to events in his life – past or present; or they can be to sounds or images or other words. Dreams often represent the dreamer's attempt to bring to awareness, complex and emerging feelings, so, just as with a child's attempt to begin to put words to his experience, the language and shapes that emerge may come through word-play or symbolic form that is not logical. It is important not to hurry to make the images concrete and 'left brain'.

> The counsellor asked Jake what the deserted seashore meant to him. He replied with an important memory. 'I remember a beach like that when we were on holiday after father had left home to live with another woman.'

Ask the client to tell you a dream in the present

As if it was happening now, using 'I' and the present tense. This makes the experience more immediate.

> 'I am walking along a deserted seashore. I am feeling nervous and frightened, the sky is dark and overcast and the waves are crashing on to the shore. I can now see someone approaching in the distance, As she comes closer I can see that it is my mother, only much younger than she is now, she is crying and calling out, saying you must help me I'm dying, only you can help me ...'

As Jake retold the dream, his energy was completely different. He was full of emotion and vitality, unlike the dull, distanced way he initially told the dream. As he continued, it became clear that he was interested and curious to understand the meaning of the dream and he started to make connections quite naturally.

Work with the experience as if it were a real story the client has told

As the dream is recounted you will certainly be able to see many themes and figures emerging, such as changes in voice tone, physical reactions, modifications to contact, etc. You can then bring awareness to the client.

> Jake's counsellor said, 'Can I pause you for a moment Jake? I'm noticing that you are sitting very still and tense as you are telling me and your voice is becoming very small, you look as if you are holding yourself in.' After this intervention, Jake became aware of his bodily retroflection and helplessness in the face of his mother.

Suggest the client express the dream non-verbally

This can involve enacting the dream by taking on different bodily postures, moving around, or making a noise. It could also mean working with plasticine or sketching a picture representing the dream.

The counsellor suggested that Jake take some paper and coloured pens to draw a representation of the dream, then stand back and look at the picture from a distance. He was invited to see what message the picture seemed to convey. What was missing in the picture or what he would like to add? How did he imagine the figure walking along the beach was feeling? What might have happened to her?

Suggest the client retell the dream from the perspective of each character or object

This experiment is based on the belief that every feature of the dream is a part of the dreamer – some parts are known, some unknown and perhaps rejected. It is sometimes interesting to start with something in the dream that the client is least identified with, such as an expanse of landscape or a peripheral detail. This can bring a surprising insight. However, if there is some aspect of the dream which carries a very strong interest or charge for the client then start with that and work through to the part which is the most distant or difficult. As the client works through the different characters in the dream, he will often have spontaneous realizations, sudden insights or identifications. This can help to clarify what meanings or symbols are present but out of awareness.

'I am the seashore that Jake is walking along. I have been here for a long time, I stretch for miles and very few people ever walk upon me. I am cold and lonely.' As Jake was speaking as a 'lonely seashore', he started to look sad and tears came to his eyes as he said 'I do feel lonely these days.'

Sometimes clients will find it difficult to identify with a frightening, aggressive or unpleasant aspect of the dream. In fact, clients often have the most difficulty in identifying with parts that are most strongly disowned. They may need gentle encouragement to take on these particular roles. This can be especially rewarding, as many of these projections contain enormous energy and power which has been bound up in the disowning and projecting.

This is also a moment to pull back and let yourself be aware of something significant that might be missing from the dream. Sometimes the client will name it himself: 'There were no people in the library', or 'The boy didn't have any feet.' However, often the person whose dream it is does not notice an obvious missing aspect and it is appropriate for the therapist to say, 'But where were the other people?' or 'Didn't the car move?' and so on. Perls believed that missing parts in dreams implied missing parts in the personality.

Create dialogues or experiments between the characters or objects in the dream

Jake was encouraged to role-play a conversation between himself and his mother in the dream. As the experiment progressed, it became apparent that nothing Jake could say (in the dream) helped or satisfied his mother and he became increasingly frustrated until he suddenly snapped out of the experiment turned to the counsellor, saying 'It's just like my real mother. She was always expecting me to look after her and take care of her needs. I hated that pressure.' When they debriefed from this experience Jake said that he had never before contacted such ordinary anger at his mother's neediness (which he had known since he was a child).

Experiment with creating a different outcome for the dream

This is especially useful for nightmares. You could ask the client to imagine themselves being stronger or more powerful or invoking an image or person to support them. They would then re-run the dream (possibly several times), seeing how the ending changed or resolved.

Jake imagined his father walking down the beach towards them. As he arrived he took Jake's mother in his arms, comforting her and telling her that he would take care of them both. Jake came to realize that his father was the person who should have been helping his distressed mother and that Jake had felt the burden of guilt. He then went on to realize how angry he was that his father had deserted them all those years ago.

Invite the client to create a sculpt using the elements of the dream

If you are working in a group, this is an ideal way of including the group members and allowing their conscious and unconscious wisdom to relate to the dream. It is particularly useful for exploring issues of psychological closeness and distance. The client allocates the characters and significant objects in the dream (including himself) to the group members and then positions them around the room in relation to one another using his feelings and instincts to guide him rather than his thought. Then each group member speaks from the character, saying how he feels to be in that position, what he needs and so on. Then either the dreamer is invited to re-position the characters as he wishes, or the characters themselves are invited first to say where they would prefer to be and why. They take the new positions and then repeat the process, one by one, each saying how they feel.

Even if the client is not part of a group, the exercise can be adapted using cushions or objects from the room to represent the different elements, and positioning them around the room. Then the client either speaks from each element and goes through the process of adjusting closeness and distance, or stands back and looks at it (taking a meta view), experimenting with placing the characters differently.

See the dream as a message about the therapist or about the therapy

In this sense, the dream may be a retroflection on the part of the client, of something that is difficult to express. As you listen to the dream, imagine what message could be contained in it for you. For example, is the dream about being cared for, frightened or let down, or of sexual attraction to a mysterious stranger? Does this have any resonance for you about what happened at the last session, for instance? Is the dream of the client trying to tell you something that he cannot easily acknowledge in the here-and-now?

> The therapist reflects: I replayed the last therapy session I had with Jake and tried to remember if he could have seen me as needy. I remembered that I had told him of a forthcoming holiday I was taking and wondered whether he had seen this as my neediness (for a break). Alternatively, I wondered if he himself was perhaps feeling needy or abandoned at the coming separation, left alone with the seemingly overwhelming demands of his current life.

The techniques outlined above are also suitable for working with fantasies or daydreams, which may also represent desires, conflicts and unfinished business that are at the edge of the client's awareness. Bear in mind also that you may have a sense of what is missing or avoided in the dream (for example, an opposite polarity of feeling, a missing family member).

Finally, you may choose to consider that, as Sichera (2003) says, a dream is a portrayal or fractal of the potential encounter between therapist and client – an invitation to engage together in a poetic exploration. Together you and the client create a new language for what emerges, engaging with the dream as a vehicle for developing contact.

RECOMMENDED READING

Amram, D. (1991) 'The intruder: a dreamwork session with commentary', *Gestalt Journal*, 14 (1): 61–72.

Bate, D. (1995) 'The oral tradition and a footnote to dreams', *British Gestalt Journal*, 4 (1): 52.

Baumgardner, P. (1975) *Legacy from Fritz: Gifts from Lake Cowichan*. Palo Alto, CA: Science and Behavior Books. (**See Chapter 2**.)

Downing, J. and Marmorsteing, R. (eds) (1973) *Dreams and Nightmares: A Book of Gestalt Therapy Sessions*. New York: Harper & Row.

Grey, L. (2005) 'Community building viewed from a group dream perspective', *Gestalt Review*, 9 (2): 207–15.

Higgins, J. (1994) 'Honouring the dream – an interview with Dolores Bate', *British Gestalt Journal*, 3 (2): 117–24.

Perls, F.S. (1966) 'Dream seminars', in J. Fagan and I.L. Shepherd (eds), *Gestalt Therapy Now: Theory, Techniques, Applications*. New York: Science and Behavior Books. pp. 204–33.

Perls, F.S. (1976) *The Gestalt Approach and Eyewitness to Therapy*. New York: Bantam.

Perls, F.S. (1981) *Gestalt Therapy Verbatim*. Moab, UT: Real People Press. (**See pp. 77–230**.)

Sichera, A. (2003) 'Therapy as aesthetic issue', in M. Spagnuolo Lobb and N. Amendt-Lyon (eds), *Creative Licence: the Art of Gestalt Therapy*. New York/Vienna: Springer Verlag. pp. 93–9.

15

USING SUPERVISION AND IDENTIFYING YOUR PERSONAL STYLE

CHOOSING A SUPERVISOR

Being in supervision is an ethical requirement of all practitioners. You will need a supervisor as soon as you start to practice, and ideally even before you start, so that you can prepare yourself well and think about your needs as a beginning practitioner. An important issue is to choose a supervisor who, as with a therapist, will suit your needs. We suggest you meet initially with a supervisor to discuss whether you are a good fit together. You will need to identify, as far as possible, whether the following considerations are met:

◆ Some appreciation by the supervisor of the implications of the stage of training or post-qualification you are at.
◆ A recognition of your particular growing edges and your style of learning.
◆ A sense of being received, accepted and understood.
◆ A feeling of rapport or relational engagement.
◆ A sense of collaboration: that the supervisor is also willing to struggle with issues in partnership with you (rather than being an 'expert' who directs you).
◆ An ability to challenge you in a way that stretches you rather than demoralizes you.
◆ A sense of humour.

If you have already had supervision, then you are better placed to be proactive and ask for what you want. You will already know what style of supervisor would be most useful based on what did and didn't work in your previous experience. You may also wish to agree to have a limited number of sessions before you decide an ongoing contract.

You need to decide which of the three most common structures are most suitable at this stage in your professional development:

◆ Individual supervision: this is more flexible, confidential, potentially less shaming, and can more easily be tailored to what you personally need.

◆ Group supervision: this offers more diverse feedback, peer support or challenge and a chance to learn from, and contribute to, others being supervised. It may also have the potential to evoke issues of competition or shame, which may or may not be useful learning. Within this group format, there are several possible structures. It might be an individual format with the supervisor working with each person separately and managing the contributions of the others. Or it might be supervision 'by the group', where the supervisor facilitates the group in learning to develop their reflective and supervisory skills, teachers where necessary and manages the group process.

◆ Peer supervision: this is more collegial, less structured (and cheaper!). It is suitable for practitioners who feel confident and are fairly experienced. The challenge for peer group members is to remain 'on duty' professionally – supporting and challenging each other to the best of their ability and not lapsing into social mode. Peer groups need very clear contracting about how they will work, and the roles and responsibilities of participants.

If you are in the position of having a supervisor allocated to you, we suggest you spend the first session agreeing your tasks and goals (and that of their employer), contracting for what you want (from what is on offer), discussing how best to manage the 'arranged' relationship, and having clear agreements about responsibilities and how you will discuss difficulties. You will then be able to make the most of the supervision and, if necessary, plan ways to get any extra support you may need.

> **Suggestion:** Remember an activity, hobby, sport or skill that you feel competent about. Take a moment to write down the process of how you learnt it. How long did it take, what helped you most, was anyone with you, what role did they play, how did you deal with setbacks? If you could do it again how would you change the learning process?

MAKING THE MOST OF SUPERVISION

Arriving with an agenda

Sometimes it is appropriate just to arrive at Gestalt supervision and see what emerges. You will also find that supervision sessions can profit from some planning before a session, especially if you have a particular issue you want help with. The following are some headings that may help you organize what you want to bring.

The client and his story

◆ What happened in a session, the emerging themes, storyline, the client's history, a description of the client and his body process.

The assessment of the client

◆ Assessment and diagnosis (especially with new clients).
◆ Planning considerations.
◆ Risk and suitability issues.
◆ What is happening in the wider field that might be having impact.

Practice tasks

◆ Skills and strategy issues (improving a particular intervention or exploring new strategies).
◆ Conceptualization (e.g. talking about your work in theory terms).
◆ Professional and practice issues (keeping notes, doing accounts, raising fees).
◆ Ethical issues that have arisen (or might arise).
◆ An overview of your case-load (the types of client you are seeing, maintaining a balanced profile a terms of issues, gender, etc.)

The relational process between you and the client

◆ What is happening in the co-created 'between'.
◆ The working alliance.
◆ Relational ruptures.
◆ Transference and counter-transference responses.

Your personal issues and development

◆ Particular issues with a client (e.g. feeling stuck, demoralized or confused).
◆ Identifying material that you are reluctant to disclose (e.g. mistakes, 'untherapeutic' attitudes or feelings).
◆ Growing edges that need attention (e.g. to focus on self-disclosure, identify transference, bring in body perspectives).
◆ Reviewing your overall development as a therapist.

The supervision process itself

◆ Issues with your supervisor (e.g. feeling misunderstood or defensive).
◆ Recurring patterns in the supervisory process (e.g. the supervisor becomes over-directive or you become over-submissive or rebellious).

- Parallel process in the supervision (e.g. the supervisor and you seem to be enacting a relationship similar to the one you have with your client).
- Reflection on the sort of supervision issues most often arising, and which ones might be missing.
- Help in distinguishing supervision issues from therapy issues that might be evoked.
- A review of the supervision, its aims and goals and how it is working (see below).

Life issues that are influencing you

- Your own circumstances, problems, stress or illness that are affecting your ability to be focused, available and present.

Celebration

- Last but not least, an account of your successes, good interventions and confirming feedback from clients, including feelings of achievement and growth (you may need to ask for help in disclosing these!).

It is very worthwhile to discuss with your supervisor your particular needs at each stage of your development. For example, if you are a beginning practitioner, you will need a fair amount of guidance about what to do and how. A more experienced practitioner may ask to be challenged in terms of differential formulations of the issues or encouraged to experiment with more adventurous interventions. A very experienced practitioner may need more of a shared mutual space to reflect, consider new theory integration or to consider the relational subtleties of transference and counter-transference.

Deciding to be truthful and vulnerable

It is our experience that if most of the criteria above are fulfilled, it will serve you best to aim for honesty and allow yourself to be vulnerable in supervision, to admit your mistakes, disclose the 'untherapeutic' responses you have felt towards clients and name your conflicts or reactions to the supervisor's input. We often find that supervisees attempt a version of what Perls called self-image actualization, where they try to become the good supervisee who makes few mistakes and tries to impress the supervisor. We encourage you to honour the spirit of Gestalt and allow yourself to be who you are – mistakes and all – and trust that this will make you a better Gestalt psychotherapist. We have often found in our own supervision, that the most learning has come from disclosing our clinical errors, our negative reactions to the client (or when we are unusually positive, or frightened or erotically interested). This will place you in a better learning frame and promote a strong working alliance with the supervisor.

In receiving supervision, it is important to be able to articulate the emotion and the effect of the feedback and ask if you need something more. It can help to check that you correctly heard the feedback by asking or clarifying, then give your reaction to it, especially if you are disturbed, and perhaps ask for time to process it before responding.

'I'm feeling criticized and anxious. Does that mean you think I am an incompetent therapist?'

'Could you also say something I did well as I'm feeling like I am no good.'

'I'm aware of feeling both scared and excited by what you said.'

'You are going through that list of suggestions too fast for me and I need more time to think about them.'

The potential for shame is very often part of the supervisory field – for the supervisee who exposes his work but also for the supervisor who expects herself to be effectively helpful. It can be really useful to name this overtly between you as a way of normalizing these feelings.

Taking a transcript to supervision

Taking a live recording, transcript or a written account to supervision is an excellent way of bringing more of the actual client (rather than your story). Having played the recording, you can consider larger 'macro' issues of overall effectiveness, style of work, transference patterns, what was avoided, growing edges, etc. You can also consider individual 'micro' issues or particular interventions, such as:

1. What might be going on for your client; what was the issue?
2. What was your feeling, thinking, and bodily response?
3. How would you describe the relationship between you and the client at that moment?
4. What was your thinking behind the intervention?
5. What was the effect on the client of your intervention? How useful was it?
6. How did you understand the effect?
7. What other options did you have for an intervention?
8. From what theory did the intervention arise?
9. What was difficult, confusing, exciting?
10. What do you want to explore furthers about this in supervision?

Here is an example of an intervention and response from a transcript brought to supervision:

Therapist: What are you feeling now as you tell me this (in response to the client telling a ('story about' being angry)?

Client: I'm feeling fine.

Below are the answers the supervisee gave to the ten questions above.

1. The client seems to be very much in their thinking.
2. I am feeling anxious (maybe resonating with the client's unacknowledged feeling?).
3. Our relationship has a sense of disconnection.
4. I intended to surface the avoided feeling.
5. The client deflected or didn't understand. Not very useful.

6. My hypothesis is that the client didn't have enough support for the expression or feeling (or I was mistaken!).
7. I could have asked him to tell me what he was noticing in his body.
8. My hypothesis involved a possible retroflection.
9. I was uncertain about whether to ask the question again in a different way or to change the topic.
10. I would like to think more about when it is appropriate to confront a possible deflection.

KEEPING THE 'GESTALT' IN GESTALT SUPERVISION!

Much of what we have said so far applies to the good use of supervision of any sort. We would like to focus now on a specifically Gestalt approach to supervision; how you can use your supervision as a reflective space that will also anchor and embody the principles of Gestalt practice so that the dynamic fields of therapy and supervision are in creative dialogue. If your supervisor is not a Gestaltist or you are in an integrative supervision group within a placement, you may need to engage your supervisor and colleagues in a dialogue about what is important in your Gestalt orientation.

EMBODYING GESTALT PRINCIPLES

In addition to the principles we have already covered, we would like to emphasize the following fundamental aspects of good Gestalt supervision.

Emerging experiences

The process of raising awareness is a key part of exploring the issue that you bring to supervision. As you introduce your client, you avoid doing so in a distant theoretical way. You try and make it 'experience near', so that you pay attention to your own feelings, thoughts and sensations as you speak; you take an interest in your supervisor's response as they listen; you notice what happens between you and your supervisor and are curious about your patterns of relating and whether they are echoing the patterns between you and your client (the so-called parallel process); you take enough time to allow new thoughts, images or associations to 'bubble up'. In this way, you keep a lived sense of the co-created realationship, the here-and-new process, and the embodied experience of both you and the client.

If you are conceptualizing the client with a view to assessment and planning, you will start with the phenomenological method – bracketing your prejudices and carefully describing the 'facts' of the client's presentation, noticing when your formulation becomes coloured by your assumptions or emotional responses. Only after this will you form tentative diagnostic pictures and possible treatment directions.

Dialogue

In the same way that you are committed to entering a 'dialogic relationship' with your client, you and your supervisor are committed to a similar engagement, where both parties bring themselves as authentically as possible, being willing to enter into contact without controlling the outcome. Experiment with simply entering a dialogue about the supervisory issue with your supervisor in which you pay close attention to your here-and-now feelings, impressions and images, trusting that what needs to emerge will do so.

A field perspective

You will consider the local and larger field conditions relevant to the event or issue you are bringing – both past and present, in both the therapy and supervisory dyads. For example, current field conditions may include cultural difference, concurrent political or social events, the weather, the economic situation, the closure of a bus route, the new grandchild of the client's wife, and so on.

Larger field conditions that may also be influential include the historical relationship between the cultures of therapist and client, the client's previous experience of therapy or what happened between the two of you last week (or might happen in the near future). Your job will be to notice what seems important to the client and also what might be missing from his expressed experience.

SELF-SUPERVISION WHEN YOU'RE STUCK

There are times in every journey with a client that you feel completely stuck. This may or may not coincide with the client also feeling stuck, but you believe that the work is not moving. There are two questions you can ask yourself when this happens. Has the client reached an impasse that he needs to stay with or is it a difficulty in your approach that needs to be resolved before progress can continue? It is easy for a therapist, especially at the beginning of her training, to see stuckness as a failure on her part and to become despondent about ever getting it right. One of the strengths of Gestalt therapy is its positive attitude towards such stuckness. Gestalt does not see an impasse as an obstacle to be overcome – rather as a difficulty to be understood.

The best strategy initially is to 'stay with' the stuckness (following the paradoxical principle of change) and be curious about what message or understanding it might be communicating. We would advise you therefore to avoid the easy trap of thinking you are not a 'good-enough' therapist and rather direct your energy to understanding the nature, geography and possibilities contained in stuckness. Indeed, it is sometimes the most important point in therapy as the client brings into the here and now the actual difficulty (and stuckness) that brought them to therapy in the first place.

We suggest three areas of self-supervision at times when you need a fresh perspective:

First, the working alliance and therapeutic relationship:

- Check the original contract you made with the client. Are you both doing what you agreed or has one of you switched to a different agenda? (For example, you think the client 'ought' to be working on something they haven't agreed to work on. Or has the client decided some other issue is more important but hasn't flagged this?)
- Imagine a metaphor that may describe the stuck situation and explore its significance (e.g. like being in a fog, or slowly drowning).
- Take the problem back to the relationship with *you*. How is the problem being enacted in the counselling relationship? If this stuckness is a communication to you, what might it be? How might you be contributing or triggering the stuckness?
- Ask yourself if you are in the grip of unrecognized counter-transference. Is the stuckness familiar or unfamiliar? (Do you often feel like this with clients or only this particular client?)

Second, the process of the client:

- Ask the client how she is finding counselling at the moment. Is she feeling there is little movement too? What does she make of it?
- What is her metaphor for her stuckness?
- Does the client have an introject or core belief which is interrupting her (e.g. that she is a person who can never succeed at anything)?
- Does she have enough support to make difficult changes?
- Does she fear change?
- Is her stuckness really a communication of distress to the counsellor, and only requires a consistent affectively attuned response with no demand for being different?
- Where is she stuck on the cycle of experience? For example, is she aware but has no energy? Does she have mobilized energy but no sense of how to apply it? And so on.

Third, your own process:

- If the client does not appear concerned (even though you are!), consider whether your own expectations of progress have got in the way.
- Have an imaginary discussion with your client using an empty chair. Exaggerate your reactions, for example, 'I'm completely and absolutely fed up with this situation/you because …' If you could say *anything* to the client without consequences, what would it be?
- As you become more experienced you will develop your capacity for awareness of the process during the session itself. You will be more able to reflect on what is happening as it happens, remember your last supervision advice, or think of your growing edges. Many therapists (including ourselves) also find they can, at times of stuckness, deliberately invoke a valued supervisor, hear their words, advice, injunctions, or even speculate 'What would she have said or done in this situation?'
- Check whether you are working too hard, have too many difficult clients, have lost focus and concentration or are not looking after yourself properly.
- Imagine what may occur if you were creatively indifferent with the client in the moment.

INTERPERSONAL PROCESS RECALL (IPR)

IPR is a method of supervision developed by Kagan (1980). It is based on the idea that we 'know' and notice much more in the therapy sessions than we allow ourselves to recognize. The process is similar to the one we described earlier, when discussing the advantages of taking transcripts to supervision. However, IPR's reach is less towards thoughtful reflection and more towards deeper intuition and implicit knowing.

IPR helps counsellors become more aware of and attuned to the dynamics of the counsellor/client relationship that they may be discounting because of a tendency towards what Kagan called 'diplomatic behaviour'. It is especially useful for identifying momentary counter-transference experiences that tend to go unacknowledged. The method involves careful exploration of a session, through *immersion* in recall of the process – ideally with the help of a recording.

You listen to a recording of a part of a session that you have pre-selected as significant. As you listen, you tune into your own internal process, stopping the tape when you remember having felt or thought something at the time, that you did not pay sufficient attention to.

IPR can be done on your own, in which case you have to be your own inquirer. Better still, however, is to have a supervisor or colleague who will support you in the process. When you stop the tape (or, by agreement, your supervisor might also stop the tape), the inquirer guides your reflection, by asking such questions as:

1. What thoughts/feelings/sensations were you having?
2. How do you think your client was feeling? How do you think he was seeing you? What was he wanting from you?
3. Is there anything you were not saying?
4. What would have been the risk in saying what you wanted to say?
5. What do you wish you had said to him/her then?
6. How do you think he/she would have reacted if you had said that?
7. Were there any other considerations you had?
8. Did he/she remind you of anyone in your life?

This exercise is a real opportunity for you to listen from a less hurried, more reflective space and to bring to the surface what was not in full awareness or what was preventing you from being the most effective therapist you could be.

CARRYING OUT A REVIEW (OR ... LETTING YOUR CLIENT SUPERVISE YOU)

As part of being a competent therapist, you are frequently reviewing, assessing, readjusting and re-contracting with a client (sometimes all in one session). From time to time, you will also hold more deliberate review sessions. This is, of course, a normal part of practice. However, we see another perspective to such reviews where your client can also be a partner in your self supervision. Having first hand experience of the therapeutic relationship with you, the client's own reflections can be a great opportunity for learning.

You may want to suggest a review to the client in advance and ask them during the week preceding the review to think about how therapy has been going for them.

At these review sessions you can:

◆ Revisit the original contract for working (what the client wanted when they first came).
◆ Check whether the client and you think it is still relevant or how it is progressing.
◆ Consider how your joint assessment of the problem has evolved over time.
◆ Ask the client how they have found being in therapy with you so far, what aspects of it have they found particularly useful, what aspects unhelpful, whether there is anything they would like you to have done differently or would have liked to have done differently themselves.
◆ You can then discuss any changes that need to be made.
◆ You can agree a further short-term contract, a continuing long-term contract or a date for leaving.

All these areas will provide material for you to reflect upon, as well as identifying issues for you to discuss with your supervisor. We would suggest a review in this man-ner about every three months, but it can be more or less frequent and more or less formal. Miller et al. (2008) suggest that what makes good therapists into great ones is their willingness to seek and act on feedback from the client about their effective-ness. After ending with a client it can also be very useful to offer a follow-up review in six months or one year's time for the client to return to touch base or to evaluate their situation since leaving therapy. Some counsellors offer this follow-up session free to enable them to assess effectiveness after discharge.

In this way, the formal review becomes part of your research into your practice (see Chapter 16) and an invaluable part to your development.

Of course, exactly the same principles apply to the supervisory relationship. You and your supervisor will review your work together, explore what has been most and least useful, monitor your case-load and agree growing edges for your development.

DEVELOPING YOUR PERSONAL STYLE

One of the most interesting (and complex) tasks early in your career is discovering what sort of Gestalt therapy suits your personality and philosophy, and this is an area where your supervisor may be very helpful. Later on you may wish to review your style and stretch your style or boundaries.

The starting point will be what you bring personally to the role of therapist. Consider the following polarities (these are only a few). Where do you stand on them? Is there a way that you would like to be different?

Cautious.........................Risk-taking
Self-disclosing...................Opaque
Body-focused...................Cognitively focused
Strategic.........................Process led
Supportive.......................Confronting
Intuitive.................. ....Practical
Phenomenological..............Interpretive
Directive........................Emergent

Do you naturally look at the 'big picture' of the client's life and existential issues or do you more often focus on the moment-to-moment unfolding of the process, small body movements, the use of one word rather than another? Polster (1998: 267) describes how two of his teachers differed at each end of the content/process continuum. 'Paul Goodman was highly oriented to content, repeatedly searching for the storyline of the patient's life … [whereas] … Paul Weisz worked at the other end, staying faithfully with the "how" of each moment of experience in exquisitely fine detail.'

All these and many other questions have answers that will be unique to you. We offer some questions here, aimed at helping you discover and develop your own personal style.

◆ What are you like when you are at your most therapeutic, what qualities do you exemplify, how do you act?
◆ How do you use your body process, do you disclose your physical responses, make guesses based on your own bodily reactions?
◆ What style and therapeutic approach have you found most useful in your own personal therapy? What has been least useful? Why? Do you think most people would have the same reaction as you?
◆ How would your clients describe you as a therapist? Is that a description you like? Is there anything you would like to change?
◆ What aspects or qualities do you have in your personal life that you do not bring into your professional life as a therapist? Why not?
◆ Which clients or issues do you find most difficult and which are most easy?
◆ What sorts of skills or techniques do you most use? What would be a stretch for you to do and what could you never imagine doing?

Suggestion: Design an ideal well-rounded competent therapist. What qualities would he or she have? Do you already have those qualities? How could you develop them?

Your clinical work can be a time for your own growth as well as that of your client and you may decide to keep flexible by experimenting with new ways of being and working. Over the years, we (the authors) have both gone through many different evolutions in our personal styles. Some have been easy and natural, some more challenging.

Keep in mind that transitions in style (like any process of change) are often accompanied by temporary periods of doubt and uncertainty.

The shape, form and nature of the therapeutic relationship you have with the client will of course be hugely influenced by what you bring and how you respond to the encounter (including your unresolved problems). Identifying your own therapy issues and your particular personal style will be a good guide to start appreciating how much of this is in and out of your awareness. (There is an apocryphal saying: 'The therapy is finished when the client has the same problems as the therapist and both of them are unaware of it!') On a more serious note, the obvious implication of the mutual impact of relational therapy is that as therapists, we must, at times prioritize our own personal therapy, self-awareness and support. We can then aim to bring to the therapeutic encounter a clear, resilient and insightful presence.

RECOMMENDED READING FOR SUPERVISION

Carroll, M. and Gilbert, M. (2005) *On Being a Supervisee: Creating Learning Partnerships*. London: Vukani Publishing.

Gilbert, M. and Evans, K. (2000) *Psychotherapy Supervision – An Integrative Relational Approach*. Buckingham: Open University Press. (**See Chapter 4 – 'Creating an Effective Learning Environment'**.)

Houston, G. (1990) *Supervision and Counselling*. London: Rochester Press.

Inskipp, F. and Proctor, B. (2001) *Making the Most of Supervision, Part 1*. London: Cascade Publications (order online).

Kearns, A. (2005) *The Seven Deadly Sins*? London: Karnac. (**See Chapter 7 – 'Shame in the Supervisory Relationship'**.)

Maclean, A. (2002) *The Heart of Supervision*. Washington, DC: Topdog-g Publishing. (**See Chapter 3 – 'Windows on the Processes of Supervision'**.)

Resnick, R. and Estrup, L. (2000) 'Supervision – a collaborative endeavour', *Gestalt Review*, 4 (2): 121–37.

Wyman, L. and Cohen, A. (2007) 'Supervising the revisited Fritz Perls: reflecting on "real Gestalt"', *Gestalt Review* 11 (1):52–8.

Yontef, G. (1997) 'Supervision from a Gestalt therapy perspective', in C.E. Watkins, Jr., ed. *Handbook of Psychotherapy Supervision*. New York: Wiley. pp. 147–63.

RECOMMENDED READING FOR PERSONAL STYLE

Bloom, D. (2008) 'Borders and bridges', *British Gestalt Journal*, 17 (2): 5–7.

Korb, M. Gorrell, J. and Van de Reit, V. (2002) *Gestalt Therapy – Practice and Theory*. New York: Gestalt Journal Press. (**See Chapter 6 – 'The Therapist'**.)

16

THE REFLECTIVE
PRACTITIONER

At the end of this chapter we recommend some excellent overviews of the wide range of possible research methods that can enhance your therapy practice. What we intend here is to offer some ideas to stimulate practitioners' interest in the need for research, outline how to start a Gestalt-friendly project and, most of all, to encourage taking *a research attitude* to the practice of Gestalt therapy.

WHAT IS RESEARCH?

In many ways, creative living itself is a process that requires ongoing research, for example deciding which restaurant is most suited for a special occasion, which school is best for your child or what sort of further training you need. In other words, it is about finding out new and useful information about something that matters to us.

At its simplest, research is a systematic study of a particular subject that leads to increased knowledge and understanding. In a psychotherapy setting it also needs to be useful in clinical practice. Good research is a creative process involving gathering reliable data, knowing how to analyse and understand it and drawing meaningful and useful conclusions.

In the types of research we discuss below, as in good Gestalt therapy, it is also at best a transformative experience for the researcher. The process of researching will involve an exploration towards new understandings and new directions. It will be a holistic, phenomenological, field-sensitive and dialogic process.

WHY IS RESEARCH IMPORTANT?

There are many reasons – some pragmatic and some aspirational:

◆ Many government bodies, institutions, employers and clients, use published research findings to decide which therapy is most effective and how long it should take. This can lead to long-term planning decisions about which therapies will be encouraged, promoted and officially recognized.

◆ It is an ethical and professional imperative to know what type of therapy works best for which client and what type of interventions may be beneficial or harmful.

◆ It is also professionally important to have (and if asked, provide) reliable evidence to show our clients that the therapy we are offering is effective and, further, that it is effective to their particular presentation or need.

◆ Research has been the source of many new ideas and has led to important developments in the field of psychological therapies (e.g. most recently, neuroscientific and infant research). Research evidence can help us keep our practice and training current and up to date with new understandings.

◆ Taking a 'research attitude' encourages a spirit of reflective practice that has been identified as increasing effectiveness in practice (e.g. van Rijn et al., 2008).

THE GREAT RESEARCH DEBATE — EFFECTIVENESS IN PSYCHOTHERAPY

In recent years there has been a crystallization of two opposing trends in the world of psychological therapies. The first trend is towards relational therapy (which has been the heart of Gestalt therapy for many decades). The second trend is towards 'evidence-based', short-term, manualized therapeutic treatments. Different strands of research have supported the two different trends and there continues to be a hotly contested debate as to which research is most valid.

However, the psychotherapy outcome research of the last half-century has discovered repeatedly and convincingly that all the major approaches to therapy are effective (see, for example, Luborsky et al., 1975, Elliot, 2002). As Cooper (2008a) says in a conference lecture,

> The research consistently suggests that the kind of therapy that a practitioner delivers makes little difference to outcomes. More important is the client's level of motivation, how much they get involved with the therapeutic process, and how able they are to think about themselves in a psychological way. After that, the key ingredient seems to be the quality of the therapeutic relationship, with warm, understanding, trustworthy therapists having the best results.

Meta-studies of outcome research reveal the importance to effective therapy, not of the elegance of the therapeutic theories and methodology, but of certain 'common factors' largely related to the type of relationship between the client and the therapist. Sometimes called the 'healing relationship', it is characterized by mutual respect and empathic understanding on the part of the therapist leading to the client feeling accepted and confirmed, despite showing their flaws and vulnerabilities (Asay and Lambert 1999; Wampold 2001). It also involves mutuality of relationship and shared understanding of the goals and processes of the therapy. We link this to the evidence offered by Miller et al. (2008) on a research attitude to practice which emphasizes the importance of asking the client what they find most helpful in the therapy, and then doing more of what works with each particular client. This seems to us to be part of that respectful relationship of shared aims and intentions. For a few presenting issues, some approaches may work rather better than others, but generally speaking any coherent approach, competently and confidently used by a therapist who is responsive to the client's views, will have a beneficial effect.

The current dispute is whether research evidence better supports manualized, short-term, outcome-focused psychotherapies aimed at symptom reduction (such as CBT), or whether it supports relationally orientated psychotherapy such as Gestalt, psychodynamic and person-centred, which are not outcome focused, are sometimes of longer duration and aim for more comprehensive holistic change.

Symptom-reducing psychotherapies have been supported by large numbers of randomized control trials, which test therapeutic interventions on comparable groups with comparable symptoms. The major criticism of this sort of therapy research is an intrinsic paradox: the more reliable and quantifiable it is and the more rigour is applied to minimize the influence of variables, the more unrepresentative it is of actual clinical practice in a non-experimental setting.

Relational therapies also have good research evidence for effectiveness on a large range of factors, often producing more wide-ranging effects, especially on an improved general quality of life in clients. The major criticisms here are the smaller numbers of research studies and, more importantly, the fact that each therapy is co-created uniquely with each client and therefore does not lend itself to studies that compare standard therapeutic methods. In terms of Gestalt research, the most detailed is that of Greenberg and his co-researchers (e.g. Greenberg and Watson, 2006) and the most impressive is Strumpfel (2004), where he reviews 60 studies involving at least 3,000 clients with varied diagnoses. They show overall that Gestalt therapy performs as well, or better, than other therapies in all cases. However, most of the research is qualitative and process-based and as such is not seen by the funding bodies to be as 'scientifically' valid as the symptom-reduction-based evidence.

The debate is also skewed by the fact that most academic researchers subscribe to a CBT approach and publish more studies on the effectiveness of CBT. These greater numbers of studies are used to imply that CBT is more effective.

The much-favoured 'evidence-based practice' started with the best of intentions – to gather all the sound data about what works for a particular condition in order to find the best treatment. But it left the 'human' variables out of the picture and has led to the design of manualized approaches. This seems to us to be a case of 'research evidence as fixed gestalt', rather than continuing to be flexible and responsive to 'what is'.

So how can Gestalt contribute? Gestalt's emphasis on reflexivity – being aware and responsive to experience – lends itself well to collecting 'practice-based evidence', in other words, learning what is effective from studying therapeutic work in action. We believe that we are ideally placed to explore the more detailed focus of what works in practice, what interventions are most useful and how. We return to this later.

TWO DIFFERENT WAYS OF KNOWING: PHILOSOPHIES OF RESEARCH

The widespread lack of research interest in Gestalt and the comparative lack of published research evidence from relational practitioners largely stems from their attitude towards 'scientific' or what is called quantitative research. Such traditional scientific (or positivist) research starts from the assumption that people can be studied objectively and impartially. Research in this modality is 'at a distance'. It attempts to be objective and often deals in numbers and figures – hence the name 'quantitative'. It is an attempt to uncover the truth that is 'out there' to be discovered.

However, in recent years, a different research perspective has become more accepted, based on what is sometimes called 'post-positive' or 'post-modern' thinking and is certainly the major position of Gestalt theory. It starts from the assumption that there are multiple realities, that truth is potentially different for each person and that the process of investigation inevitably influences what is found. The implication is that each researcher is inevitably embedded within their unique context (or field conditions). The questions they ask, therefore, the way they enquire or investigate and the meanings they make will all be particular to them. Research in this modality is participatory, collaborative and subjective. Broadly called the 'qualitative approach' it places importance on the quality of experience, not just on the measurability of data.

> **Suggestion:** You have decided to buy a new car. Several car magazine surveys recommend a particular model to be reliable, pleasing to drive, competent and good value. How influenced are you by such surveys or numbers (quantitative evidence)? On the other hand, would you say that this made little difference to the likelihood of your buying the car and you would decide only after the experience of a long test drive (qualitative evidence)?

Both types of research method, quantitative and qualitative, are useful for different purposes. Quantitative surveys and comparisons can make useful discriminations and provide data for effectiveness, while qualitative research can provide context and depth of understanding. While Gestaltists will clearly favour qualitative methods, we suggest that often a synthesis of both is useful as we believe both have value and represent different aspects of the same whole. In order to successfully make such a synthesis, it is also useful to appreciate that there are two different motives for carrying out research, represented in 'pure' and 'applied' research. Pure research is based on a desire to explore and learn. It produces (at best) rich information, deeper relationships and uncovers new territory. In Gestalt practice this is the arena of phenomenological investigation and creative indifference – there is no investment in any sort of outcome and the only motivation is to be interested and open to what unfolds. Applied research, in contrast, is based on a desire to make a difference, to be useful in some way. In Gestalt practice, this is the endeavour to improve practice, refine interventions and develop better understandings of what is useful or how best to help the client.

The Gestalt practitioner as researcher potentially straddles both these types. In pure research mode she will adopt a position of creative indifference, following her energy and that of the client, looking for a depth of understanding but allowing meaning to emerge naturally.

In applied research mode, she will be evaluating her interventions and looking at effectiveness. She is attempting to ensure that her therapy is useful to the client and will make a beneficial difference to their life. This evaluative approach will be necessary for those who offer short-term contracts and who may need to demonstrate effectiveness to the client and to a funding agency.

EVERY GOOD GESTALTIST IS ALREADY DOING RESEARCH

We would argue that a good Gestalt therapist is already carrying out research as, together with her client, she seeks and uncovers new information, new knowledge and new meanings. The reflective space of supervision will be part of this process. She is also a clinician, and therefore seeks to apply her new knowledge and understandings in the service of the improvement of the client's life (and sometimes her own).

Every time you see a client, you are trying to gain the best understanding of his presenting issues, how he relates to his life and how he and you are forming a relationship. You do this by investigating using the phenomenological method, asking questions, monitoring your own and your client's responses and then forming initial partial understandings. As a result of this, you make clinical interventions, notice their impact, learn from what happens and refine or adjust your initial understanding. You then make a further intervention based on this new understanding. On the basis of the client's response, you then adjust your working hypotheses ... and so on.

For example, after a therapy session is over, you may sit quietly, recall what happened, look for patterns, themes or change points and reflect on your part in them. You may then realize that you had missed the impact of something the client had said, re-run the session in your mind in this new light and come to a different understanding. You might then discuss this in supervision, re-evaluate your intervention strategy or investigate further next time, by checking how the client felt or thought about the last session.

EXAMPLE

After her depressed client had gone, Naomi reviewed the session and wondered why the relationship had seemed so sticky towards the end. She went through her interventions and realized that she had unwittingly provoked a shame response when she had inquired about the client's unemployment. She wondered in supervision about whether she had an investment in a return to work and if this was somehow a transference enactment. She decided next time to check if the question had been difficult for her client and to ask whether she had come across as critical.

From a Gestalt perspective, every session with a client is a co-constructed research inquiry. Although the primary task is to understand the *process* of the client, the relational nature of the endeavour means that the therapist also needs to take into account her own perspectives and responses. This research process can be one of learning for the therapist as well, and usually leads to change, for both therapist and client.

To summarize: reflective Gestalt practice is a continuing cycle of investigating the clinical issue, gathering impressions or data with your client, making comparisons, finding themes, connections or generating new ideas, then going back to the issue with fresh eyes, to experiment and explore again.

RESEARCH METHODS

Although most psychotherapy research is oriented to before-and-after treatment outcomes, 'process research' is a different approach and inquires about the impact of moment-to-moment interventions, trying to determine which moments in the therapy process are most important and most effective. Greenberg and his colleagues have published important research in this area, especially on two-chair work (Greenberg and Malcolm, 2002). Such research uses either questionnaires to therapist or client to describe what happens in sessions or transcribed tapes to identify content and emotional response (ideally both are used). Interpersonal process recall (described in Chapter 15) is also used to identify the participants' experiences. Such methods can also be easily used to determine the congruence between the clinician's and the client's opinion of the key change moments in a session and how they were important.

There are other methods that particularly lend themselves to Gestalt research, for example heuristic research, collaborative or research communities, hermeneutic research, grounded theory, interpretative phenomenological analysis and appreciative inquiry. Most of these methods are phenomenologically orientated, include the subjectivity and influence of the researcher, and are collaborative and emergent (for full descriptions of such methods we offer suggested reading at the end of the chapter).

We choose to focus here on one particular method called *action research*, which we have found most suitable for introducing our students to a research method.

> Action research is a participatory, democratic process concerned with developing practical knowing in the pursuit of worthwhile human purposes ... It seeks to bring together action and reflection, theory and practice, in participation with others, in the pursuit of practical solutions to issues of pressing concern to people, and more generally to the flourishing of individual persons and their communities. (Reason and Bradbury, 2001: 1)

The basic method is a repeating cycle of *planning–action–observing–reflecting*. It is grounded in practice and provides a structure for the sort of reflexivity and collaborative inquiry that we described above as the essence of Gestalt therapy. Here is an example:

A client criticizes herself for being unable to stop thinking about a boyfriend who cruelly rejected her.

⇒ You see her body response as she talks and decide that she needs to contact her retroflected anger (**Plan**).
⇒ You then make a suggestion to pay attention to any feelings of anger when she thinks of the rejection (**Action**).
⇒ You notice that when she attempts to do this she becomes more self-critical – now of her inability to be assertive; you notice also that you too are beginning to feel frustrated with her (**Observation**).
⇒ You wonder about the meaning of both those consequences (**Reflection**).
⇒ You then decide to give up the attempt to work on anger and focus instead on the client's self-criticism (**New Plan**).
⇒ You listen empathically and silently to her as she blames herself (**Action**).
⇒ You now hear that she begins to remember when she felt rejected by her father as a child (**Observation**).
⇒ You realize that making links to her childhood is the first priority for her (**Reflection**).
⇒ and so on …

As another avenue of exploration, you may want to undertake a *personal reflective inquiry* into an aspect of practice. For example, you notice that you are reluctant to confront another client who, in contrast, seems to be blaming everyone else in her world for own misfortunes and you feel ineffective and stuck.

⇒ You decide to monitor your internal experience as you sit with the client (**Plan**).
⇒ You notice that, as she speaks, you feel annoyed with her constant blaming but start to feel anxious when you think about disclosing this. Your anxiety turns to fear as you get ready to speak, and you end up instead simply making an empathic comment (**Observation**).
⇒ After the session, you spend some time thinking and feeling about what confrontation means to you. You become aware of a belief you have that 'the client won't like me if I'm not sympathetic'. You wonder if your reluctance to confront is true with other people as well (**Reflection**).
⇒ You decide to monitor your skill in confrontation with all your clients (**Plan**).
⇒ In the course of the week's work you notice that the clients you confront are all ones that you really like (**Observation**).
⇒ In your reflection time you think again about the link you are making between confrontation and liking. You understand that your original urge to confront your client was really a desire to blame her (**Reflection**).
⇒ You decide to ask her permission to give her some feedback and simply comment on what you have noticed. You decide also to pay attention to your breathing as you do so, to regulate your support (**Plan**).

In the first example, the reflective practitioner may understand something about working relationally with this particular client. In the second, she is on a journey of self-discovery about potency. Both experiences involve reflecting, taking action, experimenting and learning about effectiveness.

Here is a format for a simple piece of personal action research for inquiring into and developing your practice:

1. PLAN
   Look at your practice and come up with an area you would like to inquire into – for example, 'Why do I find long silences in the therapy room difficult?' or 'How does my desire to help clients to feel better get in the way of effective confrontations when they are distressed?'
   Think about how you will investigate this and make a plan of action – e.g. during the next long silence, I will monitor any introjects that arise, notice my physical tensions and ask the client how the silence is for them.

2. ACT
   Carry out the experiment.

3. OBSERVE
   Gather data or information.

4. REFLECT
   Think about the experience (after the session or in supervision), see what learning there is and notice what new inquiry or question arises. Then continue with the cycle.

SECOND- AND THIRD-PERSON INQUIRY

This simple form of clinical research in your practice, if carried out with your client as a learning partner (so-called 'second-person inquiry'), is identified by Miller et al. (2008) as one of the key routes to becoming a better therapist. If you are exploring the impact of particular interventions on the therapy, for example, you could ask the client for his experience. 'Third-person inquiry' involves consulting a neutral third party for their observations or reflections. This could include consulting a supervisor or colleagues or, if the client is interested, the opinion of his family or work colleagues.

Described in its simple stages, this sort of research can sound rather mechanical and reductionist. However, if the therapist allows feelings, sensations, imagery and metaphor (both her own and her client's) to be part of the data and the reflection, the process becomes part and parcel of the rich conversation of the therapeutic engagement.

CARRYING OUT CLINICAL RESEARCH

In carrying out this sort of action research individually or as part of a larger research project, the first and most important starting point of all is the attitude you bring. Of the many useful qualities the Gestalt practitioner brings with her, the most fundamental to good research are the spirit of openness of mind, non-defensiveness, curiosity and engagement, together with a creative indifference to a particular outcome and a willingness to explore and learn.

The second requirement is for reflexivity, the therapist's capacity to notice her own feelings and responses, to reflect critically on what she is bringing to the process, as well as observing her impact on the focus of the research. This emphasizes the importance of taking into account the influence of the starting assumptions of the researcher, the interactions of the studier and the studied and then the necessary readjustment in the light of this ever-changing awareness. Good relational psychotherapy in this sense is the essence of the reflexive approach.

Being reflexive means we are aware of the personal, relational and cultural field in which we live and operate, and how these affect the ways we understand the world and the starting position of our research. It is another way of saying that there is no 'neutral' position from which we can start research; we are always biased and uniquely making our own meaning. In offering our findings we can only declare our bias in a spirit of openness and honesty to allow the reader (or client) of the research to have their own opinion about our starting biases and our conclusions. This transparency about the values and beliefs of the researcher which inevitably influence the research findings is what Etherington (2004) calls 'researcher reflexivity' or 'critical reflexivity'.

The third quality is the desire to make your research useful as well as valid (and convincing). In order to do this, it needs to fulfil the following requirements. You must gather or collect information using an accepted method. You must be systematic. You must consider reliability. While the criteria for this sort of research are very different from the statistical requirements of quantitative research, you still need to think broadly about whether your conclusions are in principle useful to the wider field, whether your area of exploration is coherent, whether your method and the scope of your inquiry is properly described and understandable. You must also outline your motivation and assumptions and show critical reflexivity.

RESEARCHING YOUR OWN PRACTICE

Consider for a moment how you would answer the following questions a client might ask you on a first visit:

'How successful are you in treating my type of problem?'
'Are there any risks?'
'How many sessions will I need?'
'Are you the best person to help me?'
'What is your success and failure rate with this type of problem?'
'What is the research evidence for your approach?'

Many Gestalt practitioners would struggle to answer these questions, and while this is an inevitable consequence of an approach that values organismic self-organization and the power and novelty of awareness and contact, it can also be an excuse for poor practice and a failure to provide the client with the best and shortest therapy.

Suggestion: Imagine you wish to refer someone, say a good friend, to another therapist. How do you decide who would be the best person and what would be the best therapeutic modality? Do you go by seniority, qualifications, reputation, or whether you have met and liked them? Do you check the research evidence for their approach?

In your own practice, how much do you analyse your treatment failures, how much do you actively learn from your successes?

Examples of a research question in your own practice might be large topics such as 'Am I an effective psychotherapist?' 'Which clients am I most effective with?' or 'Which of my interventions are most effective?' However, we suggest you choose a question that is more limited in scope, such as, 'What is the effect on the client of my self-disclosure?' or 'Does focusing on my own body process lead to more client body-process awareness?'

For many students in training, the two potentially major research projects are the process report – the analysed transcript of a section of an actual client session – and the single case study, which describes in reflective depth a therapeutic journey with one client. The analysed tape transcript is already a useful basis for an action research project around improving your clinical skills. On the other hand, the purpose of the case study (as research) is to gain an understanding of the experience, process, inter-actions, belief systems, lived experience and responses to the therapeutic process. It is more a 'pure research' project, with increased awareness and understanding as the main goal. However, inevitably, the knowledge gained will inform and improve the work of the therapist, especially if you and your colleagues share the themes that emerge from your case studies. Frequently, an in-depth case study or group of case studies give rise to the questions that will form the basis of fruitful action research projects.

The ongoing personal journal that is a requirement of many training courses and is also part of the personal clinical reflections of a clinician can be part of reflexive practice and a research endeavour in itself.

A START TO RESEARCHING YOUR EFFECTIVENESS AS A PRACTITIONER

We believe it is important to have some sense of your effectiveness as a therapist. We have already argued that the most relevant Gestalt research area is that of process research. We also support assessing outcome. Thus, while we are not advocating that you become overly outcome-focused, we believe it necessary and possible, while remaining within the reflexive and responsive approach of 'practice-based evidence'. This will serve as a guide to avoid ineffective practice, and also to counter undeserved self-criticism (and, less commonly, undeserved self-congratulation!).

The following questions may help you reflect on effectiveness with any particular client you are reviewing. They should be taken as a general perspective over time, not simply as a spot-check, as most courses of therapy inevitably go through periods of difficulty, confusion and dissatisfaction for both counsellor and client as challenging issues are worked through.

Progress checklist

◆ Is the client is satisfied with how therapy is progressing?
◆ Do you agree!? (And does your supervisor?)
◆ Are you are meeting the aims identified at your last mutual review?
◆ Is your relational stance or counter-transference appropriate to the clinical situation?
◆ Does the feedback the client receives from his friends, family or work support his own self-assessment? (NB: Remember that some of the client's social network or family may not like the changes the client is making.)
◆ Is his level of functioning generally improving and does he show increasing resilience and self-empowerment?
◆ Do his changes reflect a respectful and relational attitude to the wider community?
◆ Is he is making more meaningful contact with you?
◆ Is he is assimilating his learning, and starting to be more creative?

Another way to evaluate your effectiveness would be to take part in some larger-scale project such as CORE (Clinical Outcomes in Routine Evaluation). This is a well-validated, standardized assessment of the client before and after therapy and includes a self-assessment by the client of his state of emotional health and well-being, using four different scales. The comparison of the pre- and post-therapy scores offers a measure of 'outcome' in relation to whether or not the client's level of distress and dysfunction have changed, and by how much. It then allows comparisons across a wide range of therapists and modalities and against national benchmarks (see Scheinberg et al., 2008: 314–17). You may choose to become involved in the *CORE Practitioner Research Network*, a UK-based project that is currently producing encourging data about the effectiveness of Gestalt therapy (see *British Gestalt Journal* website – research section).

LARGER RESEARCH PROJECTS

We offer below a series of stages to help you think through research possibilities:

1. The first task is to decide on a research question. There are three basic types of questions: comparisons, associations and open-ended investigations (see Horowitz, 1982, for more detail). For example:

    (i) Contrast group studies: the random allocation of subjects to different conditions, such as therapy or control groups. For example, is one therapy more successful than another?

    (ii) Relational or correlational studies: examining the level of association or correlation between different factors, e.g. correlations between different orientations and outcomes. (For example, what is associated with therapeutic success, which are the most helpful interventions?)

    (iii) Descriptive studies: the observation and classification of 'what one finds' within a single case or through a series of interviews. (For example, what is the experience like for the client or therapist? (and what can be learned from this?))

2.   The next task is to identify your starting assumptions, motivations and biases, including such factors as age, gender, social status, ethnicity, religion, politics and sexual orientation, and also attitudes to the research subject, the implications of particular outcomes, and so on.

3.   Decide which method/s you will use: qualitative, quantitative or a combination of both. For example, if you need to find out some hard data in order to make a decision, you may need quantitative research. If you are wanting to find out as much as possible about something, qualitative might be better. If you are wanting to assess something about the relationship between people's experience of something and their level of change, a combination would be necessary.

4.   Consider the ethical implications of the research, including client welfare, dignity, confidentiality, informed consent, beneficence, etc.

5.   Carry out the research and reflect on the process regularly, using supervision and revising the methodology in a responsive way.

6.   Assess the validity and reliability of your findings. For example:

Quantitative: Objectivity, reliability, validity, rigour, generalizability, reproducibility.
Qualitative: Neutrality or transparent subjectivity, dependability, authenticity, transferability, auditability.

7.   Make sense of the findings, including using the existing research literature.

8.   Use the findings constructively to improve your professional evidence base or your practice, consciously making changes if relevant, and practising them.

EXAMPLE

Consider how you might investigate the effectiveness of Gestalt therapy.

a)   You could conduct an in-depth interview with a client. You could also gather several accounts from several clients and compare them. This would lead to a rich story of individual experience. It would be idiosyncratic, influenced by the mood of the client at the time, shaped by the way you asked the question and their need to fulfil or deny your expectations, etc. It would give you a subjective impression of effectiveness. (Qualitative)

b)   You could ask each client to fill in a rating scale of effectiveness from one to ten after each session, after therapy had terminated and one year after ending. You could then produce a percentage figure. This would give you statistics and a numerical rating. (Quantitative)

EVALUATING RESEARCH LITERATURE

Crucial questions to ask (or how to adopt a critical attitude to published research)

One of the skills we believe essential is to be able to critique the mass of published research so you can reach an informed opinion as to the validity of the conclusions or implications. Much research is deeply flawed, methodologically unsound, unrepresentative and, at worst, deliberately biased to prove a point, make a reputation or to promote an idea.

The following questions can be a useful way to start analysing any research you read and provide a basis for a questioning attitude.

◆ Who is funding or facilitating the research?
(For example, who is the agency funding the research – a multinational drug company paying for research on the effectiveness of anti-depressants over psychotherapy?)

◆ Where has the research been published?
(For example, in a recognized peer-reviewed journal or in a newspaper with a political agenda?)

◆ Has the research finding been confirmed in other similar studies?

◆ What bias or motives do(es) the researcher(s) have for doing the research? Are these declared and explored?
(For example, are they trying to demonstrate the superiority of their own approach?)

◆ What assumptions (implicit or explicit) underlie the research design?
(For example, that a small sample is representative, that six sessions constitute 'psychotherapy', that questionnaires are completed truthfully.)

◆ How convincing is the operationalization of the key concepts?
(For example, is 'effectiveness' defined by changed behaviour or symptoms, therapist opinion, clients' subjective report, six-month follow-up questionnaire, etc.?)

◆ What was the methodology and how well was it carried out?
(For example, were the clients who left the study before the end factored in?)

◆ How were the variables managed?
(For example, was allowance made for ethnic bias? Were relational factors taken into account?)

◆ How representative was the sample or area studied?
(For example, were all the respondents well-adjusted counselling trainees?!)

◆ How generalizable are the results?
(For example, was the sample sufficiently large? Is the study applicable to most people?)

◆ How else could the results be interpreted, and what other explanations could there be?

(For example, could the clients have improved even without treatment?)
◆ What is the impact on you of the results? Are you likely to be affected by them professionally? Personally?
(For example, do you have an investment in the outcomes being true?)

CONCLUSION

And so, while our deeply held belief and knowledge is that good therapy is unique, dynamic, relational and emergent, we also need to find ways of researching our practice – combining the best of qualitative and quantitative research methods. Our research must help us, collectively and individually, to evaluate and increase the effectiveness of our practice, while providing robust evidence that will influence the policy-makers, fund-holders and purchasers of therapy.

In order to do this, we need not only to understand and be able to critique emerging research, but to develop a research attitude that is extended and articulated beyond the implicit research that a good Gestalt practitioner is already carrying out.

RECOMMENDED READING

Barber, P. (2002) 'Gestalt, holistic research and education', *British Gestalt Journal,* 11: 78–90.

Barber, P. (2006) *Becoming a Practitioner Researcher, a Gestalt Approach to Holistic Enquiry.* London: Middlesex University Press.

Bond, T. (2004) *Ethical Guidelines for Research.* Rugby: BACP.

Brown, J. (1997) 'Researcher as instrument', *Gestalt Review,* 1 (1) : 71–84.

Brownell, P. (ed.) (2008) *Handbook for Theory, Research and Practice in Gestalt Therapy.* Newcastle: Cambridge Scholars Publishing.

Cooper, M. (2008) *Essential Research Findings in Counselling and Psychotherapy: The Facts are Friendly.* London. Sage.

Etherington, K. (2004) *Becoming a Reflexive Researcher – Using Our Selves in Research.* London: Jessica Kingsley.

Finlay, L. and Evans, K. (2009) *Relational Centred Research for Psychotherapists.* West Sussex: Wiley–Blackwell.

Goldacre, B. (2008) *Bad Science.* London: Fourth Estate Ltd. (See also: www. badscience.net.)

Greenberg, L.S. and Elliott, R. (2002) 'Emotion focused therapy', in F.W. Kaslow (ed.), *Comprehensive Handbook of Psychotherapy.* New York: John Wiley.

Lebow, J. (2006) *Research for the Psychotherapist.* London: Routledge.

O'Leary, Z. (2004) *The Essential Guide to Doing Research.* London: Sage.

(Continued)

(Continued)

McLeod, J. (2003) *Doing Counselling Research,* 2nd edn. London: Sage.

Miller, S., Hubble, M. and Duncan, B. (2008) 'Supershrinks', *Therapy Today,* 19 (3): 4–9.

Parlett, M. (ed.) (2002) *British Gestalt Journal Special Edition on Research,* 11 (2): 78–119.

Scheinberg, S., Johannson, A., Stevens, C. and Conway-Hicks, S. (2008) 'Research communities in action: three examples', in P. Brownell (ed.), *Handbook for Theory, Research and Practice in Gestalt Therapy.* Newcastle: Cambridge Scholars Publishing. **(See pp. 299–309.)**

Spinelli, E. (2005) *The Interpreted World: An Introduction to Phenomenological Psychology.* London: Sage. **(See Chapter 7 – 'Phenomenological Research'.)**

Stevens, C. (2005) 'Gestalt students at Tate Modern: a qualitative research study', *British Gestalt Journal,* 14 (2): 103–8.

Stevens, C. (2006) 'A heuristic-dialogical model for reflective psychotherapy practice', in D. Lowenthal and D. Winter (eds), *What is* Psychotherapeutic Research. pp. 171–83. London: Karnac.

Strumpfel, U. (2004) 'Research on Gestalt therapy', *International Gestalt Journal,* 12 (1): 9–54.

Yontef, G. and Jacobs, L. (2007) 'Introduction to Gestalt therapy', in R. Corsini and D. Wedding (eds), *Current Psychotherapies.* Belmont, CA: Brooks Cole. **(See pp. 353–8.)** (For free downloadable PDF of this chapter go to the Pacific Gestalt Institute website: http://www.gestalttherapy.org/faculty-publications.asp)

17

ENDING THE JOURNEY

The basic problem not only of therapy but of life is how to make life liveable for a
being whose dominant characteristic is his awareness of himself as a unique individual
on the one hand and of his mortality on the other. (Perls, 1970: 128)

The ending of any therapeutic journey is an important separation and potentially stirs
up all our beliefs or fears about isolation, loss and death. There is always the danger that
the client and the counsellor will collude to avoid these issues and not reach proper
closure; as Perls reminds us, facing the reality of our mortality is hugely challenging.
There is also the opportunity, however, for the client to end choicefully and appropriately,
becoming the author of his own life as he fully accounts for the significance of the event
and makes the experience of a complete ending. Some people find that the end of the
therapeutic journey can be the most profound part of the whole experience.

PATTERNS OF ENDING

There are various ways that people avoid the pain and anxiety engendered by a loss or
an ending. Some clients avoid the difficulty by 'leaving early'. They withdraw – psychologically and sometimes even physically as the end approaches. They are the clients
who miss the last session or who are there but seem to have disengaged towards the
end. Other clients cannot bear to let go and, on the contrary, try to delay the end by
discovering new unfinished business or new therapy issues. It is not uncommon for
clients to recycle their original issues in the last stages of therapy. They appear to
return to a previous level of functioning, producing issues and problems similar to
those when they first came. We have found that this can be a way of 'trying on' old
coping strategies, to check that they will still be available when the therapy is not.
However, it may also be a way of convincing themselves and their therapist that they
are not ready to leave.

It is the therapist's job not only to help clients leave well, but also to help them
learn as much as possible about themselves in the process. Any ending, especially

one as significant as the ending of therapy, will resonate with all the client's past experiences of endings. She may put herself back in touch with the unfinished business of previously ungrieved losses. She may also turn to patterns of automatic response which have developed as creative adjustments for managing past endings and separations. Particularly relevant are the earliest relational experiences, those with primary care-takers. These usually establish relational patterns – often called attachment styles – that colour every future close relationship, with its intimacies and its separations.

> **Suggestion:** Take a few minutes to consider the endings in your own history. Consider both significant and small endings. Is there a typical way you tend to end relationships? For example, leaving quickly, not looking back or, conversely, avoiding acknowledging the actual ending, and saying 'see you soon'. Can you identify patterns in your ways of responding? There is also an ending whenever we have a new beginning or transition. Even if it is a chosen change, such as getting married or moving to a new job, there is a process of ending we need to go through. You can look at these sorts of changes when you are identifying your patterns around endings,

When you have identified your patterns and attitudes, think about what effect that will have on you as a therapist. What avoidance patterns are you likely to collude with? What might you yourself avoid?

The therapist will help the client be aware of all her experiences in relation to this ending and be alert to their significance. It will be the opportunity to resolve fixed gestalts around ending and face the necessary issues of transition.

There are many other variables that will influence the client's experience of ending:

◆ Particular transference and counter-transference issues in the therapy relationship that may lead to difficulties if not fully resolved. For example, the therapist may be experienced by the client as the vulnerable mother who can't be left.
◆ Implications from the presenting issue, for example if the client presented with relationship difficulties or bereavement.
◆ The cultural implications of endings, and rituals that may need to be observed.
◆ The current field conditions that may influence the client. For example, what sort of environmental support is available after ending? Is the client going through any other stressful changes or transitions at the same time?

A successful therapy can be seen as a process whereby client (and therapist) have fulfilled the contract and have worked through the old fixed relational patterns to achieve a mutual and congruent relationship. If this has happened, the ending will 'feel right'. However, there is a way in which this can be even more painful. Relationships of mutual authenticity are rare and uniquely nourishing. Both parties may have difficulty in saying goodbye.

EXAMPLE

B'Elanna had been in therapy for two and a half years. One day, she arrived at the session with the announcement that she had been hugely helped by the work and she was now ready to leave. It was clear that she intended to leave that day. She was genuinely astonished when her counsellor suggested that they might need a little more time to say goodbye. Exploring her assumption that they would just end without further ado, B'Elanna remembered how her mother would drop her at the railway station each term when she took the train back to boarding school. Her mother's goodbye had been brief and without a backward glance. B'Elanna realized that this was the way she also dealt with separations. As she recalled an actual memory of the school partings, she became aware of how she had suppressed her feelings of distress. She decided to do this ending differently and they agreed on five weeks in which both could make their goodbyes.

THE NATURE OF THE ENDING

Later in the chapter we outline the tasks that apply generally to most endings in therapy. However, it is useful to recognize that there are many different types of endings: planned or unplanned, chosen or enforced. Each will bring its particular challenges and opportunities.

WHEN THE ENDING IS PLANNED

The open-ended contract

Here the ending naturally arises with mutual agreement. The client often shows a new confidence or competence about old issues and maintains self-support and energy in the face of life's challenges. With this type of contract, the opportunity for the client is to choose to end in full awareness. This is often when she realizes that she is able to continue on her own and can, in effect, be her own therapist. For the counsellor, it is sometimes essential to accept 'good enough' and not expect that the client will wish to finish all the issues the counsellor has identified!

The brief or short-term contract

Please see Chapter 20 where this is covered in detail.

UNEXPECTED ENDINGS

When the therapist is forced to end

At times, the end of the therapy is brought about by factors in the therapist's life. He might fall ill, need to move away to a new location, or decide to reduce his workload or retire. In this case, if the client has any issues about abandonment (and which of us does not!) they are more likely to be stirred up. Again, it is important that the therapist help the client to voice her feelings and thoughts. The following pointers may be useful if you have to declare an unexpected and unwelcome termination.

◆ Give as much notice as possible.
◆ Allow the client to get irrationally angry or disappointed with you. This can be extremely important to allow unfinished business around other endings to surface. If the reason is a crisis in your own life, it is quite natural for the client to be concerned and sad for you. Beware of their protecting you from their anger or sadness by being too understanding.
◆ Self-disclose enough about the reason to reassure the client that the ending is not in any way connected to the therapy work.
◆ Give them a choice about the timing of the end, if possible.
◆ Offer a space in your new practice location, if you are having one, even if it is impractical for them, thereby demonstrating your continuing commitment in principle.
◆ Be strategically authentic about your own responses (see Chapter 4, section on guidelines for on self disclosure).
◆ Offer to help find a new therapist for them – sometimes it is appropriate for you to actually do the work of finding someone and facilitating the handover.
◆ Anyone who has had the experience of moving location or closing their practice for any reason, knows how emotionally draining the task is. Make sure you have lots of supervision and support during this time and don't under-estimate how stressful it is.

When the client 'disappears'

Occasionally, a client might leave therapy unexpectedly and precipitately. She simply fails to arrive at her session. Whatever reason she has – be it disappointment in your clinical ability or anxiety about the therapy, she has a right to choose. This sort of ending tends to happen at the start of therapy when the client is ambivalent about her commitment. We suggest you do not telephone the client to ask what happened. It may feel like being 'chased' into her own home and as such would seem intrusive. Normally it is appropriate to write a short letter expressing regret that she could not come and either confirming her next appointment or inviting her to phone for another (we suggest a letter rather than e-mail or text as these seem more informal and potentially lacking in privacy). If she does not respond, then you can leave it at that, or write another note saying that you assume she has decided not to pursue therapy at this time, that you wish her well and that you would be happy to hear from her in the future if she changes her mind.

Remember that occasionally a client's disappearance (especially after few sessions) can mean that she has got what she came for and is feeling better. If she is not from the world of therapy, and is not, therefore, familiar with 'the principle of good endings' she may simply feel that she does not need to have more counselling (in the same way as she would not return to her GP after successful treatment). In any event, you may need to find the best way to finish for yourself and stop 'holding on', perhaps using supervision to work through any unfinished business.

If you have been seeing the client for some time, this changes the scenario somewhat. It might be more appropriate to say more in your letter. However, it is important for you to be circumspect about what you say outside the consulting room. Even if you have a good idea why she has not come, it is a symbolic breach of boundaries to refer explicitly in a letter to the content of the sessions; your therapeutic interventions take place in the consulting room. It is also potentially a real breach, because a letter could be opened by someone else. Choose your words carefully. It is possible to say, for example, that you think there has been a breakdown in communication and you hope that she will come and talk it over with you.

When the client wants to leave 'prematurely'

We believe wholeheartedly in the client's right to decide. What is more, she might easily be right. It may be that you both need to trust her process. However, it is also true that you have the right to fight for the 'potential client' – the vision of the growthful possibility that you see in her. Your commitment to the dialogic relationship enables you to challenge her desire to leave if you think she is avoiding a difficulty. Some clients will of course end, or threaten to end, when they are angry or feel missed by you but are unable to articulate this. Open a discussion about what brought her to her decision. Some of the following questions may be useful:

- What has been happening recently, in her life and therapy?
- What sense has she been making about this?
- Is there anything about you or the therapy that she is dissatisfied with?
- How has she decided in the past when it is right to end a relationship, or leave a situation?
- How would she recognize if she were, in fact, avoiding an ending?
- You may also disclose your own polarities about her decision: 'One part of me is supportive of your decision to end; it is your right to choose. Another part of me wants to fight for you to stay and continue our work.'

It is almost always inappropriate and disrespectful (and even unethical) to say, or imply, to a client who clearly wants to leave, that she will not be able to cope or is not functioning well enough to be 'on her own'. It is appropriate to say something like, 'I'm fine with you leaving but I'm aware of how sudden your decision has been. I wonder if you'd be willing to explore it.'

THE TASKS OF ENDING

In our experience, the following tasks are common to most therapeutic endings. The process of leaving will involve shuttling back and forth between the tasks as the end approaches. If the work has been long-term, it should take several weeks or even months. You may need to raise these topics yourself in the sessions before the end if the client seems to be avoiding them.

Raise awareness of the ending

This might seem like an obvious task, but it is surprisingly important. There is evidence that one of the most important factors in working through a bereavement is for someone to be able to describe the significance and meaning of the death. The same is true of any significant ending, including therapy. We believe that the client needs to have a meaningful narrative about how the ending of therapy fits with their journey. You can encourage this by inviting them to reflect on what brought them to you in the beginning, what unfolded for them and how they are now.

We all potentially deny the existence of endings in many ways. Sometimes, we agree with clients that they can return for follow-ups if they feel the need. This can be a valid offer. However, it can also be an avoidance. It is hard saying goodbye to someone with whom we have been in a significant and intimate relationship. Yet this deprives our clients, not only of the opportunity to terminate 'cleanly' but also of the true experience of the final and important stage of therapy – discovering that they can manage on their own. If you have both agreed that an ending is appropriate and a date for an ending has been set, it should usually be kept despite any emergence of new (or old) symptoms. The client can be invited to explore what these symptoms might mean for her in relation to the ending.

Be aware of the significance and implications of the ending

Both counsellor and client need to account for the many ways that the therapy has been significant in the client's life.

- 'This is the place I have come every Tuesday at 3.00 p.m. for the last four years.'
- 'You are the first person I ever told about my mother's madness. It has felt as if I have let you know all about me, not just the surface parts.'
- 'I have got used to being able to come and discuss it here when problems come up in my life. I shall have to do that for myself.'

On both sides, there may be a simple acknowledgement of:

- 'I like you. I shall miss having you in my life.'

EXAMPLE

B'Elanna was surprised at first when her counsellor asked her about previous endings in her life. Had there been any major, difficult ones? She did not think so. Gently the counsellor expressed his puzzlement 'None at all? What about your marriage?' B'Elanna shook her head emphatically. 'That was just a relief – it had all been so awful.' 'What about leaving your home and country?' Again a denial: 'Oh it was bad there. I was glad to get away.' As the counsellor named many endings that B'Elanna had experienced, each one was met with a dismissal. In each case she said the lost person or situation was not worth grieving. As they explored the subject further, however, B'Elanna began to recognize the pattern. She had grown up needing to be independent and strong. When war had come to her country she had been forced prematurely to put 'childish needs' of grief behind her. She had then followed this way of coping with loss all her life. This awareness led her to re-examine how she would leave her counsellor and how she would deal with the sadness.

For some clients, the relationship with the therapist will be one of the most significant and intense of their life. Leaving this relationship will therefore be enormously important. It may also highlight the apparent strangeness of the therapeutic boundary. Having been so close, you will probably never meet again. This is hard for the therapist too and has sometimes led to damaging boundary violations (agreeing to meet socially, becoming friends, etc.). In our opinion, ending cleanly is very often a *necessary* conclusion to seal and contain what has been achieved in therapy.

Encourage full expression of feelings

Expression of feeling could include sadness, anger, fear, relief, excitement or a mixture of all. You can encourage this with questions such as, 'What has this relationship meant for you? What are you aware of now, as you contemplate ending with me?' This is a time when you might choose to self disclose some of your own reactions.

It might also include familiar, negative, habitual feelings such as depression, bitterness, self-pity, guilt and so on, old relational patterns that can be brought to awareness and worked through. They can include versions of familiar introjects or beliefs like: 'Everything important is always taken away from me.' 'If you had been a better therapist, I would have no pain at all.' Inevitably, clients' fixed patterns of avoidance of the meaning or pain of ending may threaten to interfere with the expression of feelings.

EXAMPLE

B'Elanna had been deeply moved by the discoveries she had made about herself in relation to endings and had spent much time in deep grief for her past. She had set her ending date for July but in early June she arrived in an irritable mood complaining about the parking arrangements. There should, she said, be a better system for telling clients where to park. Her therapist sympathized with her about the inconvenience and apologized for the lack of clarity, but she began to talk about how bad the traffic had been on the route to the session. He very gently teased her, 'It's a real nuisance coming here, isn't it!' B'Elanna stared at him and then became upset and withdrawn. The therapist realized he had made a mistake and apologized. B'Elanna received this and relaxed visibly; she started to cry, saying 'I don't know how I'll manage without you.' The therapist felt both warm towards her and aware of his own sadness. He said so. They both sat for a moment in silence acknowledging their mutual sadness.

Acknowledge and celebrate what has been achieved and acknowledge what is still unfinished

Look back on the journey you have made together – the difficulties and successes, the changes made or not made. You can ask the client to review the stages and turning points in the journey, what was most important or most transformative, as well as times when there was little movement or they felt stuck. It can be useful to share your insight about how you have seen your client's journey and the important moments. Your validation and recognition can be supportive and confirming. Also ask if there is feedback she wants from you and any she wants to give you, or herself.

EXAMPLE

B'Elanna felt shaky as July arrived. Yet she was also excited at the idea of 'doing it properly,' as she put it. In the penultimate session they spent the time looking over their work together. B'Elanna said, 'You know, the day I really started to trust you was when I was telling you how I got upset at work and you remembered what I had said about my grandfather a whole year before.' As the therapist asked her to recognize how she had changed since she came, she realized how much was different, how she felt much more alive and optimistic about her life.

Suggestion: A visualization that can be useful at this time is to ask your client to 'Imagine that you are six months into the future. How do you feel about having left therapy, what regrets do you have, if any? Is there anything you wished you had said or done or expressed?'

It is perfectly appropriate for there to be matters that are unresolved. Melnick and Roos (2007) question Gestalt's emphasis on the completion of unfinished business and believe that we can combine withdrawing energy with staying internally attached to the lost person. They speak of 'hanging on and letting go' (p. 102) and assert that there is much learning and growing that comes from living with the internal attachment to a lost significant other.

Plan for the future

Towards the end of your mutual review, identify future issues. What issues or situations can she expect to arise in the coming months and how will she manage future crises or difficulties, especially ones like those that brought her into therapy in the first place? If you have had a long relationship with her, you will have been internalized as a resource. Your modelling, your voice, your care and attention will be part of her inner landscape. What other resources are in her life that she could call on, now that therapy is ending? What new social networks or activities might she develop?

EXAMPLE

B'Elanna took seriously the therapist's suggestion to consider how she would face the future. Carefully, she thought about what sort of challenges she might have to meet and how she might cope with them. The therapist was relieved to hear her thinking in this way, as in her past she had shown a marked lack of desire or ability to plan for herself or ensure her security. As he shared this with her, she recognized how she used to believe that she didn't have any worthwhile future for herself. As they linked this deep sense of insecurity to her early childhood in a wartorn country, both therapist and client felt deeply moved – both at what she had been through and also that she had regained her self-support to the extent of caring for her future life.

Of course, it would be impossible (and missing the point!) to try to anticipate too much. The client is going on with her own journey and part of the anxiety and excitement of it is the unknown.

Say goodbye

Deciding how to end should be a shared decision. Together you can work out what is important or needs to be marked. Sometimes, clients like to work out a special ritual, for example offering some small gift or token to remember them by.

EXAMPLE

B'Elanna did not want to create any particular ritual. She said that it was important to her to simply stay in relationship right up until the moment of goodbye. She predicted that in the last session she would cry and just be inconsolable, but in the event they also laughed together as well – remembering times they had shared and celebrating the journey they had made. Tears filled B'Elanna's eyes as she faced the therapist to say goodbye. The therapist felt moved also and showed it. As she walked down the path from the consulting room B'Elanna turned and stood still for the moment. They smiled warmly at each other. Then B'Elanna turned and walked away while the therapist closed the door. The therapist knew he would probably never see her again; he felt satisfied but melancholy and reflected on how hard it was to let go of such intense relationships.

Withdraw energy

The final task is the withdrawal of energy from the therapy relationship in order to enter the 'fertile void' of the cycle of experience and be available to re-invest in new relationships and emerging figures. This is a task that both counsellor and client will carry out alone in the days and weeks following the final session.

A caveat: Bereavement is often called 'grief work' and, in our opinion, fully addressing and being with a parting of this nature is certainly 'work'. As well as being potentially satisfying and transformative, it can be exhausting, and both the client and the therapist should make sure that they are well supported during this time.

THE THERAPIST'S LOSS

We have, of course, been focusing on helping clients identify their patterns around endings. But inevitably, as we said earlier, the therapist has her own patterns. We also struggle with issues of attachment and loss; we also react to the echoes of death in every ending. It is crucial for our clients' sake and also our own that we get to know our own responses in this regard for two major reasons:

♦ We need to ensure that our own patterns of modifying contact around ending do not get in the way of our client doing what she needs to do. We must be sure that we are neither ignoring the importance of the ending stage nor refusing to let go.

♦ A successful therapist will have to go through many endings of successful and rewarding relationships during the course of her professional career. All the more important that we know how to do this in a way that makes us wiser and more complete, so that we are not having to put energy into maintaining old patterns of avoidance.

The running example above was of B'Elanna, a client who fully addressed her ending. It could as easily have been written about a therapist, who at each stage or task had to confront himself about the significance and importance of the loss of this client relationship.

We invite you to do some more exploring about your own patterns, in order to make sure that your endings are as uncontaminated as possible.

> **Suggestion:** See if you can recall your first day of school. Can you remember how you felt before you went? How much were you helped to prepare for it? Often people find that this experience of separation marked a pattern of their response to future changes and adjustments. (If you have no early memories, recall instead your first day at secondary school or at your psychotherapy or counselling training institute.)
>
> How might this experience influence your attitude to endings, how will it affect your work as a therapist? What have you learned since then – both in theory and in your experience – that has enriched your process?

RECOMMENDED READING

Houston, G. (2003) *Brief Gestalt Therapy*. London: Sage. (**See Chapter 6 – 'The Ending'**).

Mackewn, J. (1997) *Developing Gestalt Counselling*. London: Sage. (**See pp. 209–14.**)

Melnick, J. and Roos, S. (2007) 'The myth of closure', *Gestalt Review*, 11 (2): 90–107.

Murray Parkes, C. and Sills, C. (1994) 'Psychotherapy with the dying and the bereaved', in P. Clarkson and M. Pokorny, *The Handbook of Psychotherapy*. London: Routledge. pp. 494–514.

Philippson, P. (2009) *The Emergent Self. An Existential-Gestalt Approach*. London: Karnac. (**See Chapter 6 – 'Death and Endings'.**)

(Continued)

(Continued)

Roos, S. (2001) 'Chronic sorrow and the Gestalt construct of closure,' *Gestalt Review*, 5 (4): 289–310.

Sabar, S. (2000) 'Bereavement, grief and mourning: a Gestalt perspective'. *Gestalt Review*, 4 (2): 152–68.

Worden, J.W. (2008) *Grief Counseling and Grief Therapy: A Handbook for the Mental Health Practitioner.* 4th edn, New York: Springer Publications.

PART TWO

MANAGING CHALLENGING ENCOUNTERS

18

ASSESSING AND MANAGING RISK

There are many times when a client presents with a life issue, a condition or a way of behaving that is particularly challenging for the therapist and may require special attention to risk, or a specialized treatment approach. Among these clients are those with psychotic process, self-harming behaviour, dissociative or regressive processes, depression and anxiety. In their more severe forms, they often imply a need for the therapist to take specific courses of action that strongly deviate from usual Gestalt practice. A more behavioural and directive approach may often be necessary, with more focused interventions around risk and safety issues (including even the safety of the therapist). They are clients who can evoke difficult and disturbing responses in the therapist, challenge boundaries and need more strategic thinking and management.

These clients (who often already have a diagnosis on Axis I in DSM IV) tend to have global difficulties in functioning, may be in great distress and frequently cause suffering and disturbance to therapists, family and friends.

The other challenging category of clients includes those who have inflexible personality styles or personality disorders (Axis II of the DSM). These clients are often functioning adequately in the world but may come complaining that they are misunderstood or are unhappy about their relationships; sometimes, they say that others are complaining about their behaviour. In our experience, the challenge of clients in this category tend to fall mainly into the area of transference and counter-transference rather than risk or emergency, so we refer you to Chapter 12 and also to the recommended reading on working with personality disorders at the end of this chapter. Having said that, some people with personality disorders can also present unexpected emergencies, especially at times of crisis, or occasionally later on in the therapy if the client has been moving too fast and the old creative adjustments are breaking down.

While we do not have the space to look at working with the large range of Axis I and Axis II issues, we will outline ways of assessing and managing risk so that you will know what particular action you may need to take (and when). In the next chapter we will look in detail at depression and anxiety, which are the most common presentations where risk can often be an issue.

We also believe that practitioners who have clients with serious issues in these areas should consult the relevant literature, get expert help through supervision with specialists in the field and consider referral for psychiatric consultation. In the recommended reading section we suggest a variety of helpful literature from both within and outside Gestalt. In addition, we suggest that therapists become familiar with a standard diagnostic system such as DSM IV (or the forthcoming DSM V) or ICD 10, if only to be able to access non-Gestalt literature and to be able to communicate meaningfully with other professionals.

Lastly we want to make the point that working in a more strategic and directional way with disturbed clients can be seen as a violation of the Gestalt maxim to stay with 'what is' and allow a natural process of unfolding. However, we believe that this is not necessarily a contradiction and agree with Yontef and Philippson (2008: 271) who say:

> Growth may be a spontaneous outcome of focusing, intimate contact in therapy and so forth. Or it may be part of a systematic program of instruction and experimentation. But even in the latter case, it is based on self-recognition and self-acceptance while moving towards growth ... in many clinical situations, the work may focus on building a repertoire of psychological tools, getting mastery over destructive behaviour ... This learning can be done cooperatively ...

ESSENTIAL CONSIDERATIONS

In Chapter 5, we gave suggestions for the assessment of risk at initial interview. We now explore in more detail some of the issues that should be considered when deciding whether to take on a 'disturbing' client. We have developed five steps to help you to understand the situation and decide how to proceed.

1. **Assess** the immediate picture.
2. **Gather** relevant information.
3. **Rate** the risk.
4. **Take** a course of action.
5. **Monitor** the ongoing process.

Assess the immediate picture

It is surprising how often practitioners – with a desire to stay with and follow the client – do not give themselves permission to take charge of the session and ask what they need to know in order to make an assessment. Some clients will present at the initial meeting with many overlapping issues and, depending on the potential risk, you must decide if there is a need to take immediate action. The first priority is to assess whether the situation is high risk:

◆ Is the client is about to lose their job/relationship/accommodation/children/money/liberty if some action is not taken straight away?
◆ Is the client on the edge of collapse or general loss of functioning?
◆ Is the client suicidal or self-harming?
◆ Is violence any part of the picture?
◆ Is the client suffering from an untreated medical condition? Many symptoms that accompany organic problems are emotional or psychological (e.g. thyroid disorders).
◆ Could the symptoms be pointing to substance abuse or an energing serious Axis I condition?

If the answer is 'yes' to any of these questions, your prime concern is to prevent further decline or loss of ability to function competently in the world. It is important to think out a concrete, pragmatic way of addressing the problem that may involve discussing risk management with the client (and sometimes insisting on discussing it), practical advice, education, or contacting the GP or the community mental health response team.

Even in the absence of emergency, there may be other important questions that take precedence as you decide whether – and how – to work together.

◆ Is there a practical issue that needs to be addressed first? Every presenting situation is inevitably a gestalt of biological, cognitive, emotional and somatic factors in a context of historical and present field conditions, such as over-stressful work environments or relationships (e.g. living with a partner who is ill) which may require practical action before deciding a 'psychological' treatment plan.
◆ Do you *want* to work with this person? Have you enough training and supervisory support? Are they suitable for your style of psychotherapy? Are your premises suitable? For example, it is not advisable to work from home with more seriously disturbed clients. Both you and your client may feel better contained if you meet in an agency building, a medical centre, etc. A client may scare you or may be difficult to relate to, and you may not wish to take him on. It is important to take your own responses seriously and not be grandiose in imagining that you can treat everyone who comes to you.
◆ Does the presenting issue make sense to you? In many situations it is important not to make a decision to work with the client at the initial interview but to have supervision first. In any case, we generally recommend offering a short-term assessment contract, for example four sessions with a review. This gives you the option of referring on at the end of the period. It can also be useful to decide whether the disturbance fulfils the criteria of an Axis I or II disorder, or is what you might call 'just difficult' for a variety of other reasons.

Gather relevant information

When you have formed an initial picture of the client's situation, you need to set about identifying areas of particular concern or details that need further investigation. It can be useful to write down these issues in specific terms, including any questions on which you need more information. This helps to protect you from a feeling of being overwhelmed or confused by the emotional impact or disorientation that sometimes accompanies the assessment period with high risk clients. Having some clear points that you wish to address in the next session will help provide a containing structure.

Good assessment is also a matter of exploring the origin and meaning of a symptom or problem. We suggest that a careful history of the presenting complaint is a way to gain clarity.

The following questions can easily be modified for any topic of concern:

- When did the problem first occur (for example, suicidal thoughts, self-harm, drug abuse, avoiding food or bingeing, thoughts about going crazy?)
- What else was going on at that time in your life?
- How did your family or friends react (or how do you imagine they would react)?
- How often has this happened through your life and what sense do you make of it?
- When was the problem at its worst in your life?
- Did you ask for, or get, any help with it?
- When was the last time it happened/or was most difficult?
- How did you handle it or try to help yourself?
- What made you seek help now, at this time?

Obviously, you would not ask these questions one after another as in this list! If the client is sufficiently self-supported, he may be comfortable with answering these questions in one session. You may, however, need to gather this information over the course of several sessions. It is essential to remember the client's inevitable sensitivity and vulnerability about the issues. Sometimes practitioners feel themselves to be constrained by fear of provoking further distress from asking details about certain areas – for example, suicidal thoughts, hallucinations or abusive relationships. However, many clients will find it a relief to be able to share their story with someone who is not afraid to ask (and hear) about distressing material. Indeed, listening with respect, openness and acceptance can in itself start a similar process in the client towards himself.

Rate the risk

Once you have identified specific areas of concern, you can then read specialist literature, and discuss it with your supervisor. This will avoid you having to 'reinvent the wheel' and will provide more support for you. For example, there is a lot of very useful descriptive and predictive information about the risks of different types of mental health problems, when suicidal thoughts are most likely to be acted on, or the particular implications and dangers of different kinds of drugs, to name only three areas.

Assessing severity

A useful start is to locate the client's presentation on a rough continuum of

Mild --------------------**Moderate**--------------------**Severe**

Mild disturbance is when a client has disturbing symptoms that cause subjective distress but don't significantly interfere with day-to-day activities (although it may take extra effort to do the things the client needs to do).

Moderate disturbance is when a client has disabling or disturbing symptoms which periodically interfere significantly with day-to-day activities.

Severe disturbance is when a client has persistent disabling or disturbing symptoms most of the time and is often unable to function normally in day-to-day activities. It may also mean that the client is at immediate risk of causing harm to self or others.

The more disturbed end of the continuum is a reflection of how difficult (or impossible) it is for the client to respond effectively to what they are facing or are experiencing. It also flags the importance of considering your own self-protection and restorative care at the end of a difficult session.

A rating of severity will also enable you to:

◆ Decide how much to introduce strategic planning for behavioural interventions (for example, to consult or refer to a specialist, suggest a course of behaviour such as taking time off work temporarily, or teach anxiety-reducing techniques, etc.);
◆ Organize the therapy around stabilizing, containing and grounding (for example, for clients who are continually overwhelmed or distressed);
◆ Decide how much responsibility you need to take to avoid deterioration (for example, how much to insist on a psychiatric referral or a risk-management plan).

Rating suicidal clients

You should treat all threats of suicide seriously even if you suspect the client is manipulating you, as you may provoke escalating behaviour if you do not. Very occasionally, people have decided to kill themselves as a clear rational decision (when suffering from a terminal physical illness, for example). However, most suicide threats arise from a confused, conflicted state of mind and can be seen as a communication of some sort (often anger towards another person – sometimes towards you), which cannot be expressed openly and is retroflected into suicidal impulses. This idea can sometimes help you to see that the person is making an attempt at *life* (to be heard or seen), rather than an attempt at death.

There is a common misconception that asking questions about suicidal intent is likely to provoke it. This is not borne out by the research. Indeed, discussing the possibility of suicide in an open, non-judgemental way can give the person a sense of relief and support. It is important that you do not react with fear, anxiety or disapproval when your client alludes to the subject. You should first decide if there is any immediate action that ought to be taken to prevent loss of life, and then you will need to form a clear and detailed assessment of the degree of risk before planning a strategy. To do this you will return to the 'Gathering Information' stage. The following are questions additional to those described earlier in this chapter that may help you to make a clearer decision.

◆ Has the client ever made an attempt to harm himself in the past? If so, when and what happened?

◆ What were the precipitating factors (being rejected by a lover, for example) that led up to this previous episode (do these exist at the present time or are they imminent)? You can ask the question, 'If this [the same precipitating factor] happened now, what would you do?'

◆ What stopped them from dying before? Was it an intervention from another person, if so, how did that happen?

◆ Have they made any plans to carry out the suicide? Have they decided how, and in what way, they would actually do it?

◆ Who would be affected by their death (and how)? Who in their social world do they think would be most upset? Bear in mind that the threatened suicidal behaviour may be part of a systemic issue in the client's family or social network.

In general, the risk of suicide is somewhat higher when the person has made a detailed plan. Uncomfortable as it may seem, therefore, it is crucial to ask specific questions such as 'Have you thought about how you would actually kill yourself? What pills exactly would you take? Where would you get them? When and where would you take them?' Specific details are more worrying than vague intentions. Evidence of a detailed plan should be considered as a more serious risk.

Take a course of action

Managing the suicidal client effectively needs to become your highest priority while the risk is acute. In situations of imminent danger you may need to contact a family member, GP or community mental health team. In less immediate, but still high-risk situations, you may need to see the client more frequently or offer brief telephone contact to provide a holding environment. Some therapists advocate a 'no-harm' contract with clients. This notion is somewhat controversial in the Gestalt approach but it can have some positive advantages (for a discussion of the debate, see Mothersole, 2006). One such contract might be to ask the client to agree not to attempt to kill himself before your next session with him, or, in extreme cases, to speak to you on the phone beforehand (make sure the agreement is about speaking to you, not simply phoning you – if you are not in, he has not fulfilled the contract). You can help him to draw up a list of emergency support numbers that he will phone if he feels suicidal, starting with the Samaritans, who can be relied upon to answer and to offer an empathic ear. Such agreements may help your client find a way to survive without trying to kill himself. He can then see the contract as containing and holding – evidence of your commitment to his life rather than any attempt to restrict or impose your will.

Even if you believe that the client has the fundamental right to make choices about his own life and death, we believe you have an obligation as a Gestalt therapist to attempt to preserve life (see Chapter 21 on Ethics). This may mean temporarily changing your therapeutic approach in order to manage the crisis. At these times, supportive, containing work with strong boundaries is often necessary. Do not attempt cathartic, empty-chair or confronting work unless you are absolutely sure of the client's ability to manage it. Occasionally, despite your best efforts, the client might still decide to kill himself. While this is enormously distressing, it is a time for you seek support rather than blame yourself, and to remind yourself that ultimately we do not and should not have control over our clients' decisions.

Referring on

We strongly suggest that a part of every assessment of a disturbing client is the consideration that you may need to refer him on (if only for a second opinion) and we advise that you seek supervision to make this determination. Chapter 1 contains some suggestions for referring someone on to another agency or practitioner. However sensitive you are in your manner, this process often generates understandable suspicion on the part of the client that they have been judged and found unacceptable. You can minimize this by strongly focusing on conveying your respect and compassion for this person in difficult circumstances who has taken a risk in sharing their vulnerabilities with a stranger. You can also say that of course you want the best help for them, so it is not a case that they are too difficult, but of finding someone who specializes in this area of difficulty.

Planning the therapy direction

By the time you have decided to offer a contract for therapy, you will have carefully considered the issues of risk, the particular needs of the client and also your level of confidence and competence. You will have discussed the client with your supervisor and have decided to proceed. You will have thought about this particular client's needs and decided if any issues must be addressed first or, conversely, left till later. You will also have considered whether the type of Gestalt relationship you offer needs to be adapted. Clients in a high risk category may also need a more considered use or grading of the offer of a dialogic relationship, as a therapist with strong presence can often seem quite overwhelming to a fragile client. We suggest you then return to Chapter 6 on Treatment Considerations to help you to decide the best (unique) strategy for your client.

Working with disturbed clients, especially those with long-term chronic difficulties, is often slow, with only gradual incremental change. It is also challenging, usually long-term and there may be many issues around dependency. This will no doubt be a difficult (but fascinating) journey of learning and discovery for you. It is working with our most disturbed and disturbing clients that we learn most about ourselves (and often learn to face our own unacknowledged disturbances or shadow aspects).

Monitor the ongoing process

In addition to thinking carefully about treatment direction, you need to pay attention to how you will monitor the situation in ongoing work. You will need to be alert to signs of symptoms temporarily worsening in response to life circumstances or to the challenges of the therapy. Is the client perhaps having more frequent thoughts of self-harm, drinking more, being erratic in attendance, considering stopping their medication, not sleeping or eating properly, becoming more isolated, becoming unresponsive to you? These are all signs that you need to reassess the risk, temporarily pause your strategy and respond to deal with what is emerging. It is a time to discuss with your client your concerns and find a way to minimize risk. You can also create together a plan of action in this time of increased difficulty. In this way, you are both monitoring the situation and supporting his growing ability to function healthily.

How to bring someone back to the present

It may occasionally happen that your client becomes regressed, dissociated or out of relational contact. She may need help to regain her self-support. The following are suggestions for helping a client return fully to the here-and-now so that she can leave your consulting room with adult resources to negotiate the outside world (for instance, to drive home).

You should leave at least 10–15 minutes before the end of the session to carry out any of the following suggestions, although it is often enough simply to say, 'You need to come back here to the room now so that, before you go, we have time to talk about what happened.' Otherwise, you may need some or all of the following interventions (not necessarily in this order):

◆ Take the client through as many contact functions as are available: 'What can you see in the room, what colours and shapes? Can you hear the noise of the birds, the clock, the traffic? Listen for a moment – how many different sounds can you distinguish?'
◆ Ask simple here-and-now questions: 'How are you feeling right now? What are you aware of in this room? Are you aware of me sitting opposite?'
◆ Speak in a deliberate, slow and firm voice.
◆ Resensitize body awareness: 'I'd like you to pay attention to your body sensations now, notice your breathing, the weight of your body on the seat, your feet on the floor, be aware of the chair you are sitting in, feel your whole body, notice any tension or relaxation.'
◆ Gently but firmly insist she comes back to the room with you. For example, for clients who are having a flashback – 'This is a memory you are having, I want you to leave that behind and come back to the room *now* with me. Pay attention to my voice.'
◆ Remind her of where she is: 'You are here in this room with me.'
◆ Be reassuring in what you say: 'It's OK to leave that now, you can come back to it at another time, but now you must stop and focus on me in this room.'
◆ Ask about what she is doing after the therapy session, to invoke thinking and anticipation: 'What will you be doing after we stop, this afternoon, evening, etc.?'
◆ If it seems necessary or appropriate, offer normalizing activities such as suggesting she walk around the room with you, offer a glass of water or even a cup of tea (in England any way!).

◆ Debrief about what has happened. Talk about what you have just witnessed and ask her to tell you what has just happened. Using words and descriptions usually puts more distance from an experience. Make sure you are satisfied that the client has returned to full self-support before leaving the room. Ask how she will get home, how she will look after herself, how to contact you in an emergency (all things that require 'adult' awareness and planning).

LOOKING AFTER YOURSELF

In Chapter 7 we have already looked at ways of supporting yourself; however, there are specific issues that it is vital you are watchful for when working with more disturbed clients.

One consequence of seeing disturbed and disturbing clients is the risk of vicarious traumatization, burn-out, secondary stress disorder and compassion fatigue. Research shows that around 50 per cent of clinicians who work with traumatized clients report feeling distressed or very distressed, sometimes for long periods of time. Such responses can be common when the therapist has herself experienced childhood or recent trauma.

Our ability to be dialogically inclusive, somatically resonant and available to receive our client's felt experience is both the healing environment and the possible cause of vicarious trauma. It is also the prelude to burn-out, where your interest, compassion, energy and availability for contact is diminished. Counter-transference responses can also be strong, especially where the therapist feels pulled into an abusive re-enactment.

> **Suggestion**: Reflect on your most difficult clients. How often do you feel emotionally drained, exhausted, or isolated after a session? Have you experienced physical symptoms of discomfort after a session or other feelings that seemed distressing and unusual? How often have you wanted to block out the pain of the abusive story you were hearing?

There is often shame or a reluctance to bring these issues to colleagues or to supervision as it seems to imply weakness or incompetence. On the contrary, we believe it to be simply a consequence of a committed, sensitive and resonant clinician going beyond her self-support.

Here are some suggestions for self care

◆ Draw up a list of your supports – Family, friends and colleagues you can call on.
◆ Identify activities that are soothing or supportive or de-stressing, such as exercise, yoga, meditation, music.

- See if you need to be in personal therapy or organize more supervision.
- Decide whether you need to say no to new cases which are especially stressful.
- Develop a ritual that marks the end of a session or the end of a day's work (this can include meditating, airing the room, playing music, and so on).
- Keep a diary where you express your left-over feelings, or at least identify them.
- Remember the slow nature of this kind of work and check your original estimates of the level of progress you would have expected by now.
- Supporting yourself extends also to the therapy session. At times it is reasonable to ask the client to pause in his story to allow you time to process it. This can be good modelling also for the client, who may feel he has no right or ability to slow down or regulate his emotions.
- Make sure you have enough professional or personal support after sessions (such as arranging a supervision session or a confidential conversation with a colleague to debrief).

RECOMMENDED READING ON WORKING WITH AXIS II DISTURBANCES

Benjamin, L.S. (2002) *Interpersonal Diagnosis and Treatment of Personality Disorders*. New York: Guilford Press.

Brownell, P. (2005) 'Gestalt therapy in community mental health', in A.L. Woldt and S.M. Toman (eds), *Gestalt Therapy – History, Theory and Practice*. Thousand Oaks, CA: Sage.

Delisle, G. (1999) *Personality Disorders: A Gestalt Therapy Perspective*. Cleveland, OH: Gestalt Institute of Cleveland Press.

Greenberg, E. (2005) 'The narcissistic tightrope walk: using Gestalt therapy field theory to stabilize the narcissistic client', *Gestalt Review*, 9 (1): 58–68.

Kearns, A. (2005) *The Seven Deadly Sins*? London: Karnac. (**See Chapter 2 – 'Fragile Self Process'.**)

Sperry, L. (2003) *Handbook of Diagnosis and Treatment of the Personality Disorders*. Levittown PA: Brunner-Mazel.

Stratford, C.D. and Brallier, L.W. (1979) 'Gestalt therapy with profoundly disturbed persons', *Gestalt Journal*, 2 (1): 90–104.

RECOMMENDED READING ON WORKING WITH PSYCHOSIS

Brownell, P. (2005) – See above.

Harris, C. (1992) 'Gestalt work with psychotics', in E.C. Nevis (ed.), *Gestalt Therapy*. New York: Gardner Press. pp. 239–62.

Howdin, J. and Reaves, A. (2009) 'Working with suicide', *British Gestalt Journal*, 18 (1): 10–17

Prouty, G. (2004) 'Pre-therapy and pre-symbiotic experiencing: evolutions in experiential approaches to psychotic experience', *International Gestalt Journal*, 27 (2): 59–84.

Spagnuolo Lobb, M. (2002) 'A Gestalt therapy model for addressing psychosis', *British Gestalt Journal*, 11 (1): 5–15.

Spagnuolo Lobb, M. (2003) 'Creative adjustment in madness', in M. Spagnuolo Lobb and N. Amendt-Lyon (eds), *Creative Licence – the Art of Gestalt Therapy*. Vienna: Springer-Verlag.

Stratford, C. and Brallier, L. (1979) – See above.

RECOMMENDED READING ON SELF-CARE

Meichenbaum, D. (2007) 'Stress inoculation training: a preventative and treatment approach', in P.M. Lehrer, R.L. Woolfolk and W.S. Sime (eds), *Principles and Practice of Stress Management*, 3rd edn. New York: Guilford Press. (**See www.melsissainstitute.org for a copy on this Chapter**)

Rothschild, B. (2006). *Help for the Helper: The Psychophysiology of Compassion Fatigue and Vicarious Trauma*. New York: W.W. Norton & Company.

Smethhurst, P. (2008) 'The impact of trauma – primary and secondary: how do we look after ourselves?', *British Journal of Psychotherapy Integration*, 5 (1): 39–47.

19

DEPRESSION AND ANXIETY

Depression and anxiety are increasingly common manifestations of psychological distress in our society. They are both responses to life circumstances that seem unmanageable or overwhelming. One type of response is to withdraw, isolate and shut down (a depressive reaction). The second response is to over-mobilize, worry and agitate (an anxious reaction). Both involve negative beliefs or attitudes and a loss of connection or control. There is often a sense of hopelessness. Clients have a diminished capacity to self-manage and creatively adjust to their situation.

Several research studies (e.g. Lambert, 2003) have now shown that Gestalt therapy is an effective treatment for many specific conditions such as severe depression and anxiety, and has a larger life-enhancing effect in the treatment of depression compared to cognitive behavioural approaches (Watson et al., 2003).

COMMON STARTING POINTS WHEN WORKING WITH ANXIETY AND DEPRESSION

An assessment of risk is crucial, as both conditions are potentially serious and can lead to a breakdown of functioning, self-harming behaviour and even suicide (see Chapter 18). Depending on the severity of the problem, you will want to think about whether to involve the GP, enable a psychiatric assessment or prioritize practical strategies to minimize the risk of deterioration. Clients often present in a serious crisis, with a breakdown of relationships, employment or general functioning. They are highly distressed, often completely focused on their symptoms and desperately wanting relief from them. Even if you consider that there is no risk, clients may initially need practical strategies or support to deal with the current crisis before they are able to engage in more psychological work (we return to this topic later).

First we will outline three areas of focus that are relevant to both depression and anxiety, before we deal with each presentation in detail.

Holding the hope

Many clients have lost any hope or expectation of improvement. Outcome research (such as Seligman, 2002) has identified the importance of hopefulness, resilience and optimism as client factors which are supports against depression. Melnick and Nevis (2005: 11) also describe the importance of encouraging 'optimism as a process ... a way of encountering the unknown', and of helping the client to develop this as an orientation towards the future.

It is clear, therefore, that in the early stages it is very beneficial for the therapist to hold a positive attitude to what is being offered therapeutically. It will also be conveyed in your confidence and in how you demonstrate your capacity to tolerate the impact of the hopelessness and distress of the client. Your steady interest, dialogic attitude and willingness to engage will all start to signal this positive approach. With clients who need more verbal reassurance, you may wish to say something like:

> 'Problems of anxiety usually respond well to this sort of therapy.'
> 'I believe that together we can find a way forward about your depressed feelings.'
> 'I'm optimistic that I can be of some help to you' (this must be true, of course!).

In this light it can also be useful to bring to the client's attention the efforts they have made so far that have helped, their persistence, their courageous commitment to therapy and any small moments of change, relief or connection they report.

Apparently overwhelming symptoms are often the result of unfinished business or a response to a seemingly insoluble current situation or crisis. Many clients are unaware of this, however, and see the symptoms themselves as the problem to be solved rather than a response to a 'situation'. It can be useful, therefore, to reformulate the symptoms as carrying a message or as potentially meaningful responses to a particular set of circumstances (or as an unintegrated part of themselves).

> 'I wonder if your anxiety is telling you something about your life-style?'
> 'Is it possible that your depression is a way of expressing something you don't know how to face?'

As well as potentially refocusing the client on more fundamental issues, this can also evoke a curious, reflective position that can be the start of a more creative or open attitude to their situation.

The issue of labels

Psychiatric diagnoses are very problematic. Some clients find it very helpful and containing to have a name for their condition. They find having a label normalizing (e.g. 'I am suffering from depression' or 'I have an anxiety disorder') and a relief to discover that their distressing and confusing experience is not unique to them and has been lived through and understood by others. One client said, 'Oh *that's* what's wrong with me. I thought I was going mad.' For other clients, labelling is experienced as the worse sort of objectifying and pathologizing and they experience it as a denial of their uniqueness. We stress (as does the DSM IV) the need to see the *person* as primary and to hold the holistic frame of 'a person with a problem' (e.g. a person with depressive or anxious symptoms).

You will need clinical experience to help you decide which is best in each situation, but in general we advise against offering or confirming psychiatric labels and instead have found much benefit in explaining that we believe everyone is different and that regardless of what label they have been given (for example by their GP), we see them as unique. It is often useful to ask 'What does the label of depression/anxiety disorder mean to you?'

Identifying secondary gain

There is often some 'secondary gain' in long-standing conditions where depressed or anxious behaviour attracts some benefit (such as getting care and sympathy, not having to deal with a situation, not having to go to work, etc.). In other words, the symptoms are part of a 'hardened' creative adjustment (Yontef and Jacobs, 2007: 342) to unmet need. This can have a resisting effect on the progress of recovery, as, out of awareness, the client can be reluctant to give up the benefits of the illness (even though it is very distressing). This is a subject that needs a diplomatic touch but you can invite the client to notice how there may be some other consequences to their distressing condition. An exploration of this kind can lead to a significant uncovering of another need, the fulfilment of which has seemed unattainable (e.g. to be met and understood). Stress how meeting this need is important for everyone, and wonder how else he or she could get it met. It may be vital that that you focus on answering that question before the client will be motivated to address the original problem.

> **Suggestion**: Identify your most common negative mood or state. What secondary gains do you get from such a state? Remember when you were last ill, unable to work or over-stressed with work. What were the advantages? See if you can identify which of these benefits you can't get without an 'excuse'.

WORKING WITH DEPRESSION

A client who presents with depression will often describe miserableness, loss of energy and motivation. He may also complain of loss of enjoyment or meaning in life, negative thinking and disturbed patterns of sleep and appetite. These 'symptoms' may be the result of many different factors or field conditions that get classified into a simplistic label of 'depression'. It is arguable that such a diagnosis has little useful meaning and is an unhelpful generalization that only serves the 'illness model' so favoured by the drug companies that prescribe anti-depressants (see Leader, 2008). We prefer the more relational term depressive response (rather than an 'illness'). This may follow life events such as bereavement, trauma, developmental stage adjustments and ongoing crises that have become overwhelming. It can also result from learned help-lessness or the unrecognized and unmourned losses of early separations or dysfunc-tional attachment patterns.

The strength of a Gestalt therapeutic approach is that it is not restricted by any particular theoretical position. Rather, it is about identifying the particular process issues involved for the unique individual in his unique situation (expressed in the co-created relationship with you), such as retroflection, low body energy, negative beliefs, withdrawal and a loss of meaningful relational contact. This means that the label of depression is less important and, as you read the following sections, you can focus on the aspects that are most relevant to each case. For many presentations of depres-sion, no specialized treatment considerations are necessary. The therapist will carry out a Gestalt assessment, identify areas that need to be attended to and form a plan of action in a standard way as suggested in Chapters 5 and 6.

However, we have found the following areas particularly relevant to working with depressed presentations:

◆ Increasing self and relational support.
◆ Completing unfinished business.
◆ Identifying unhelpful beliefs.
◆ Attending to body process and breathing.

Increasing self and relational support

Many clients have lost a sense or ability to make meaningful relational connection, have stopped seeing friends, feel alienated and find little value in social relations. This is particularly true when the initial trigger is around bereavement or shame (such as following a loss of employment or status). Your relational availability may be the first step to reconnecting and can be the springboard to encourage the client to re-connect with other people and experience the support of human contact. There is a particular need to offer a steady embodied presence, to demonstrate inclusion and to provide a strong container for difficult or unmanageable feelings.

◆ For clients whose initial response to their dilemma is to withdraw and hide, how-ever, a therapeutic relationship where they are 'seen' and understood can be poten-tially shaming, as they may imagine that the therapist will have the same criticism or negative judgement that they have for themselves. You will need therefore to be sensitive to grading your dialogic presence to avoid them feeling too 'seen'.
◆ Identify the support needed to best facilitate a naturally resolving condition (such as bereavement or a life transition). See the guidelines in Chapter 7.

- Identify the field conditions (for example, social deprivation, discrimination or alienation) that may be a primary influence in the presenting issue and encourage action to change the situation (rather than finding a different personal readjustment). (We realize, of course, that therapy as social action deserves another book.)
- Encourage contact with supportive friends or consideration of supportive activities.
- Make sure the client has considered the effects that erratic eating or sleeping patterns can have on his mood.

As we stress throughout this book, the way the client organizes his life is also played out in the therapeutic relationship. His depressive presentation will be a combination of his life situation, his organizing principles and how you and he co-create your relationship. This will show in the ebb and flow of how the therapeutic *between* becomes 'depressed'. Your own reactions and responses, your counter-transferences of anxiety, rescue, irritation or hopelessness all become useful information about how you and he co-create the problem and shed light on how he co-creates it with others.

EXAMPLE

Susan's regular appointment was at 2.00 p.m. on a Tuesday afternoon. The therapist came to dread the sessions, in which Susan bemoaned her lonely life and wept quietly through her story. The therapist felt alternately disconnected or exhausted and struggled with a strong urge to sleep. She put this sleepiness down to the post-lunch dip. However, one week, Susan had to re-arrange the session and they met at 9.00 in the morning. With dismay, the therapist noticed the same responses within five minutes of the start of the session. She recognized that she was 'depressing herself' as she sat with her client; they had co-created the deadened relationship of Susan's early life. She realized that she needed to understand this process and find a way to bring it into awareness for both of them.

Completing unfinished business

Depression can often be provoked by a sense of loss of control over one's life; feeling helpless to affect or influence what is happening. If the client identifies recent traumas where they experienced a loss of control, they may well be evoking echoes of past times of helplessness, which may contain unfinished business. Greenberg and Watson (2006) have identified what they call 'depressogenic emotional schemas' which are the legacy of previously unresolved traumas or experiences. Here, the client has formed an emotionally based depressive template or self-organization involving negative self-evaluations, negative feelings and negative expectations about the world and himself within it. You may therefore need to identify and bring into awareness unresolved traumas and work on older issues (see Chapter 11).

Identifying unhelpful beliefs

The depressed client usually has powerful negative introjects, core beliefs and repetitive thoughts such as: 'Everything goes wrong for me.' 'Its all hopeless.' 'I'll never succeed.' 'It's my fault.'

Often these beliefs start from an accurate and realistic assessment of a situation such as 'I failed at …' 'It was unfair …' − but the beliefs then become unbalanced, over-generalized, or catastrophizing. These patterns of thinking become self-perpetuating as the depressed client starts to believe that his life is hopeless or meaningless and that there is no point in trying to succeed. He gives up making an effort, stays at home, avoids people and stagnates. He then feels more isolated and miserable, has a sluggish body process and thus confirms his belief in the misery of life.

Working with negative beliefs is often thought to be the province of CBT (and somehow 'un-Gestalt'), but we have always found that Gestalt therapists are highly competent to work with cognitive schemes or core beliefs:

- Using the phenomenological method, identify and raise the client's awareness of his here-and-now thoughts and associated feelings; notice the words, metaphors, and self-descriptions that point to underlying core beliefs. Explore how he came to hold these beliefs and be curious as to whether he has really considered how appropriate or relevant they are now. Clarify generalizations by gathering evidence and looking for exceptions. Deconstruct and challenge unhelpful introjects.
- Identify more positive, hopeful beliefs that in the client's best moments have seemed true: 'I can reach out for support.' 'I will get through this' (sometimes called positive self-talk). Reframe positively, e.g. 'You did survive', 'You have got through this before and you will again.'
- Some research suggests that people who are depressed actually have an accurate view of the world but it is untempered by appreciation of its beautiful side. It may be that what is needed is a confrontation of the negative *focus* rather than trying to argue about the content of his thoughts. Invite him to notice what he is making figural and what he might be missing.
- Identify what beliefs he has about your attitude to him and start to make the connection about his expectations or projections. Possibly disclose your actual responses as information, but be wary of trying to convince him that he is not as bad as he thinks. It is contrary to the paradoxical theory of change (and it won't work!).

Attending to body process and breathing

The body energy of the depressed person is usually low, retroflected and collapsed. As we mentioned above, this can be a part of a self-reinforcing cycle of negative thinking, feeling and acting. Work to enliven breathing and body sensation can be of great help.

◆ Find ways to energize and sharpen any emerging figures. A characteristic of depression is a loss of interest and energy. Chapter 13 on 'Body Process' and Chapter 9 on 'Experimenting' offer many approaches to encouraging energetic connection and regaining lost liveliness.

◆ Work on retroflected energy (see Chapter 10).

While relaxation and mindfulness techniques have traditionally been used for anxiety conditions, they are increasingly being found to be helpful in the treatment of depression.

◆ Teach one of the many protocols for aware breathing (see Recommended Reading). For example:

> Find a position in which you can sit comfortably, your back straight and supported and your feet on the floor, so that you have a feeling of just sitting. Come to a sensation of your body and watch the movement of your chest and your belly, slowly rising and falling as you breathe deeply. Just notice your breath coming and going in a rhythmic pattern without judgement or opinion. Have a sense of being breathed – effortlessly – a simple being here in the moment, keeping your attention on the movement of the breath in your body. As you notice that your attention has turned to thoughts or feelings, simply bring yourself back to the breath. Don't worry how often you have to do that, it is part of your learning to be with yourself, in the moment, without judgement.

We now turn to working with anxiety, a phenomenon in its own right, but also often experienced alongside depression.

WORKING WITH ANXIETY

The anxious client experiences bodily tension, palpitations or sick feelings in the stomach, increased heart-rate, shallow breathing and often intolerable feelings of fear and agitation in the absence of any real, here-and-now threat. This is also often accompanied or provoked by fearful thoughts or beliefs. In its simplest form, anxiety starts as a normal response to threat; energy for action builds but does not discharge or subside.

It is important to find out whether the client's experience of anxiety is a chronic state or whether it dates from a particular time. If it is chronic and not incapacitating, the therapy may need no specialized treatment sequence other than symptom management when necessary and the usual assessment and treatment considerations discussed in the book so far will apply. It is useful to distinguish between several types of anxious presentations as this helps you to think with your client about the meaning of their experiences. Some are part of a cycle, the anxiety resulting from an attempt to resist problematic behaviour (Obsessive Compulsive Disorder and phobias), which itself arose from an attempt to control the anxiety. Some are related to current or past stress or trauma (for more about trauma, see Chapter 11) but some seem to be without source and are simply reinforced by persistent negative thoughts.

Remember also that the onset of anxiety may link to some organic or medical cause (such as over-active thyroid or medication) or to diet (such as excess of caffeine or some drugs) and this should always be checked first.

Commonly the anxiety seems to have emerged without obvious cause and although the client may report that it has a particular focus (perhaps. about leaving the house, collapsing or failing at some demand), it is usually the case that the apparent focus is only the tip of a deeper issue that will emerge as therapy continues.

We believe the following areas to be particularly relevant:

◆ Managing the symptoms.
◆ Managing avoidance.
◆ Identifying anxious cognitions.
◆ Attending to body process.

Managing the symptoms

It is impossible to do therapy with a person whose anxiety is incapacitating. If this is the case, then the initial therapeutic task is to increase self-support, reduce the level of distress to manageable proportions and facilitate a productive engagement with the problem. It is not an attempt to 'remove' the symptom, but to allow a 'safe emergency' or 'window of affective tolerance' so that the client is available to respond and relate to their issues, rather than just attempting to avoid or 'survive' the symptoms. If your client starts to feel overwhelming anxiety as she describes an event, you may need to interrupt the process with techniques for grounding her in the here and now so that she can learn to reliably manage her overwhelming emotions or symptoms.

Focus on breathing

'Exhaling and inhaling more deeply can transform anxiety to excitement' (Perls et al., 1989 [1951]: 167). Breath is an important regulator of energy and emotions. Indeed, simple attention to breath can be transformative for an anxious client. Learning to control or influence erratic breathing can prevent an escalation of anxiety from becoming a full-blown panic attack. When people are frightened or startled, their breathing usually becomes rapid and shallow. You can notice a client's breathing change as she begins to tell you about a difficult situation or starts to become anxious in the session. At times, you may need to make an active intervention.

◆ If a client seems to be holding his breath either through retroflection or fear, he can be encouraged to breathe *out* rather than simply to breathe. This releases the tension and creates space for the revivalizing in-breath, which will naturally follow.
◆ When a client is anxious, his breathing often becomes shallow and faster, causing oxygen deprivation or he starts gulping air so that he become over-oxygenated. All these actions can make him dizzy or lightheaded as if he is about to pass out. He may then label this state as a real threat rather than a physiological reaction to erratic

breathing. If this happens in the session, you can take him through a breath-management sequence. Give the instructions in a slow, even voice, guiding him until the rhythm is established. Reassure him that this sort of breathing is supposed to feel unusual to start with.

> Count slowly up to four, breathing in through your nose and allowing your abdomen to expand, as if it were pulling the air down into it (keeping your chest still), hold for a count of three, then slowly breathe out to a count of seven, imagining you are gently blowing out a candle. At the end of this out-breath, slowly inhale again to the same count of four.

◆ Ask him to repeat this sequence several times and check how the anxiety has changed.
◆ If the client is too panicky to follow this you may suggest he breathes into cupped hands or a paper bag (one you have prepared earlier!). Tell him to keep both his nose and mouth covered and to continue for three to four minutes.

Encourage your client to practise these techniques if he gets anxious between sessions.

Working with imagery and mindfulness

Many clients find it useful to create a 'safe place' in their minds. Using guided visualization, the client is invited to imagine a place (ideally one that they have actually seen or experienced), which is utterly peaceful, supportive and safe. Typically, clients choose a beach, mountaintop, or a favourite peaceful place. You then suggest they fully explore in their imagination how it would feel to be there – the sun on their skin, the noise of the breeze, the sensation of peace and calm in their bodies and so on. There are many different variations of this kind of calming imagery (for a good example, see Perry (2008: 16). Mindfulness techniques (a reformulation of the Gestalt awareness continuum) are now well recognized as helpful for anxiety and we refer you to Hooker and Fodor (2008) for an excellent overview with many guidedprotocols.

Practical behaviours

◆ You may need to help your client find practical ways of altering the field conditions that are creating or aggravating the anxiety, for example by changing a job or the level of responsibility, changing how they structure the day, and so on.
◆ Encourage activities that facilitate the release of tensions and the build-up of 'feel-good' endorphins. Regular aerobic exercise such as fast walking, running, dancing and vigorous sports are excellent in this regard.
◆ Find calming activities such as walking in a park, meditating, relaxation exercises, slow breathing, listening to music.
◆ Focus on how you and he co-create an 'anxious' relationship. This will show in the ebb and flow of how the therapeutic *between* becomes 'anxious'. Your own reactions and responses, your counter-transferences of anxiety or irritation all

become useful information about how you and your client co-create the problem, and shed light on how he co-creates it with others. This can be a here-and-now relational phenomenon or it could be a repeat of history. Frequently, anxiety can be traced to childhood, when an anxious parent's warnings are introjected, or an unconfident or inconsistent parent created an atmosphere of anxiety and vigilance. You will need to offer a steady embodied presence and demonstrate an ability to contain and tolerate difficult or overwhelming anxious feelings and body states.

Managing avoidance

When clients identify a situation or issue that they believe is the 'cause' of their anxiety, avoidance is understandably often the first response. This temporarily reduces the distress, but does not solve the problem, and usually then leads to other disadvantages (such as an inability to face important situations). It is relieving but dysfunctional. The avoidance then becomes a habitual way of responding to the first signs of anxiety, thus confirming the impossibility of facing what is feared. This is the road to phobias and Obsessive Compulsive Disorder. While it is normal to avoid something that is dangerous and to feel anxious if the threat remains, clients typically feel anxious about events that do not contain this sort of danger, such as being outside, talking in public, being in crowds, shopping, etc.

A process of education may be needed to help the client understand how the avoidance is contributing to the problem and how you need to find a way together to understand and face what is feared.

- When you have reached an agreement about stopping the avoiding behaviours and staying with the feelings that arise, you are in the territory of impasse work (see Chapter 11). This will also involve finding ways to reduce the anxiety or charge as he starts thinking or remembering the feared situation (see relaxation exercises below). It can include many types of 'desensitization' techniques that encourage the client to first become familiar with his feelings and then start to process them differently (see Chapter 9, 'Designing graded experiments'). He can then start a different relationship with what is being avoided.
- For clients with a phobia, it can be useful to reformulate the feared object as the 'container' of a disowned and projected part of the self – some polarity that out of obedience to an introject or fear of its destructiveness has been suppressed out of awareness. Two-chair work can be a useful technique for helping a client to explore these polarities (see, e.g. Philippson, 2009: 31–4). Invite the client to 'become' the feared object and explore its qualities.
- Often we have found that there is retroflected rage underlying incapacitating anxiety (panic, phobia, etc.). Gradually facilitate your client to identify, own and express all of his feelings in the safe container of the therapy room.
- Help the client to find meaningful different action that can be taken as an alternative to the habitual avoidance or dysfunctional action.

EXAMPLE

Delenn, manager of a large charity, was referred by her GP for her anxiety, which was leading to overworking, lack of sleep and constant worrying that she had not done enough. From the first meeting, Delenn said she appreciated 'everyone's concern' but that she had far too many responsibilities to spare the time for counselling. She said that too many people were relying on her and it would all fall apart if she relaxed. The therapist started by talking about anxiety and its causes and effects. She gently challenged Delenn to face the fact that she was on the road to collapse or burn-out. Reluctantly her client agreed with her; indeed as she felt the non-judgemental interest and presence of the therapist, she felt tearful and realized how unsupported she had been. She agreed to come for a series of sessions.

The therapist started by teaching her some relaxation techniques, to which she responded very well. She was encouraged to re-discover some activity or hobby that she had enjoyed when she had been less stressed (in her case, photography). She also made an agreement to structure her day better, delegate some work and make sure that she was having regular meals. Then they were able to start exploring the anxiety itself – where her need to 'save the world' had come from. Slowly, Delenn began to make links to her past – she was the eldest child of four who had taken over running the house at the age of nine when her mother became chronically ill with Alzheimer's disease.

Identifying anxious cognitions

As with depression, anxiety conditions are normally associated with powerful negative introjects, core beliefs and repetitive thoughts: 'I'm out of control', 'I can't manage', 'It's all too much', 'I'm going to faint and die.' With the anxious client the focus is on the future – either imminent or more distant.

Anxious beliefs are typically over-generalized, exaggerated or catastrophizing. They become self-perpetuating and lead to a cycle of anxiety, where the expectation brings on the symptom, which then reinforces the belief. For example, a client who is shopping starts to worry that she will have a panic attack and collapse in public. This produces bodily symptoms of anxiety, The client focuses on her anxious symptoms and her fears of collapse increase, thus heightening her anxiety, and so on, in an escalating cycle until she does collapse (which then confirms the belief that she is likely to collapse in public). She then decides to avoid going out, which succeeds in removing the worry but means she now can't go shopping.

◆ As the client is describing a situation – or as she begins to get anxious with you – ask her to be aware of what she is saying to herself. What thoughts or fantasies does she have? What is the worst that could happen? Get her to be as explicit as possible. Try and identify the core beliefs that underpin her feelings, then introduce a grounding exercise to bring her to the here and now. Ask her to sit in a different chair and consider how realistic the thoughts and beliefs are. Ask her to design supportive or positive statements to say to herself when she is getting anxious – hopeful beliefs that in her best moments have seemed true. 'I can cope with anxious feelings and still be competent', 'I can reach out for support', 'I will get through this' (sometimes called positive self-talk). Reframe positively, for example, 'You did survive', 'You have got through this before and you will again'.

◆ Suggest the client keep a diary of her anxiety. This will raise her awareness of the anxiety process, which in itself can be transformative. It will also show how it relates to certain situations, certain places or certain people, certain times of the day. Over the course of a week she can keep a record of what was happening when she was anxious, the situation, the time and a rating (out of ten) of the severity. This will have two effects: it will make the field conditions sharper and help to identify the negative thoughts, introjects or core beliefs that go with the anxiety. This often forms a clearer figure of the actual problem (rather than the imagined one) and gives you more detail to assess the most influential factors that provoke or maintain her anxious state. Keeping a diary also requires the client to access a here-and-now orientation which strengthens her capacity to cope.

◆ Explore what underlying beliefs are associated with the issues, problems and situations that the client is bringing to therapy. Ask how she came to hold these beliefs and be curious about any historical links to past events or relationships. If these are identified, sometimes simply being aware of the difference between past and present can change the client's experience.

EXAMPLE

Lyta realized that her anxiety in the face of authority figures could be traced to the bullying and cruelty of a primary school teacher. After telling her story with emotion and energy, she was invited to stand up, breathe deeply and say: 'That is over now. I will never let that happen to me again.' She gave a deep sigh, visibly relaxed and said she felt a weight had been lifted.

◆ Identify the message or instruction the anxiety is carrying. Sometimes it is an introject from a parent about not being excited, or about the need to 'be perfect', to 'never fail', which almost guarantees failure and consequent anxiety.

Attending to body process

In Chapter 13 we described many ways of working that are also useful in working with anxiety. Most useful will be finding ways of encouraging over-mobilized or retroflected body energy to purposeful action.

◆ Encourage the bodily expression of any movements that seem interrupted (gestures, body postures) and create experiments to encourage or develop the movement. Often you will notice the anxious client begin to shift, become agitated or retreat and retroflect their energy. Ask the client to sense into the emerging movement or position in their body as they feel their anxiety (or other feeling), then follow what the next movement might be.

> **Suggestion**: Think back to how your family expressed or avoided excitement and energy in your childhood. Now remember a recent situation you experienced that made you anxious. Notice your bodily response, your breathing, thoughts, and any messages you are telling yourself.

◆ Muscle or body relaxation techniques can be used for anxiety in the session or as a technique to practise at home or in stressful situations. Remind the client that relaxation is a skill like any other; it needs practice and takes time. For example:

⇒ Find a position in the chair you can feel comfortable and supported. Close your eyes and start to notice your body and how it feels. Concentrate on your breathing, noticing the rising and falling of your chest. Focus only on the in and out of your breathing … Let your breath be slow and calm.

⇒ Say the words 'I'm calming down' or 'I'm relaxing', as you breathe out.
(Do that for a few minutes.)

⇒ Now bring your attention to the soles of your feet and slowly tense, them, hold for a moment and then slowly relax, breathing in as you tense, and breathing out as you relax. Now bring your attention to your lower legs and slowly tense them, then relax. Then your knees … your hips and pelvis (repeating this sequence slowly until you have covered all the body).
(Several minutes)

⇒ Bring your attention back to your breathing.

⇒ Now move your attention to your shoulders, arms and legs, hands and feet. Notice how it feels to stay connected with yourself as you come back to meet the world. (Calibrate the speed and duration of the exercise to what suits the client.)

◆ Lastly, your client's apparent anxiety may be due to unrecognized or unexpressed excitement. It may be appropriate to invite her to reframe her symptoms, to breathe into them and celebrate the exciting scariness of a new endeavour.

There are many useful books suitable for clients, which go into great detail about relaxation techniques and practical ways to manage anxiety. We make some suggestions at the end of the chapter.

FACING EXISTENTIAL ISSUES AND LIFE EVENTS

We conclude by describing a situation that is common to both depression and anxiety and indeed is the backcloth to all our experiences: the human condition. Many clients present with anxiety or depression in response to a realization of the existential issues that face us all (but are usually ignored), such as aging, illness, the inevitability of death, the uncertainty of life, the experience of feeling connected and yet deeply alone. Or they are facing one of life's challenges such as the loss of a loved one, redundancy or a serious accident. The therapeutic task here is to encourage the broadest perspective on these issues.

◆ Start with exploring whether there are recent events that have preceded the depression or anxiety. Do a recent lifeline (See Chapter 5), outlining changes, transitions, losses and stresses and invite your client to talk about their significance to her.
◆ Identify the client's spiritual/religious belief system. Ask how the crisis is seen in her belief system, what spiritual or religious support she has sought and why it hasn't helped. What else could she do within that belief system? (See Chapter 22.)
◆ Support the client to stay with the impasse or crisis. Transformations or life adjustments are often preceded by difficult and apparently impossible situations and the task is often just to find ways of tolerating the anxiety or hopeless feelings to allow a readjustment or working through, rather than finding a relief of the distress. Sometimes the best strategic response is to be available and stay with what emerges. The client may be in a period of natural withdrawal which Roubal (2007) calls a 'depressive adjustment', where in an impossible situation effective action cannot be taken for resolution (such as an untreatable life-threatening illness), and a person withdraws energy from fighting or resisting while they are finding a new adjustment or re-engagement. As with bereavement, this may be a natural process requiring only time and support.
◆ Recognize the universal nature of the presenting issues. We are all challenged by the issues we have listed above – we are all going to die but we normally don't know when; we are all embodied in time and space; we all experience separateness and loss. It is very important that we are aware of this and ensure that we have our own support for facing the issues. In that way we minimize the danger of colluding with our client in avoiding these challenging truths.

Suggestion: Take a few minutes to reflect on what in your life gives you meaning and purpose. Is it family or friends, your job, helping others, connection with nature, a feeling of being alive in the moment, a spiritual or religious path? Or is it the expectation of a better future, money, designer clothes, success or power (just to put the other point of view!)? How do you support yourself when life seems unrewarding or you have lost your way?

RECOMMENDED READING ON DEPRESSION AND ANXIETY

Greenberg, L.S. (2002) 'Working with emotion', *International Gestalt Journal*, 25 (2): 31–57.
Greenberg, L.S. and Watson, J. (2006) *Emotion-Focused Therapy for Depression*. Washington, DC: American Psychiatric Association.

(Continued)

(Continued)

Hooker, K.E. and Fodor, I.E. (2008) 'Teaching mindfulness to children', *Gestalt Review,* 12 (1): 75–91.

Leader, D. (2008) *The New Black.* Harmondsworth: Penguin.

Melnick, J. and Nevis, S. (2005) 'The willing suspension of disbelief: optimism', *Gestalt Review,* 9 (1): 10–26.

NICE (National Institute for Clinical Excellence) (2007) Guidelines on Depression: http://www.nice.org.uk/guidance/index.jsp?action=byl D&o= 10958#documents [For position of national UK government-funded body].

Roos, S. (2001) 'Theory development. Chronic sorrow and the Gestalt construct of closure', *Gestalt Review,* 5 (4): 289–310.

Roubal, J. (2007) 'Depression – a Gestalt theoretical perspective', *British Gestalt Journal,* 16 (1): 35–43.

Shub, N. (2002) 'Revising the treatment of anxiety', *Gestalt Review,* 6 (2):135–47.

SELF-HELP BOOKS (which are also useful to read if you are new to these conditions)

Baker, R. (2003) *Understanding Panic Attacks and Overcoming Fear.* Oxford: Lion Hudson.

Bourne, E. (2007) *The Anxiety and Phobia Workbook,* 4th edn. Oakland, CA: New Harbinger Press.

Perry, A. (2008) *Claustrophobia. Finding Your Way out.* London: Worth Publishing. (A very useful self-help book with many suggestions equally useful for general anxiety.)

Rowe, D. (2003) *Depression: The Way Out of Your Prison,* 3rd edn. East Sussex: Routledge.

Weekes, C. (2000) *Essential Help for your Nerves.* London: Thorsons.

Williams, M., Teasdale, J., Segal, Z. and Kabat-Zinn, J. (2007) *The Mindful Way Through Depression.* New York: Guilford Press.

WEBSITES THAT ARE USEFUL AND REPUTABLE

http://www.patient.co.uk/showdoc/27001314/#related_s

http://www.rcpsych.ac.uk/mentalhealthinfoforall/problems/anxietyphobias/anxietyphobias.aspx

PART THREE

GESTALT PRACTICE IN CONTEXT

PART THREE

20

BRIEF THERAPY

Gestalt counsellors are increasingly working in settings where there is a limit to the number of sessions allowed and where recognized outcomes (often behavioural) are demanded. Many agencies also require progress reports and a rating of success in achieving the initial desired outcome. This is particularly highlighted in the short-term context of the GPs surgery, mental health placements, funded care or Employee Assistance Programmes (EAPs).

In these settings, some clients present with vague or unclear desires to 'feel better' or because they were referred by someone else who 'thought it would help'. Others present with specific goals or outcomes in mind, for example, 'I want to stop feeling anxious all the time/have a better relationship with my life partner'. In brief therapy we have to balance the attitude of creative indifference and congruent Gestalt practice with a need to focus the work for the time available. With the first group of clients, we may need to be more directive than usual in order to help to clarify, understand the issue, and identify what might help. With the second group, we may need to discuss with the client how much, as a Gestalt practitioner, we are prepared to focus on a particular desired outcome. With both groups, we must stay aware of what can realistically be addressed in the time.

Both groups highlight the tension in Gestalt practice about how much to be directive or goal focused. We discussed this same issue in Chapter 3 and there is no doubt that in brief therapy settings it is particularly acute. We strongly believe, however, that the Gestalt practitioner *can* offer focused or directed work that stays true to the principles of creative indifference, phenomenology and staying with 'what is'.

In fact, Gestalt counselling already *does* have goals, but they are usually *process* goals, for example, of raised awareness, healthy functioning, choicefulness, authentic relationship and completing unfinished business.

Therefore, when a client presents with a request for a particular desired outcome, for example, 'to help with my depression', the counsellor can clearly agree to focus on the 'depression' and support the client to move in the direction she chooses. However, she will not usually agree a particular behavioural outcome (e.g. to 'stop feeling depressed') as she believes that such a rigid contract would be artificially limiting and not be in the best interests of the client. Equally, clients who come with a particular ideal picture or fantasy of how they want to be different (for example, to 'be happy' or 'free from stress') are attempting to achieve a pre-determined outcome and are therefore inhibiting the natural growth and change of the whole person (what Perls (1969) called 'self-image actualization' rather than 'self-actualization').

The important question is not about defined directions or intention, but whether the therapeutic agreement also allows for new unanticipated outcomes, as clients frequently find that what they actually want only emerges after some weeks of therapy and is then often different from what they believed they wanted. We believe that the key lies in sharpening the figure of the client's issue. Brief therapy then becomes an exciting and potent intervention. Ideally, it would not be 'time-limited', but 'issue-focused', whereby therapist and client stay attuned and alert to the client's needs and circumstances, and negotiate a contract for one, then four, then perhaps twelve sessions, only extending it when necessary. It is interesting to note that in a setting where there is a limit of say, twelve sessions, people usually come for the full twelve, even if six would have been adequate. Thinking of the counselling as 'issue-focused' rather than for a set number of sessions, can mean that the work is focused on the client's need, not on the set structure. It also will ensure that you do not fall into the trap of seeing short-term as second best to long-term (for example, 'I can *only* offer you six sessions'), rather than presenting the contract as a positive opportunity ('I can offer you up to six sessions', said with enthusiasm).

It is necessary to be clear about the advantages and disadvantages of brief work. For some clients, a brief contract may avoid the stigma of 'illness', pathology or dependence. It is less costly and may focus and motivate facing a difficulty. It also more obviously demonstrates effectiveness (or the opposite!). We have found that clients can achieve quite dramatic changes after a relatively short time. However, we have also found that important material is sometimes only revealed after several months or even years of a trusting relationship (especially issues of sexual abuse and shame). We are dubious, therefore, whether profound insights or deep shifts of perspective about larger life issues can be properly assimilated in a short-term engagement. This is usually true also where the work involves exclusive focus on a change of ingrained behaviour such as drinking or drug abuse. Yoy may say. 'This is an issue where specialist help might be more useful', and suggest a referral to a more suitable practitioner.

> **Suggestion**: Remember, for a moment, some of the important changes you have made in your experience of therapy and therapy training. How many of these could have been achieved in four or even twelve sessions? What are the reasons why some of them could and some couldn't?

DECIDING WHO IS APPROPRIATE

A variety of factors are indicators of when brief counselling will be most appropriate and effective. We suggest you check in the initial session/s whether the client:

- Can engage with you sufficiently in the first session for you to have a sense of some relational connection starting to form.
- Has a willingness to see and accept some responsibility for the part he may play in the presenting issue.
- Accepts that he will need to be active in the change process.
- Has good enough support to do the work.
- Has the ability to agree a focus for the work that can be addressed in a limited number of sessions, even if it is actually part of a deeper problem.
- Understands and agrees with your description of the way you might work together.

We realize that having answers to all these questions can be unrealistic with some clients and within some agencies. Some presentations do not lend themselves to a brief setting as they cannot meaningfully be addressed in just a few sessions. However, your work can be enormously important in preparing the ground for a referral to longer-term therapy. You aim to engage the client's interest in himself, support his motivation and offer a positive experience of therapy so that he chooses – either straight away or at a later date – to move on to longer term treatment. Examples are clients with eating disorders, persistent drug or alcohol addictions, dual diagnosis or other long-standing issues.

ENGAGING IN THE WORK

As with any therapeutic beginning, the task is two-fold – to develop a working alliance and to agree a focus for the work, having together assessed the problems and what is possible. Overall, we believe that a respectfully negotiated assessment and contract are compatible with the Gestalt approach, and indeed are essential to ethical effective practice. This is a delicate balance to manage at the best of times, but even more so in brief work, where by the end of the first (or at most the second) session you are aiming to be able decide the key issue for the work and determine if the client and his issue is suitable. What is more, you are doing this while ensuring that the client has plenty of time and space in which to tell her story and feel that you are listening with sensitivity and a dialogic attitude!

The counsellor may need, at times, to develop quite an assertive style and be willing to direct the flow of the session more than she might in a long-term context. Some counsellors send out a pre-session questionnaire for history and aspirations, together with a leaflet explaining the process of counselling to maximize the time available. It is always a good idea to start with: 'This is an initial session to see if I can be useful to you.' At the end of the session you can then more easily tell the client whether you believe you can help him, or need another session to decide, or whether you will need refer him on (see Chapter 1).

Then you will need to clarify the issue and agree what is possible in the time. Questions you might find useful (in brief work but perhaps also at other times):

'What were you hoping for/expecting/thinking when you decided to come and see me?'
'How do you understand the problem that brought you here?'

'Do you have some sense of how counselling can help?'
'What would be a successful outcome for you?'

History-taking may be quite brief, although we strongly urge you, for reasons of safety, to ask about any risk factors (for instance, previous history of self-harm, mental illness, etc. see Chapter 18).

We also find it crucial to identify unsuitable types of presenting issues which we loosely call 'issues of circumstance'. These are complaints about other people or circumstances ('my husband treats me badly'), where the client assumes no self-responsibility and the only solution they want is a practical one or for someone or something else to change. Sometimes, the client has been sent by their GP, partner, employer and has only come because they have been told to, and are expecting you to 'make them different'. These are issues not initially suitable for therapy or, at best, are deserving of practical or supportive counselling (which you may or may not be willing to offer). Asking the four questions above usually clarifies the issue or at least moves you into finding an issue that *is* suitable.

In addition, we have found great benefit in finding out how the client believes change happens, why he has come for counselling at this moment in time and how he has managed similar crises in the past.

If your client is confused or distressed you may sometimes need to allocate one or two sessions just to identify the issue that needs to be tackled or the direction of the work. This may well involve prioritizing the issues to find what needs to be addressed first. Working on one or two issues to the exclusion of others may be justified (even though it is more directive and less dialogic). Always check at the end of the assessment: 'What are your impressions after this hour?' 'What are you making of this process so far?' 'How has it been to talk with me?' 'Has it been useful?' This is important as it can give you some sense of impact and effectiveness of one session and what adjustments you may need to make.

'WORKING THROUGH'

For this phase of the therapy we believe that if the contract is properly crafted, it will be possible to complete it, so that even if the client leaves with unfinished issues, he will have had the experience of achievement and success which will not only enhance his current life but make him likely to use any future therapy well. Houston (2003) simply calls the phase 'middle'. It is a time to be moving forward with the work in a timely manner, while holding the beginning (the contract) and the end clearly in view.

As with all Gestalt counselling, you will have been offering from the start a dialogic attitude and using phenomenological inquiry to raise your client's awareness of himself in his situation. Even in brief work, a phenomenological approach, resting on the principle of paradoxical change, can often be enough. In addition the following may be especially relevant:

◆ Emphasize the link between how meaning-making affects behaviour (that is, how core beliefs influence outcomes in his life). See the useful discussion in Whines (1999: 10).
◆ Gather only as much information as is necessary to move to the next moment. Beware of getting captivated by the story and losing the focus.

◆ Find the specific manageable figure for each session (for example, 'to be more assertive', needs to be refined down to *particular* situations where the client is under-assertive). Find the relevant ground to that figure ('What feelings go with that, how do others react, when do you get angry?', etc.).

◆ Keep a tight focus on relevance of the material or figure brought, bearing the contract in mind and making a point of making links to it often. Sharpen the figure to keep the emerging material relevant.

◆ Offer experiments to clarify or expand the emerging figure (*not* to find a solution), for example, 'Let yourself fully know that emerging feeling as you imagine that situation.' In other words, trust the process of raising awareness.

◆ Minimize transference phenomena, by naming, confronting or self-disclosing (see Chapter 12 on ways of working with transference).

◆ Practise tight (and loose) sequencing (Polster, 1999: 208). This useful skill either narrows or widens the focus. With tight sequencing, rather than exploring the moment itself, the therapist attends to its transition into the next, tracking carefully the unfolding of the process and its dynamic potential (e.g. 'So now you are starting to breathe more slowly'). Loose sequencing, on the other hand, can be noticing important missing pieces in the narrative and inquiring into that (e.g. 'But where was your mother at that time?').

◆ Past or present crises such as job loss or bereavement may become figural and you may need to interrupt the ongoing theme temporarily, to allow the crisis to be understood in the light of present awareness. However, it is important to make a link to the overall contract at the end of the session. If something emerges that clearly and appropriately supersedes the original contact, make an overt agreement to discontinue the previous contract and agree a new one. In this way the contract can be the ongoing container and boundary of the work.

◆ There is also merit in 'independent practise' (or 'homework'), where the client agrees to do a task between sessions – perhaps to practise a new type of behaviour or to keep a record of anxiety responses.

◆ It is important always to keep the ending in sight and to 'count down' the sessions. 'So this is our fifth session and we have three more', adding, 'And how is that for you?'

Your supervision can be a place to practise this sort of focused work. Develop the skill of being open to emerging learning opportunities, while presenting your work economically – making a contract with your supervisor (as you would with your client) to address the major figure and stay focused on it.

AGENCY CONSIDERATIONS

While some therapists offer brief therapy in private practice, this is usually freely chosen. In agencies there is less flexibility and both client and counsellor are subject to the, perhaps unwelcome, limits imposed from 'above'. This situation gives rise to several considerations right from the start.

◆ When, for example, a GP or employer refers a client, it is crucial to explore the referrer's motivation, expectation and the expectations they generate in the client. These can be accessed by asking: 'What were you told about coming to see a counsellor? Did the doctor explain how counselling could help you? What were you expecting would happen here?'. Where the counselling takes place in a medical practice there may be a high expectation that the counsellor will 'cure' the patient.

◆ In a setting of shared notes, it is important to decide and agree with the agency beforehand how much information, if any, you are prepared to disclose to other professionals in the agency and under what circumstances you will break confidentiality, for example in cases of suicide risk. The client should be told in the first session about the limits of your confidentiality.

◆ In an agency, you have several different relationships to negotiate. It is useful to remember that there are multiple contracts (with the agency, your client, your supervisor, your training organization as well as between the supervisor and the agency and so on). This may take careful handling as they are not always compatible.

Proctor and Sills (2005), developing the work of English (1975) (see Figure 20.1), propose a useful framework for structuring the administrative contract and broad treatment goals in brief work. It is especially useful in agency settings.

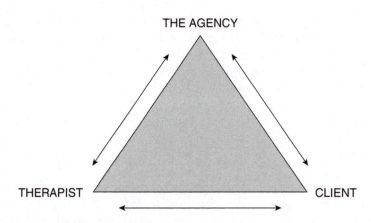

Figure 20.1 Contracts within an agency

Along each axis, the details of the agreement are made transparent between the parties, so that, for example, all three know what limits to confidentiality there are, all three are aware of what information has been provided to the counsellor about the client; all three are aware of the restrictions and rules that have been imposed by the agency. Tudor (2006) has written extensively on the complexities of three- or indeed multiple-cornered contracts.

Primary care

In primary care, 'the key aspect is to be part of the team' (Mandic-Bozic, personal communication, 2009). Often counsellors have a tendency to keep themselves separate because of their different role and approach to patient care. However, your work will go more smoothly and enjoyably if you make sure that you are in regular contact with colleagues, both individually and at team meetings. Doctors and health visitors have a wealth of information about patients and everyone can collaborate to decide how to respond to critical issue, which can be very supportive. You can also 'educate' people about the criteria for a good referral. Some counsellors like to prepare an information sheet about what they offer, but face to face meetings, where possible, create better and more cooperative relationships.

Be ready to offer support to doctors as well as clients. Mandic-Bozic says 'GPs have 7 or 8 minutes per patient and on top of needing to diagnose, prescribe and complete computer records, they also get impacted by the transferential and psychological issues in that short time. So when they approach a counsellor with a referral, that can often start with a parallel process'. Counsellors need to connect with doctors over this, offering support and helping to contain the issues and plan the next step.

You will need to be able to articulate your formulation of the problem, your treatment plans and intended outcomes in a way that makes sense to other health professionals in the team, so be prepared to create a shared language, staying approachable and open to other perspectives.

It may be useful to become familiar with the structure of the Primary Care Trust, attend meetings if they are held, and be interested in the management challenges they face. Also, contact the association Counsellors in Primary Care (CPC) for support, ideas and workshops.

ENDING

In Chapter 17 we devote an entire chapter to endings in therapy. However, the ending in brief work has a particular significance. In agency work, the end is often predetermined before assessment and in that sense is not freely chosen. This may bring up issues for either or both of you about powerlessness or abandonment, about being controlled or restricted by an insensitive external authority. It is important to allow (or put words to) these issues with the client, but also to avoid letting the space be contaminated by any unfinished business or opinions you have.

On the other hand, the benefit in this sort of ending is that it replicates many life events – very often endings 'happen to' us, rather than being chosen. At either end of our life is a major transition or 'ending', the timing of which we do not choose (our birth and our death). Perhaps the most powerful association is the fact that we will all die, although we rarely know exactly when. But there are myriad other losses and endings – some desired, some not – that attend our growing up as well as our adult lives. Therefore, the opportunity for the client is to go through an ending like this in full awareness – noticing her learning towards particular responses, noticing how she feels towards her therapist and her therapy. She may discover a tendency to say 'What's the point of doing this work when we only have three more sessions?'. Or she may say, 'I need to take advantage of every minute.' She may avoid getting attached, or she may feel angry or scared: 'I'm not ready yet', or 'There's never enough.' Whatever emerges, it is important that the client's feelings and reactions are linked to the contract and to patterns in her life. In the process, it may be reparative for her to be allowed to talk about her losses and be heard.

For the counsellor, the challenge is to accept what is and is not achievable in the time. Many counsellors have to learn to discipline themselves to accept the good work they have done and not yearn to be able to have more sessions (as does the client sometimes). You may both have to mourn the loss of what cannot be achieved in the time and accept the frustration, anger or sadness that follows. Don't forget, however, the other tasks of ending: to name and celebrate what *has* been achieved and to plan for how future challenges will be met.

CONCLUSION

Working short- or long-term, is largely a matter of personal preference, except when you have an agency limitation. The disadvantage of brief work is that it can be an inappropriate and poor substitute for problems that need a longer time, especially those that require a deeper trusting relationship. However, at its best, brief therapy can be transformative, efficient, cost-effective and amply sufficient to help a client. It can also give her a good experience of the counselling process and can lay the foundation for further counselling in the future. We would encourage you to avoid the trap of wanting 'completion' and accept that, for some clients, a successful outcome for brief therapy includes leaving an open Gestalt that naturally leads to further growth and change.

RECOMMENDED READING

British Gestalt Journal (1999) 8 (1): 4–34 (several relevant articles).

Denham-Vaughan, S. (2005) 'Brief gestalt therapy for clients with bulimia', *British Gestalt Journal,* 14 (2): 128–34.

Elton Wilson, J. (2006) '*Choosing a time-limited counselling or psychotherapy contract*', in C. Sills (ed.), *Contracts in Counselling and Psychotherapy.* London: Sage. pp. 137–51.

Harman, B. (1995) 'Gestalt therapy as brief therapy', *Gestalt Journal*, 18 (2): 77–86.

Houston, G. (2003) *Brief Gestalt Therapy.* London: Sage.

Polster, E. (1991) 'Tight therapeutic sequences', *British Gestalt Journal*, 1 (2): 63–8.

Tudor, K. (2006) 'Contracts, complexity and challenge', in C. Sills (ed.), *Contracts in Counselling and Psychotherapy.* London: Sage. pp. 128–30.

Williams, B. (2001) 'The practice of Gestalt therapy within a brief therapy context', *Gestalt Journal*, 24 (1): 7–62.

21

DIVERSITY, CULTURE AND ETHICS

Difference and diversity are inevitable in all counselling. In addition to differences of attitude or character, there are differences of race, culture, nationality, gender, age, ability, sexuality, class and first language. Differences fall into two categories – those that are obvious and visible such as race, physical ability, gender (and often nationality and class), and those that are not obvious such as sexuality, attitude, education, and so on.

In this chapter we mainly focus on race and culture. However, we believe that most of the ideas we raise can be generalized to other areas of difference and, in the exercises we offer, we urge you to consider all and any issues of difference in your reflection.

As we become an increasingly multicultural society, differences in race and culture between client and counsellor are more and more likely. Recognizing how much, even after several years of our own personal therapy, we (the authors) are still limiting our thinking and perceptions according to our cultural background (especially as we are from a dominant culture) can be a chastening experience as well as an exciting challenge.

RACIAL IDENTITY

Racial identity is an interwoven and integral aspect of personality. The client's core beliefs about self and others, their creative adjustments and fixed gestalts, will all be affected by the racial, cultural and linguistic norms that are an inherent part of his ground. In order for this aspect to be fully taken into account, it is essential not only for the client, but also for the counsellor to explore and own their racial identity and the effect this has on the therapeutic relationship.

It is important also to acknowledge that counselling and psychotherapy in the twentieth century were largely dominated by white, middle-class practitioners. This has meant that the values and customs embedded in their theory and practice, including

Gestalt, are largely white and middle-class. So, inevitably, are the biases and prejudices of which practitioners may hardly be aware. They are the ground of our practice. Jacobs (2006) points out that if the cultural ground holds white culture and practices, it is hard for people of colour to fully have a presence. Whether the counsellor is Black or white (we use the term Black here to represent all people of colour) or from an ethnic background which is different from the one in which she is living, she will be affected by the dynamics of the wider field, the cultural ground of the society in which she lives.

In the ground of both client and counsellor is their unique history of race, nationality and culture. All these are potentially influential, as are the dominant race, nationality and culture of the society in which the counselling is taking place. The historical relationship between the 'tribe' of the counsellor and that of the client forms part of their relational field both in and out of awareness, as do all the current tensions and integrations that are happening moment by moment.

Suggestion: How would you characterize yourself in terms of culture, race, nationality and other factors that are important to you? For example, you might say female, white, working-class, Irish. Now take a moment to think about all the other sub-cultures that have had an influence on you and helped to form the person you are now. For example, how would you describe your parents and grandparents? Did you move to a different area as a child – one with different cultural values? For each of these cultural influences, think of one value or custom that you still hold now. Then think of your clients one by one. What is the historical relationship between your two cultures (include such things as gender, education, life-style as well as culture and ethnicity)? How might that history be affecting your relationship?

DIFFERENCES IN CUSTOMS AND VALUES

Then there are differences in customs, values and beliefs. As we mentioned in Chapter 5, differences in values and attitudes can cause unwelcome prejudice in the mental health field. At the very least, they can lead to the therapist (who has most power in the relationship) imposing, in or out of awareness, his values on the client. Here, Gestalt therapists are in a strong position, as the phenomenological method of inquiry helps to avoid such imposition of values. It is important, though, to realize the potential danger of bracketing, which might allow the therapist to ignore the significance of the differences in attitudes and beliefs. Vigilance is needed as many values are so ingrained as to be deeply out of awareness. It is safer and more respectful to deliberately invite your client to share with you the values that are important to her. It is also helpful to know something already about the culture or national customs of your client, although this is not always possible (and can, in any case, lead to disrespectful generalizations). What is important is to acknowledge the difference between you, and invite your client to tell you anything she wants you to know. In that way, she does not feel that difference is being ignored or denied or that she has to 'play by your rules' in order for you to respect her. You might say something like:

> There are some important differences between us because I am a Polish woman and you are an Indian woman. I don't know a lot about your culture but I am very interested to find out. It is certain to be important in our work together and I really hope and suggest that you tell me what you are thinking and feeling about our differences as we get to know each other. I am imagining that we might also share some similar experiences.

Suggestion: Think of a culture, nationality, community or group about which you have some negative feelings or beliefs. Put your dislike into words. Are those negative feelings based on hard evidence? If so, are they a result of a custom or habit that you don't like? And if that is so, why do you not like it (that is, does it go against a value that is important to you, or is it simply that it is different, strange and uncomfortable)? Is that negative feeling or belief one that is shared by your community, society or nation? Does it have a historical root?

DIFFERENCES IN THE CONSULTING ROOM

All these influences – historical, structural and 'here-and-now cultural' – will be brought into the therapy room. They will show up in non-verbal and verbal language, choice of words, values and biases about life, and in the transference and counter-transference relationships between therapist and client.

If you were brought up in Britain, you are likely to have internalized some racist attitudes. These attitudes may be buried deeply out of awareness, but it is not possible to grow up in a culture with such a colonial history and continuing aspirations for world influence without having internalized some sense of white British superiority. This is true whether you are white or Black, although of course, the impact on you of this will have been very different. If you are white, a sense of white 'rightness' will have been deeply embedded in your sense of yourself; to be 'other' is to be 'lesser'. If you are Black, you will almost certainly have internalized a sense of oppression or powerlessness; some sense that 'other' is more powerful or somehow more entitled. This is an important field condition in the consulting room. It is especially relevant if the counsellor is white and the client Black. The therapeutic relationship already has built-in potential for power differential, and institutionalized racism reinforces this.

EXAMPLE

Jadzir's therapist became discouraged when time and time again she experienced his comments as patronizing. She was struggling with the decision about whether to give up her boyfriend (a young white man) in order to conform to the demands of her strict Muslim family. The therapist prided himself that he had really tried to understand the important cultural implications and had nothing but sympathy and support for his client. However, Jadzir's criticisms of him eventually began to unsettle him. In supervision, he realized he had been defining her reaction as transference (both of her dominating father and inevitably of the cultural stereotype of the white male). His supervisor challenged him to try to find out how he was contributing to the situation and asked him to explore his feelings and thoughts about his client's dilemma. He realized that he had put aside his desire to empower Jadzir in favour of respecting her cultural values. In a subtle way, he was minimizing the enormity of the problem for her and expecting her to make an either/or decision. In the next session, the therapist asked her if they could spend some time really looking at their relationship, so that he could understand how he was being patronizing. Jadzir was enormously relieved and together they discussed the many small ways in which his 'doing the right thing' had not supported her as she wanted.

Inequality and racial identity may, of course, still be an important focus even if both therapist and client are white or both Black.

As we prepare this second edition, we are aware of changes in the UK field in relation to racial prejudice. Younger readers will have experienced a much more diverse culture as they grew up in a country which has third- and fourth-generation Black British communities. They will also have introjected less arrogance about British superiority. Racism has recently tended to turn its face to Eastern Europe and the Middle East; troubled times politically have introduced a new sort of wariness and prejudice among different cultures, religions and traditions. The challenge offered by Jacobs (2004) to greet our fellow man and woman with care, inclusion and openness to dialogue, was never more urgent.

OTHER DIFFERENCES IN THE CONSULTING ROOM

In any meeting between two individuals, there are bound to be many differences and all of them are potentially relevant in therapy. There are some differences which have many of the same dynamics in the consulting room as racial difference. There are differences where one person is part of a group that is or has been the target of oppression, disapproval or discrimination (deliberate or accidental). They include differences of gender, physical ability, sexuality, age, religion, class and education or intelligence.

These need to be treated with the same alert attention as differences in culture. Both parties (including the person who is in the 'target group' (Batts, 2000)) need to take account of the meaning of that issue for them, examining what it is like to be in the target or non-target group – both advantages and disadvantages. If the counsellor is not yet able to overcome issues of prejudice about, say, women, homosexuality or disability, then he should not work with a client in these groups as he will risk denying their identity or reinforcing any negative beliefs they have about themselves.

Suggestion (from Batts, 2000): Think of an occasion when you were part of a 'target group' and experienced yourself as being treated as 'lesser'. (If you are white, male, straight, English-speaking, middle-class, physically able and well-educated you may find it hard to identify an experience like that and we then suggest you choose the experience of being a child, which sadly is often experienced as 'target'.) What did it feel like and what did you think to yourself about yourself, others and the world? How do you use that 'targeted' experience to limit your power? Now allow yourself to know an advantage of being in this group. See if you have gained some strength or advantage from your experience.

IN SUMMARY

In order to work effectively and usefully with issues of race, culture and difference of any kind, the counsellor must first look at the field influences of his own cultural background, his biases, his preferences, his racism, homophobia, ageism, and so on. The acknowledgement of prejudice, while uncomfortable, is important but the counsellor should not become paralysed by its discovery. For example, appropriate shame and cultural embarrassment should be tempered with equally appropriate pride in whatever cultural values and achievements you honour. The counsellor from a dominant or oppressive culture should not burden his client with his humble apologies, looking to her for understanding. On the contrary, practitioners should be willing sometimes to be the representative of the oppressive society and to receive the anger attached to that role. It can sometimes be healing for a client to be able to address these important issues with a counsellor who is respectful and interested and who can acknowledge the truth of his contribution to this transference as to any other. Equally, the counsellor from an oppressed group may need to be quite robust in receiving the projections of his clients – whatever their culture or ethnicity – and be prepared to offer a dialogic relationship while the client works through their prejudices or idealization, either of which may make him feel quite invisible.

It would be unrealistic to expect that we can know and acknowledge all the prejudices and assumptions that have been deeply ingrained in us since childhood. While some of our assumptions are accessible to conscious awareness, inevitably many will be in our unaware ground, unknown but influential. What we must ask of ourselves as therapists is the intention and good will to become aware of them, examine them and challenge them.

ETHICAL DILEMMAS

Man does not strive to be good; the good is what it is human to strive for.
(Perls et al., 1989 [1951]: 335)

Gestalt therapy was developed in the 1950s and promoted an anarchic attitude that saw moral codes as outmoded fixed gestalts that needed to be challenged. Ethics and codes of conduct were to be individually decided or negotiated. There was little interest in the potential for therapeutic harm or any discussion of morality or community values. We believe that this has led to many examples of abusive therapeutic relationships and continues to pose a significant problem for a Gestalt code of ethics and conduct.

However, we believe that it *is* possible to distil certain value implications from the Gestalt process model of health and the understanding of unhealthy or neurotic behaviour. For example, most Gestalt literature clearly favours the left-hand side of the following polarities (there are many more, of course).

Interdependence	over	Autonomy
Cohesion	over	Fragmentation
Integrity	over	Randomness
Community	over	Individuality
Honesty	over	Manipulation
Joy	over	Despair
Authenticity	over	Appearance
Life	over	Death

There are therefore many values in Gestalt theory that could support a Gestalt code of ethics (although the generation of a detailed code from these 'first principles' is beyond the scope of this book; see Lee (2004) for a collection of articles around this debate). In practice, there is surprisingly good general agreement in the Gestalt community over the necessary content of such codes of ethics and the professional adoption of recognized codes such as, in the UK, those of the Uniked Kingdom Council for Psychotherapy, the British Association for Counselling and Psychotherapy or the British Psychological Society. We would argue that this is due to the unstated but implicit values in the Gestalt theory of healthy functioning.

Suggestion: Take a moment to consider the basis of your own morality (the cornerstone of all ethics). Is your moral code the same as that of your parents or caretakers? In what ways has it changed since you left your family of origin? On what basis do you decide what is right and wrong – for example, religious or legal grounds? How do you decide when to be honest; or whether it is wrong to steal? Are these absolute values for you or are they always relative to each particular situation? What are the absolute or non-negotiable values of your theory of therapy or your clinical practice?

The notion of ethical practice is further complicated by the fact that Gestalt is philosophically relational and field theoretical. In other words, the idea of a list of absolute rules about right and wrong is antithetical to our approach (for example, that it is *always* wrong to steal, to kill, to lie). Even so-called 'situational ethics', which takes context into account (for example, that it is wrong to steal *except if you are starving*, wrong to kill *except to protect your children*; wrong to lie *except to save life*, and so on) does not really come close to the truly relational perspective, which would see each event as uniquely co-created and having a potentially unique moral determination.

A relational approach to ethics sees an ethical response to a challenging situation as being field-dependent and needs to find a solution that 'further[s] the development of both the individual and the environment' (Lee, 2007: 2). Lee distinguishes between a code of ethics as a set of rules, and a relational ethic where ethical implications and decisions emerge from the ground of a compassionate, connected and valuing relationship. We applaud this vision but believe we also need a way of determining ethical responsibilities in the usually hostile field of complaints.

Lee (2007: 7) quotes Wertheimer as saying, 'all values are fundamentally relative, changing with place and times'. Yet, with all this, the therapist has to find a way of engaging with ethical issues and ethical practice. We agree with Elton Wilson (2003, personal communication) who points out that what therapists sometimes describe as ethical dilemmas are often not dilemmas at all. They are, in fact, situations in which the therapist is (understandably) reluctant to challenge the inappropriate behaviour of (for example), a colleague, because it is difficult to do so. There is no dilemma; the right course of action is clear – but is feared. A real dilemma is one where the way forward is not clear at all. Elton Wilson identifies a series of parameters, which can be used to assess and judge the ethical considerations of a situation. We have developed her work to create Table 21.1 below.

Table 21.1   Polarities for the analysis of dilemmas and consequences

Keeping the contract	or	Breaking the contract
Legal	or	Illegal
Safe	or	Unsafe
• Protects life and limb • Protects practitioner • Protects client • Protects the community		
Just (natural justice or fairness)	or	Unjust
Promotes relational connection	or	Diminishes relational connection
Honest	or	Dishonest
Compassionate	or	Cruel
Supports interdependance	or	Creates isolation
Supports the therapy	or	Harms the therapy

True ethical dilemmas occur when there is conflict between two or more values. For example, an action might be 'right' (morally) but 'illegal' (for example, withholding case notes that would be damaging to the client's position but are subpoenaed by a court). Or the dilemma might be about an action that 'supports autonomy' but is 'unsafe' (for example, when the client insists on her right to commit an act of violence on another). Table 21.1 shows a number of relevant polarities that we identify as common to many dilemmas.

The table of course does not provide a guide for action, it only promotes an awareness of the issues common to most professional codes of ethics and conduct. A Gestalt relational approach also needs responses or solutions that foster a development of the relationship of the individual to community and field conditions.

Suggestion: It is helpful to have thought through some ethical issues on the polarities above (before they arise!), in order to become comfortable with the process of 'thinking through'. We have included some challenging examples below for you to consider.

1. A new client reveals to you he has been hiding a serious mental illness for fear that he will be rejected from the counselling course he is on. He is about to take on clients, as it is a requirement of the course, and he is insistent that it remains a secret.
2. Your client describes a home situation where you believe her three-year-old child might be at risk. Although at the outset of therapy you clearly explained that one of the limits to confidentiality was if you believed there to be risk of harm, you fear that your speaking out would irreparably damage the therapeutic trust. You know that your client's capacity to care for her child depends heavily on her staying in therapy.
3. You are told by one of your clients that her friend is in therapy with one of your colleagues and has had sex with him. She says her friend is happy with this arrangement and your client refuses permission for you to break confidentiality about what she has told you.

These examples illustrate the complex conflicts of values that are inherent in ethical dilemmas. For example, the rights of the client versus the rights of others; the legal requirement versus harm; the respect of the here-and-now wishes of a client versus the need to uphold ethics codes. None of these situations has a 'right answer'. Therapists, when faced with such dilemmas, need to think carefully through the issues to try to find the best way forward. We believe that the following checklist provides a framework and procedure, which will help you cover all the important issues.

WORKING THROUGH AN ETHICAL DILEMMA

1. Summarize the dilemma.
2. Identify the ethical issues involved.
3. Find the section of your ethics code that applies.
4. Identify the values that are in conflict.
5. Check any legal constraints (e.g. the need to report child abuse).
6. Brainstorm ALL possible decisions for action (or inaction).
7. Arrange consultation or supervision (*before* making a decision).
8. Assess the possible consequences of each decision you could make.
9. Choose the decision which would have the least damaging consequences or the best outcome overall.
10. Make a written record of your considerations and the recommendations of your supervisor (with dates).
11. Plan how to support yourself to live with the decision.
12. Take the action you have chosen.

Remember that there is usually no outcome that is without some disturbing drawbacks. You are always finding the best compromise to a difficult situation. As the decision starts to have its consequences, you may want to consult frequently with your supervisor and any colleagues who are experienced in the particular area. You may also find that your professional organization or your insurance company has a free legal helpline for advice on any legal issues.

We have endeavoured to stay true to Gestalt's relational and field theoretical perspective, which implies a trust in healthy process – the 'striving for good' that Perls names in our opening quotation. A relational approach to therapy understands that we co-create the therapeutic relationship and therefore co-create the relational patterns, transferences and experiences that happen within it. Many of these interactions are of course out of awareness, non-verbal, implicit and only consciously apparent later, if at all.

The inevitable consequence of this viewpoint is that it is much harder to claim objectivity or certainty in ethical desion making. Acting ethically, authentically and with an awareness of the wider field issues potentially requires a commitment to finding a new solution each time.

RECOMMENDED READING ON DIVERSITY

British Gestalt Journal (1998) 'Special focus on gay and lesbian issues', special edition, 7 (1).
Brown, J. (2004) 'Conflict, emotions and appreciation of differences', *Gestalt Review*, 8 (3): 323–35.

(Continued)

(Continued)

Counselling Psychologist (2007) Special Issue on Racism, 35: 13–105.

Davies, D. and Neal, C. (eds) (1996) *Pink Therapy Two: Therapeutic Perspectives on Working with Lesbian, Gay and Bisexual Clients.* Buckingham: Open University Press.

Fernbacher, S. (2005) 'Cultural influences and considerations in Gestalt therapy', in A.L Woldt and S.M. Toman (eds), *Gestalt Therapy – History, Theory and Practice.* Thousand Oaks, CA: Sage.

Jacobs, L. (2000) 'For whites only', *British Gestalt Journal*, 9 (1): 3–14.

Levine Bar-Joseph, T. (ed.) (2005) *The Bridge: Dialogues Across Cultures.* New Orleans: Gestalt Institute Press.

Lichtenberg, P. (1990) *Community and Confluence: Undoing the Clinch of Oppression.* Cleveland, OH: Gestalt Institute of Cleveland.

Ponterotto, J.G., Utsey, S.O. and Pederson, P.B. (2006) *Preventing Prejudice: a Guide for Counsellors, Educators and Parents,* 2nd edn. London: Sage.

Thompson, C.E. and Carter, R.T. (eds) (1997) *Racial Identity Theory.* New Jersey: Lawrence Erlbaum Ass.

Wheeler, G. (2005) 'Culture, self and field: a Gestalt guide to the age of complexity', *Gestalt Review,* 9 (1): 91–128.

RECOMMENDED READING ON ETHICS

Bernhardtson, L. (2008) *'Gestalt ethics: a utopia?' Gestalt Review,* 12 (2): 161–73.

Bond, T. (2000) *Standards and Ethics for Counselling in Action.* London: Sage.

Gremmler-Fuhr. M. (2001) 'Ethical dimensions in Gestalt therapy', *Gestalt Review,* 5 (1): 24–44.

Jacobs, L. (2004) 'Ethics of context and field: the practices of care, inclusion and openness to dialogue', in R. Lee (ed.), *The Values of Connection.* Cambridge, MA: Gestalt Press.

Lee, R.G. (2002) 'Ethics: a gestalt of values', *Gestalt Review,* 6 (1): 27–51.

Lee, R.G. (ed.) (2004) *The Values of Connection – a Relational Approach to Ethics.* Cambridge, MA: Gestalt Press.

Melnick, J., Nevis, S. and Melnick, N. (1994) 'Therapeutic ethics: a Gestalt approach', *British Gestalt Journal,* 3 (2): 105–13.

Pope, K. and Vasquez, M. (2007) *Ethics in Psychotherapy and Counselling: A Practical Guide.* San Francisco, CA: Jossey Bass.

Swanson, J. (1980) 'The morality of conscience: valuing from a Gestalt point of view', *Gestalt Journal,* 3 (2): 71–85.

22

SPIRITUAL COUNSELLING

It might seem strange that we are including a chapter on spirituality in a book devoted to counselling and psychotherapy. As practitioners we are trained to work with 'earthly' issues and, in the main, we are not trained to address our clients' spiritual needs. Indeed, it may be grandiose to suppose that we can. However, there are three important reasons to include spirituality. First, our clients' spiritual paths are often inextricably entwined with their personal lives – they hinder or help each other in a myriad of ways. Second, it is important for us as counsellors to discriminate when a problem or need of a client is of a spiritual nature and not the province of psychotherapy or counselling. Indeed, it may be necessary to recommend the client to a source of spiritual guidance. Third, Eastern spirituality has played a significant part in the shaping of Gestalt theory and practice since its origin, and many Gestalt principles have much in common with spiritual practice. The Eastern spiritual traditions emphasize equanimity, surrender and connection with a greater reality. For example, Zen Buddhism stresses living in the present moment (the here-and-now) and mindfulness (being holistically aware of what you are doing). It also advocates the avoidance of 'thinking about' in favour of simple awareness (lose your mind and come to your senses), adopting equanimity (creative indifference) and the experience of *sartori* or small enlightenments ('aha', peak, or I–Thou moments).

This influence has waxed and waned in the Gestalt world over the years and has always been the other polarity to the directive, individualistic, materialistic flavour of early Gestalt theory and practice. In more recent times, the increasing influence of field theory and the dialogic method has reintroduced a more connecting, communal and ecological emphasis. It has also led to a greater interest in the potentially spiritual nature of the field and of the spiritual elements of a dialogic meeting.

> **Suggestion:** What in your view is the most important meaning or purpose of human existence? Happiness, creativity, status, success, intimacy, raising a family, helping others, living a religious life, finding a spiritual meaning or connection? How open are you to being with a client with a radically different worldview to your own?

We believe there are two important distinctions to be made in any clinical understanding of what are loosely called spirituality issues.

The first distinction is the difference between exoteric and esoteric spirituality. Exoteric (or religious) is concerned with belief in a personal god, adherence to rituals, customs, codes of conduct and morality. Esoteric spirituality, on the other hand, has minimal interest in dogma or belief and is concerned with practices that lead to a direct experience of spiritual connectedness. In Eastern religion and to a lesser extent Western religion, there is a clear division between the outer form of belief or ritual and an esoteric or mystical dimension that stresses personal experience.

> The esoteric aspects of spirituality are those practices designed to give the aspirant a direct encounter with the Divine. (Ingersoll, 2005: 137)

Exploration or questioning of exoteric issues will stay within an established structure, while esoteric issues will require openness to moving beyond structures into unknown territory.

The second distinction is the two different uses of the word spiritual. In one sense, it means a personal expansion of meaning or self-boundaries or feeling 'one with nature' yet still within the frame of familiar consciousness. In the other sense, it means an experience of a radically different consciousness which is mysterious, humbling and often described as connecting with a larger presence.

Those who have had no direct experience of a transcendent spiritual connection are likely to label such experiences as imagination or evidence of psychotic illness. It is also sometimes seen as an unhealthy loss of boundaries, the 'pre/trans fallacy' of Wilber (2000: 205) where,

> Genuine mystical or contemplative experiences ... are seen as a regression or throwback to infantile states of narcissism, oceanic adualism ... and even primitive autism.

We believe that it is crucial to be clear about which of these meanings of 'spirituality' you and your client are negotiating in order to know how to best respond.

Both these distinctions are relevant to shaping the therapy. A client presenting with issues of the larger meaning of life, possible spiritual crisis or despair may be facing one of three potential situations, each of which need a different counselling approach:

◆ First, he could be experiencing an existential crisis of meaning (sometimes, we believe, inaccurately called a spiritual crisis). Here the client is well served by competent humanistic/existential Gestalt practice where the focus would be on facing the life crisis, coming to terms with the anxiety or problems of living and finding new meaning.

◆ Second, he could be experiencing a loss of faith in his traditional religious belief or practice. Here, we might explore the issue but would consider referring on to an appropriate religious mentor, sympathetic priest or elder.

◆ Third, he could be experiencing a sense of something missing from his life that cannot be satisfied by the rewards of ordinary life. These are often clients who come with a sense of confusion that they 'should be satisfied' with their successful life or with a sense that there is 'something more' that lies in a spiritual realm. For this (esoteric) issue or crisis the client needs clarification, support for uncertainty, and help in identifying practices which will strengthen his search. For some clients, it will mean finding a spiritual path or discipline to engage with (and they may or may not then leave therapy).

During the initial assessment it may be useful to ask about spiritual or religious orientation. This will allow you to have some perspective on whether this relates to the reason he is coming to therapy. A useful way to start a dialogue about this is to ask the client for moments in his life where he had an experience of spiritual meaning and the sense he made of this.

SPIRITUAL INQUIRY

If the spiritual dimension becomes figural, we find it useful to explore the context of the client's spiritual beliefs and influences. This helps the therapist to understand how much impact the spiritual ground has on the client's issues as well as its place in the client's life and whether they need additional guidance. For example:

◆ What religion or spiritual orientation were your parents or caretakers?
◆ How did this affect you as you were growing up?
◆ What were the religious or spiritual values that were important in your family?
◆ Did you rebel or challenge them – if so what happened?
◆ What current religious or spiritual beliefs do you hold?
◆ What supports you, for example, meditation, prayer, spiritual community, church, temple, etc.?
◆ Do you experience or fear discrimination or criticism about your beliefs?
◆ How important are your spiritual beliefs in your life?
◆ How do these inform or affect your current difficulties or problems?
◆ Are *my* religious or spiritual beliefs important to you? If so, how?

EXAMPLE

Odo came for therapy with a sense of disillusionment and a lack of meaning in his life. By any standards he was a successful, competent professional with a loving partner and many interests in his life. As the counsellor explored, it became clear that Odo had been searching for something that he could not find

(Continued)

(Continued)

in his life of material and emotional well-being. He had little interest in formal religion and firmly believed that although he experienced periods of meaninglessness, this was not an existential reality but a lack of connection to something he sensed but could not explain. Although he had the usual sort of relational issues from childhood, both he and the therapist did not think that this was the root of his issues. As they explored his history, however, Odo reported that at times he had felt a sense of meaning in moments of quiet on holiday visits to cathedrals, temples or places of worship. A common theme in these experiences seemed to be a sense of silence, openness and receptivity to something beyond his usual sense of 'I'. The therapist encouraged him to pursue this experience actively, by setting aside times for quiet reflection, and making visits to local organizations that seemed to invite this kind of meditative state, such as Quaker meetings, silent retreat centres, and Buddhist meditation courses. However, she advised him to try to have a bodily felt sense of which places spoke to him, rather than to use his intellect to decide. Odo decided to join a course of meditation and eventually found a spiritual teacher. For the first time in many years, he felt hopeful that he was on a journey of meaning and connectedness.

There are many reasons that lead clients to seeking counselling help. They range on a continuum from problems that they want to solve (or have solved for them!), through the mid-ground of self-knowledge and personal growth, to the other end of the continuum, a desire for spiritual realization.

Problems or distress . . . . . Personal growth . . . . . Spiritual growth

Of course, all these three needs may be present at the same time, or the client may move between these three positions as the therapy progresses. The ability of the counsellor to move skilfully along this continuum will depend on his interest and training in spiritual matters. In some cases it may be important to realize when you have reached the edge of your competence and need to suggest that the client find a spiritual teacher for that part of their journey.

AWARENESS

In its broadest sense, awareness has both an ordinary and a transcendent meaning. It includes living fully in the moment, both in a thoroughly human way and also in a way that surpasses the ordinary. This is the sense implied by spiritual awareness or awakening in Zen Buddhism, and is also contained in Martin Buber's description of the transcendent quality of the I–Thou meeting. These experiences are characterized by being compelling, mysterious and somehow beyond words. People describe a sense of connection and contact, of moving beyond the ordinary, a sense of awe in the face of something larger and all-encompassing. It is at these moments also that there is little sense of 'doing' or ego, but more a humility in relation to a larger meaning or purpose.

> ... a stage of awareness beyond the awareness of here and now; an awareness retroflected unto itself, which devours itself and dissolves into a condition of consciousness without an object ... non dual awareness, cognition of the 'ground of being'. (Naranjo, 1981: 9)

Many of the Gestalt techniques of grounding, attention to breathing, sensory awareness, openness of attitude, all lead to a state of simple awareness that can move into transcendent awareness. Gestalt's invitation to 'lose your mind and come to your senses' also accords with the common perspective that the restless thinking activity of the mind is a hindrance to spiritual awareness. Indeed, many spiritual and meditation practices start with just such self-preparation exercises as those described in Chapter 1 (which prepare you for the task of therapy). Guided visualizations, meditation, shamanic rituals, prayer, music, contact with nature, are just some examples of creating the possible conditions for spiritual experience. None of these is specifically Gestalt, but some Gestalt counsellors who are also trained or gifted in these areas can incorporate them appropriately into their work if the client requests this sort of exploration.

Suggestion: Look back over your life and identify the times when you felt an experience of strong spiritual meaning, a sense of some larger purpose of connection. What were the conditions?

By way of a caution, it is important to remember that a spiritual crisis or emergence can involve extraordinary experiences and a disorientating breakdown of ego boundaries. Without proper support, a spiritual crisis can become a psychiatric emergency or be unhelpfully labelled as such. For example, spiritual despair – the dark night of the soul – can be mislabelled as depression. Out-of-body experiences, quaking, visions, and so on, are all accepted and welcomed as spiritual in some communities and treated as psychosis in others. If the therapist does not have the option of the lens of a spiritual dimension he will usually see the client's spiritual quest as something that needs to be changed rather than lived through. You need to know, therefore, whether there is a context within the person's culture or belief system for this sort of experience.

MYSTERY AND THE SELF

The experience of spirituality is one of mystery, of standing in relation to, or in the presence of, some larger reality, when the usual sense of self is not lost but transcended.

Kennedy (1994) makes this point about the essential mysteriousness of the spiritual experience. In the same way, peak experiences, or I–Thou moments, often have a quality of transcendence of ordinary personality where the usual sense of self or identity seems minimal or temporarily absent. At the moment of full contact there is a loss of self that paradoxically feels the height of aliveness, engagement and excitement. This experience is comprehensively described in Buddhist literature as the loss of ego (in their terminology, an illusionary or a false self-perception) and is an inevitable characteristic of spiritual enlightenment.

In recent years, there has been an increasing trend in Gestalt literature to recognize the transcendent dimension of Gestalt. This includes the maturational process of Jacobs' 'urge to growth' (1989), Buber's 'I–Thou moments' (1958/1984), Clarkson's transpersonal elements, 'the soul in Gestalt' (1989), Parlett's (1991) description of the spiritual quality of presence, Williams' (2006) Gestalt-transpersonal, and many other contributions (see recommended reading at the end of this chapter). There are also spiritual programmes such as the Ridhwan School founded by A.H. Almaas that impressively integrate many Gestalt psychotherapeutic practices with a spiritual path.

Spiritual traditions and Gestalt therapy both emphasize living in the present moment, and emphasize *experience* over belief or dogma. Both demand an openness to the mystery or spontaneity of life itself and, in this relationship, find a subtler level of experience that is clearly of a different order.

RECOMMENDED READING

Almaas, A.H, (2008) For articles see website: http://www.ahalmaas.com.

Bate, D. (2001) Letter to editor: 'Gestalt and spirituality,' *British Gestalt Journal*, 10 (2): 125–6.

Crocker, S.F. (2005) 'Phenomenology, existentialism and Eastern thought in Gestalt therapy,' in A.L. Woldt and S.M. Toman (eds), *Gestalt Therapy – History, Theory and Practice*. Thousand Oaks, CA: sage. (**See pp. 73–80.**)

Denham-Vaughn, S. (2005) 'Will and Grace', *British Gestalt Journal*, 14 (1): 5–14.

Frambach, L. (2003) 'The weighty world of nothingness: Salomon Friedlaender's "Creative indifference"', in M. Spagnuolo Lobb and N. Amendt-Lyon (eds), *Creative License: The Art of Gestalt Therapy*. New York: Springer-Verlag Wien. pp. 113–28.

Fuhr, R. (1998) 'Gestalt therapy as a transrational approach', *Gestalt Review*, 2 (1): 6–27.

Harris, E.S. (2000) 'God, Buber, and the practice of Gestalt therapy', *Gestalt Journal*, 23 (1): 39–62.

Ingersoll, R.E. (2005) 'Gestalt therapy and spirituality', in A.L. Woldt and S.M. Toman (eds), *Gestalt Therapy – History, Theory and Practice*. Thousand Oaks, CA: Sage.

Kolodony, R. (2000) 'Some reflections on Gestalt meditation and spirituality', Gestal Institute of Cleveland *Voice*, 1: 6–14.

McConville, M.G. (2000) 'An interview with Mwalimulmara', *Gestalt Institute of Cleveland Voice*, 4: 17–20.

Naranjo, C. (2000) *Gestalt Therapy: The Attitude and Practice of an Atheoretical Experientialism*, 2nd. rev. edn. Nevada City, CA: Crown House Publishing. **(See Part One: Chapter 2; Part Four: Chapters 12 and 18.)**

Naranjo, C. (2006) *The Way of Silence and the Talking Cure: On Meditation and Psychotherapy*. Nevada City, CA: Blue Dolphin Publishing.

Snir, S. (2000) 'A response from a Kabalistic perspective to "The spiritual dimensions of Gestalt therapy"', *Gestalt!* 4 (3) (Fall). Available at: http://www.g-gej.org/4-3/index.html.

Sperry, L. (2001) *Spirituality in Clinical Practice*. Hove: Brunner-Routledge.

West, W. (2004) *Spiritual Issues in Therapy*. Basingstoke: Palgrave Macmillan.

Wilber, K. (2000) *Sex, Ecology, Spirituality*. Boston, MA: Shambhala Publications Inc.

Williams, L. (2006) 'Spirituality and Gestalt: a Gestalt–transpersonal perspective', *Gestalt Review*, 10 (1): 6–21.

Wolfert, R. (2000) 'The spiritual dimensions of Gestalt therapy,' *Gestalt!,* 4 (3) (Fall). Available at: http://www.g-gej.org/4-3/spiritual.html.

23

GESTALT AND COACHING

There are many ways of understanding the activity called coaching – from expert mentoring in a business setting, to teaching new competencies, to offering encouragement and even hands-on help. Our approach to coaching is that, like therapy, it is the intentional use of a collaborative relationship, for the development of the client in his particular situation. As such, like all Gestalt, it is a relational approach.

This trend towards a relational approach to understanding process and change, finds a strong voice in coaching and organizational theories. Many organizational development (OD) consultants have integrated theoretical concepts and principles from Gestalt with complexity theories to create a vibrant and dynamic attitude to working with groups and organizations. There is a growing body of literature where consultants have described the use and application of Gestalt in their organizational work (see for example, Bentley, 2001; Nevis, 2003; Denham-Vaughan, 2005, 2009; Maurer, 2005; Frew, 2006; Critchley, 2006; Cavicchia, 2009; Gaffney, 2009).

These consultants and others have challenged traditional approaches, which largely concentrated on structure, role, responsibility and business processes to understand what goes on in organizations. Interventions often focused on what was wrong, diagnosing where these errors or faults lay and then applying expert solutions that were determined to address these. They prioritized ordering and regulating, setting goals, creating new organizational design and so on. The critique of this deterministic and rational way of approaching organizations is that it is outdated and ineffective, especially in the fast-changing, globally connected world where data gathered today can be irrelevant next week.

Critchley (1997) coined the term 'bounded instability' to describe a space (either actual or psychological) where there is enough structure to provide safety and order but enough chaos to allow novelty and change. We believe that the process orientation of Gestalt can revitalize much of the existing methodology for coaching and consulting to organizations, by introducing such necessary instability to the existing boundedness of many structured approaches. (See for example, Coffey and Cavicchia

(2005) who offer a phenomenological approach to 360 degree feedback or Denham-Vaughan (2009) who describes 're-enchantment' of theories in organizations.)

A Gestalt approach sees organizations as individuals and communities of people in interaction, who co-construct their reality as they attempt to focus on the organizational tasks. Gestaltists are interested in understanding how these individuals and groups organize their experience and make contact that enables them to 'get the job done' with a sense of agency and choice. The task is to support the ability of people in an organization to grow and learn by letting go of unhelpful fixed gestalts that inhibit them from creatively adapting to the ongoing changing circumstances of the field, while maintaining a sense of continuity in those habitual patterns of relating that are helpful.

This approach is based on the concept of using our self–in-relationship as coach (or consultant) where our presence, awareness and ability to work in relationship is critical to the effectiveness of our interventions. Gestalt concepts that are especially useful in this context are field theory, dialogue, awareness and contact. Understanding that the relationship is *of* and *from* the field highlights the importance of the coach attending to the client's field and its impact and presence in the coaching encounter (see also Chapter 2).

We briefly review below some key suggestions for a Gestalt approach in organizational practice (adapted from B. Desmond, personal communication, 2009)

◆ As you work with the client, inquire into the organization as a whole in order to understand how it interacts internally and externally, where interconnections and interdependences are present or absent; how people make contact and relate in way that appears to support or inhibit activity on its tasks. Try to remain creatively indifferent, so you notice 'what is' rather than moving to 'cause and effect'.

◆ Notice what is figure and ground; what '… lies in the background of peoples' lives as well as what is uppermost' (Parlett, 1993: 117) . Notice how your client describes the way individuals/groups engage with what is important to them (figure) and what is ignored or out of awareness (ground).

◆ Take a current field perspective. View all phenomena as inextricably linked so that a change in one aspect of the field changes the whole. Since the field is co-created, this includes us as coaches, especially if we have contact with other parts of the organization. Once we are 'engaged' we are part of the field where we shape and are shaped in a dynamic and reciprocal process. This requires practitioners to be very aware not only of self in relationship with client, but also the larger organizational, social, political, environmental, and ecological fields they are interconnected with. Changes in the way you and the client relate have the potential to affect the organization.

◆ Be open to the historical and potential fields. Just as in counselling, it is not uncommon for past hurt to impact present behaviour. For example, a Head of Learning and Development and his team feared inviting the senior board to a critical workshop on developing change capability across the organization. On exploration it emerged that on a previous occasion several years before he joined the organization his successor had attempted this and was dismissed. The history and dynamics of organizational unfinished business can cast its shadow and form an unrecognized influence in the present.

Figure 23.1   The dimensions of self in coaching

Gestalt coaching skills

> The job of a coach is to put her clients in a position to be able to fulfil increasing and in some cases even contradictory expectations posed by their work, such as flexibility, performance, innovation, quality awareness, team-building, problem solving, stress reduction, motivating employees, and decisiveness. (Arnold, 2008: 78)

Gestalt coaching is a collaborative learning partnership that on the one hand, draws from the skills of mentoring, teaching or managing and on the other, from the skills and insights of counselling and therapy. It is beyond the scope of this chapter to investigate the connections and differentiations on the more directive (and business focused) side. However, because this book is about the 'soft skills' of therapy, it is important for us to look at that link and also the boundary.

What makes the difference between therapy and coaching is that the focus of coaching is the development of the client's *professional* self (see Figure 23.1). It will certainly involve a focus on his personal self – his individual patterns and issues; it might even involve a focus on his private life if that is what is most affecting him at any particular time. However, the main focus will be on the development of the client at work and it will tend largely towards growth and development rather than the healing of old issues.

This boundaried focus is both heightened and demonstrated in two other important differences between the therapy we have described in this book, and coaching. They define both what the coach does not do and also what he does. The first is the duration and frequency of sessions. Coaching sessions tend to be longer than the therapeutic hour but for fewer sessions and normally spaced at monthly or two monthly intervals. This gives time for the client to experiment and respond to developments in his organization. It also means that the type of work is different. For example, it does not lend itself to working through unfinished business from the past, or transference and counter-transference dynamics in the way that therapist and client might do. Transference exists, of course, in any relationship but a more pragmatic approach of identifying, questioning, minimizing and learning from the dynamics is appropriate to the work focus in a coaching contract.

For example, a manager seems anxious with you and appears to think that you find him inept, which is far from the truth. You may choose not to explore the depth and history of such transference but simply to reassure him that you are not feeling critical. You could then invite him to be interested in his relational feelings and expectations. As he reflects, he may recognize that this is one of his common patterns with 'authority figures' and wonder how it may be playing out in the organization. Alternatively, he may realize that in the hierarchy of his organization, it has become a habit for managers to be sharply critical of their reports. Anxiety about incompetence is rife.

The second important difference between coaching and therapy is that coaching is more clearly contained and managed by a complex contract that accounts for the complex web of roles and relationships in the organization. The counselling contract described in Chapter 1 can be nested within another schema that shows the different levels of contracting in Gestalt coaching.

The framework we suggest is based on five 'levels' of contracting process (Sills, 2006), starting with the largest contextual container and then working down the levels to the micro-moment. Our colleague Brigid Proctor likens this to a set of Russian dolls. Each one nestles safely inside the container of the previous one – each separate but contributing to a whole. The dolls capture the idea that the effective contract acts as a safe container for the creative work in the area of 'bounded instability'.

1 The contract with the world — society, the environment, the law...

This first level of contract is not one that is negotiated by the organization. It is like a personal contract or commitment that each of us makes with the world we live in. Different coaches may be committed to different values, but essentially each of us has some principles and values we will not transgress. They may be to do with harming human beings or degrading the planet. They may be to do with keeping within the law or respecting diversity. Many coaches believe that it is necessary to make clear to the client the professional organizations to which they belong, and the ethical codes to which they adhere.

Suggestion: Ask yourself the questions: What work would I need to refuse or give up? What principle would I be willing to lose my job over?

BOX 23.2   LEVELS OF CONTRACT

1 ... With the world, society, the environment, etc.

2 ... With the organization – The Administrative Contract

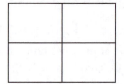

3 ... With the client regarding the desired 'developmental outcome' – The Learning Contract
The Contracting Matrix

4 ... With the client for a session

5 ... With the client 'moment by moment'

NB: Beware the 'psychological contract' – that which is out of awarness and not within our control

Contracts are reviewed regularly and updated as appropriate.

Source: Sills, 2006.

EXAMPLE

Jennie is offered the opportunity to coach the top team of a clothes manufacturer whose success is built on the exploitation of children in the Far East. She turns it down, in favour of a less financially attractive but, to her, more acceptable contact from the HR Director of Goodmac, a large engineering firm based near where she lives.

---

2 The contract with the organization and its parts or members

Below we illustrate the 'The Three-Cornered Contract' of English (1975). The model starts with a triangle:

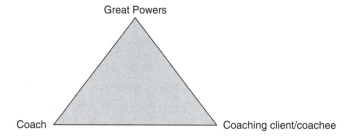

Figure 23.2 The three-cornered contract

The 'Great Powers' are the organization, the Human Resources department, or whoever is purchasing the coach's skills and has the power to dictate how the work will go. The other two points on the triangle are coach and client. The important implication is that there are certain elements that must be transparently agreed, on all three vectors of the triangle in order for any coaching engagement to be safe and effective. English's work was developed in 1992 by Micholt, who drew triangles with sides of unequal lengths to indicate different relationships of allegiance, contact or power between coach, coaching client and organizational client.

You can expand the diagram to have many points and vectors to represent multiple stakeholders and lines of authority. For the purposes of this chapter, however, we will stay with the simple three-cornered contract. It gives rise to several tasks that must be agreed on all sides:

◆ *Clarify the administrative contract.* Sometimes also referred to as the business contract, this type of contract, just as for the counselling client, deals with all the practical arrangements such as time, place, duration, fees, confidentiality and its limits (for example, what will be the required report-back to the HR Director when coaching is part of an assessment centre), and so on. These are all apparently straightforward but it is surprising how often coaches, with their eyes firmly fixed on the coaching work to come, can be unclear about them or overlook their importance. This importance is fundamental. Not only is clarity about administrative agreements essential to the world of business, but the creation of this structure significantly contributes to the provision of the area of bounded instability that Critchley describes as necessary for creativity.

◆ *Clarify the reason for the coaching.* The coaching may be put in place as part of a wider consulting intervention or as an adjunct, for example, to a leadership development programme. Alternatively, coaching may be part of the professional development that is routinely offered to managers at a particular level. It may be part of talent management or it may simply be that an executive is realizing that he wants or needs some support in managing his current or prospective role. The context – including whether the coaching is chosen or imposed, considered as a punishment or a perk – will play an important part in the nature of the administrative contract (and indeed in the development contract).

◆ *Discuss the possibility of changes to the contract and how they will be negotiated.* Any one of the three parties to the contract may at some time want to change the agreed contract. This may be unforeseen or it may be planned according to the needs of the client or the coach. Where possible, changes in frequency, duration or fees can be predicted at the initial stage of coaching so that they are part of both people's expectations.

◆ *Draw up a written contract.* This will detail the agreements between the three parties in order to ensure clarity of all the details. As there are often many stakeholders in the arrangement, it can be vital to ensure that everyone knows what is formally agreed.

◆ *Decide how the coaching will be evaluated.* It is impossible to measure success by ROI (return on investment), and yet organizations need to feel that they are getting value for money. Therefore, a realistic way of evaluating the work has to be agreed. The coach (especially if he is not known to the organization) may well need to engage in a conversation with the purchasers as well as the coaching client about the sort of coach he is and what sort of effect can be expected. This ensures that all parties are agreed on the broad outcome of the coaching and can describe what success would look like (or feel like) to them.

◆ *Clarify your coaching style.* It is important to be able to articulate one's coaching proposition – even to guide the client as to what might be most suitable. Turning down work because it is not the type of coaching we offer, is likely to make a better impression on potential future purchasers than trying to be a 'one coach fits all'. It may be especially important to give a fairly detailed explanation of the approach when proposing to work cross-culturally. The role of the coach can vary enormously between different cultures – from advice-giving organizational leader in one culture, to spiritual guide in another, to awareness facilitator in a third. For example, clients from some Asian and other oriental backgrounds may want a logical and rational approach, while those from Western cultures may expect to address their feelings (d'Ardenne and Mahtani, 1989). Another significant factor could be the different language interpretations when coach, organization and coaching client are from different cultures. The meaning of the words of a contract, the language used to describe the coach's and coaching client's roles – even the word 'contract' itself – might be full of subtle shades of meaning. Clarifying them can be part of the process of interested inquiry and contact that is so necessary in a cross-cultural engagement.

◆ *Outline the learning and development contract.* This defines the purpose and focus of the coaching and how it will proceed. It may be expressed in behavioural terms, as in the development of certain skills, or in more subjective terms, as in wanting to feel more confident or wanting to think about a career move. Coach and coaching client agree on what the focus of their work will be. Sometimes the client is not clear about what he wants and a preparatory contract to explore is agreed upon. The learning and development contract is mainly the concern of coach and coaching client. However, there are times when it needs to be part of the contract with the organization and be named as part of the three-cornered contract. For example, a coaching engagement to develop future leaders, or to facilitate a transition, or to build particular skills may be part of the condition on which the coach is hired. It is thus one of the transparent details that is known by all. Organizations frequently want to plan for some sort of evaluation at the end of coaching and this inevitably involves naming some sort of goal.

On a more Machiavellian note, organizations – sometimes knowingly, sometimes unconsciously – may use a coach, or even an entire team of consultants, as part of a plan to achieve a hidden end. We discuss this later under 'psychological contracts'.

The coach, Jennie, meets with the HR Director of Goodmac and also the Chief Executive Officer. She is told that the economic situation has led to some redundancies in the firm but that in principle the future looks good. As a result of restructuring, a new senior manager is taking responsibility for two departments and has asked for help with his new role. Jennie then meets the manager, Sarek, to discuss his needs in a general way and make sure that there is a 'good fit'. After that, there is a three-way conversation between Sarek, Jennie and the HRD. They agree a contract of five sessions over the coming 6 months, followed by another meeting to review. The broad goal is to support Sarek in his new role but the details of the sessions will be his own choice.

---

3 The developmental or learning contract

When all these measurable details are clarified, the coach and coaching client are free to move into the work. The first task, as with counselling, is to establish the working alliance (see Chapter 4). At the same time, a more careful exploration and agreement about the development contract takes place. A useful tool for clarifying the contract at this stage is the Contracting Matrix (Figure 23.3).

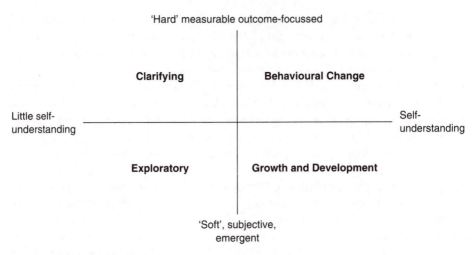

Figure 23.3 The contracting matrix

In Chapter 1, we described the polarity of hard contracts (observable, measurable outcome) and soft (subjective, experiential outcome) contracts. This becomes the vertical axis of a matrix, of which the other axis relates to the level of understanding – the extent to which the client is aware of what his issue is and what he wants from coaching. This matrix gives rise to four types of contract for coaching, which vary according to how clear the goal is and how behaviourally definable it is. It encompasses contracts for skills acquisition or performance improvement through to an emergent process of self-discovery.

We find the matrix extremely useful for broadening the perspective of a client who can only see things in terms of facts and outcome. Inevitably, as the coaching proceeds and the client's awareness increases, the contract evolves and moves fluidly between the four aspects.

At the first coaching session, Dev says that he can envisage that there will be much that he will want to work on, but his first priority is to find out the scope of his new role and what it would require of him. They agree a list of actions he needs to take and people he should talk to (Behavioural contract). Then he says that what he is most concerned with is the challenge to him personally. In future, he will be reporting directly to the board and he feels excited and nervous. He is not sure what he will need to learn, but he wants to make a good impression (Exploratory contract).

---

4 The sessional contract

◆ Make a contract for each individual session. Some coaches like to have a structured start to the session, perhaps reviewing experiments that the client had agreed to carry out since the last session. Gestalt coaches often wait to see where the client is and what is in the forefront of his mind, perhaps beginning 'So what is important today?' or 'What is figural?'

> At his second session, Dev is very clear about what he wants to focus on: his skills in influencing sideways and upwards. He has noticed that he is not very successful in this and is aware that it is important. He needs to find out what he is 'doing wrong' (Clarifying contract).

5 Moment-by-moment contracts

◆ These are the here-and-now 'instant' contracts, offered in order to clarify something or find a way forward in a session. They might involve the client saying what he wants and the coach agreeing; or the coach making a suggestion which the client accepts, as in:

'Do you want to say more about that?'
'Are you willing to pause and look at your relationship with the CEO?'
'I have a suggestion for an experiment – do you want to hear it?'
'Do you want some information about that?'

> As the session progresses, Jennie finds herself feeling increasingly steam-rollered by Sarek as he outlines his plans for his new division. After a while, she says 'I have noticed something that is going on here. Can I give you some feedback?' Sarek pauses and agrees so she explains that there is such pressure to take in all he is saying that she feels overwhelmed! Sarek is thoughtful. He realizes that sometimes he gets so anxious to get his point across that he stops being aware of the other person. He agrees to experiment with stopping his speeches regularly to ask for and listen to the response to what he is saying.

BREACHES OF CONTRACT

A breach of contract on either side is likely to be a serious matter and probably indicative of significant issues that must be addressed. There may initially be pragmatic issues to be resolved. However, for a relational Gestalt coach, breaches can be welcomed as valuable and rich sources of out-of-awareness information for both client and coach about what is going on between them, or for the client and his situation.

Before leaving the topic of contracts, it is important to remember what is sometimes called 'the psychological contract'. This means the unspoken and indeed out-of-awareness (or unconscious) emotional exchange between coach and client that is not accessible to rational, explicit contract making. This psychological level of contract can be a positive one – a mutual enjoyment and appreciation of each other, based on personal preferences or even positive transferences. Or it can be a negative process whereby both parties are trapped in a limiting or harmful dynamic, enacting fixed patterns and co-creating destructive outcomes.

> Example: Jonathan a successful and charismatic CEO claimed he wanted to be challenged but, by his voice tone and facial expression, sent the implicit message that he was too vulnerable and would be unforgiving of confrontation. His coach picked up the unspoken agenda and complied with it. She was half aware of doing so, guiltily thinking that she didn't want to lose the work. Only in coaching supervision did she realize that her bullying father was being evoked in the counter-transference. Afterwards, she was able to free herself from the unhelpful dynamic.

We cannot control this level of 'psychological contract'. We can only be alert to its emergence in enactments in the coaching room and be ready to welcome the learning it will bring, as unrecognized dynamics are brought to awareness.

GESTALT COACHING SKILLS

Once the initial contracts are established, many of the skills already described in this book form the essential coaching relationship. We offer the following core skill suggestions, which we believe are especially important:

- Offer your presence in a spirit of inclusion, ready to enter a co-creative dialogue.
- Notice your own feelings and responses and be ready to share your own experience, using the here-and-now relationship as a way of learning about the client and his organization as well as creating the possibility of 'new conversations' (see chapters 4 and 12).
- Summarize themes and reflect back what you have heard and what you notice in the here and now (bodily and facial expression, feelings, assumptions, his attitude to authority, his feelings of strength or inadequacy, etc.).
- Ask open questions, inquiring into the phenomenological world of the client, raising awareness of fixed gestalts, core beliefs, patterns of organizing the world. (see chapters 2, 3 and 11)
- Explore with the client what is happening in his organization and the wider field. Are there circumstances or events that need attention (such as global trends, media interest, a change of CEO, re-structuring and so on)?
- Suggest or co-create experiments for new behavior, allowing your intuition to play on what unfolds.

In other words, use the phenomenological method and dialogic presence to raise awareness of your client's thoughts and feelings, unfinished business and patterns, using the here-and-now relationship to learn about the client-in-relationship, the client's ways of regulating contact.

THE SCOPE OF COACHING

The spectrum of coaching covers a continuum of:

Skills .... Performance .... Transformation .... Emergence
(Acquisition)   (Improvement)   (Learning)   (Development)

Gestalt is ideal for the development end of the spectrum, as it works well with 'what is and is becoming'. However, it has very real uses in all aspects. At the skills acquisition stage, strengthening support is vital alongside experimentation and practice. These will be important also where improvement of performance is key. The cycle of experience (see Chapter 3) can be useful to help the client reflect on the natural stages of a process (either psychological or actual). He might also benefit from identifying where he is strongest and where weakest in the cycle and how he might interrupt the flow.

In the area of transformation and learning, exploring modifications to contact and fixed gestalts might be particularly useful in facilitating a client to understand his patterns. Simon Cavicchia (2009, personal communication) suggests that particularly patterns of assimilation, introjection-rejection are relevant here. Raising awareness helps the client develop the capacity to make contact with the 'novel' in service of learning.

FROM INDIVIDUAL TO ORGANIZATION

The way the client is with you may be an echo not only of his relationships generally, but also potentially of the relationships that happen in his organizational context. Your focus is the person in his structured field. Earlier in the chapter, we described a view of organizations and how change happens, which underlined the impossibility of working with the individual separate from the field. We also believe that for the client to change his professional self, he will have to think about how change happens – not just for himself, but in the wider team or organization. He can be aware that his behaviour at work is affecting (and being affected by) the way the organization functions and behaves; fully understanding his patterns of relating can create first 'local' and then larger change. The Gestalt coach can support her client in inquiring into and amplifying small movements for change, challenging the habits and customs that have been taken for granted, and experimenting in and outside of the coaching room, rehearsing or practising new conversations.

RECOMMENDED READING

Arnold, H.-P. (2008) 'Gestalt-integrated strategy development. Making the Gestalt approach available for the coaching process', *International Gestalt Journal*, 31 (2): 77–107.

Critchley, B. and O'Brien, D. (2004) 'Transformational strategy: myth or reality?' Critical Eye Review: *The Journal of Europe's Centre for Business Leaders*, www.criticaleye.net.

Critchley, B., King, K. and Higgins, J. (2007) *Organisational Consulting: A Relational Perspective*. London: Middlesex University Press.

Magerman, M.H. and Leahy, M.J. (eds) (2009) 'The Lone Ranger is dying: special issue on gestalt coaching as support and challenge', *The International Gestalt Journal*, 32 (1).

Maurer, R. (2005) 'Gestalt approaches with organisations and large systems', in A.L. Woldt and S.M. Toman (eds), *Gestalt Therapy – History, Theory and Practice*. Thousand Oaks, CA: Sage.

Nevis, E. (2003) 'Blocks to creativity in organisations', in M. Spagnuolo Lobb and N. Amendt-Lyon (eds), *Creative Licence – the Art of Gestalt Therapy*. Vienna: Springer-Verlag.

Parlett, M. (2001) Special issue on Gestalt Consultants in Organistions. *British Gestalt Journal*, 10 (1).

REFERENCES

Arnold, H-P. (2008) 'Gestalt-integrated strategy development, making the gestalt approach available for the coaching process', *International Gestalt Journal*, 31 (2): 77–107.

Asay, T.P. and Lambert, M.J. (1999) 'The empirical case for the common factors in therapy: quantitative findings', in M.A. Hubble, B.L. Duncan and S.D. Miller (eds), *The Heart and Soul of Change: What Works in Therapy*. Washington, DC: APA Press. pp. 33–56.

Barber, P. (2006) *Becoming a Practitioner Researcher, a Gestalt Approach to Holistic Enquiry*. London: Middlesex University Press.

Batts, V. (2000) 'Racial awareness in psychotherapy', Workshop Presentation, ITA Conference, Canterbury.

Baumgardner, P. (1975) *Legacy from Fritz: Gifts from Lake Cowichan*. Palo Alto, CA: Science and Behaviour Books.

Beaumont, H. (1993) 'Martin Buber's I–Thou and fragile self organisation', *British Gestalt Journal*, 2 (2): 85–95.

Beisser, A.R. (1970) 'The paradoxical theory of change', in J. Fagan and I. Shepherd (eds), *Gestalt Therapy Now*. Palo Alto, CA: Science and Behavior. pp. 77–80.

Bentley, T. (2001) 'The emerging system', *British Gestalt Journal*, 10 (1): 13–19.

Blake, W. (1969) *The Complete Writings,* ed. G. Keynes. Oxford: Oxford Paperbacks.

Bohm, D. (1996) *On Dialogue,* ed. Lee Nichol. London: Routledge.

Bordin, E.S. (1994) 'Theory and research in the therapeutic alliance', in O. Horvath and S. Greenberg (eds), *The Working Alliance: Theory, Research and Practice*. New York: Wiley.

Brown, M.T. and Landrum-Brown, J. (1995) 'Counselor supervision: cross-cultural perspectives', in J. Ponterotto, J. Manual Casas, L.A. Suzuki and C.A. Alexander (eds), *The Handbook of Multicultural Counselling*. London: Sage.

Brownell, P. (2005) 'Gestalt therapy in community mental health', in A.L. Woldt and S.M. Toman (eds), *Gestalt Therapy – History, Theory and Practice*. Thousand Oaks, CA: Sage. pp. 257–78.

Buber, M. (1958/1984) *I and Thou*. Edinburgh: T. & T. Clark.

Buber, M. (1967) *A Believing Humanism*. New York: Simon & Schuster.

Burley, T. and Bloom, D. (2008) 'Phenomenological method', in P. Brownell (ed.), *Handbook for Theory, Research and Practice in Gestalt Therapy*. Newcastle: Cambridge Scholars Publishing.

Carter, R.T. (1997) 'Race and psychotherapy: the racially inclusive model', in C.E. Thompson and R.T. Carter (eds), *Racial Identity Theory*. New Jersey, NY: Lawrence Erlbaum.

Cavicchia, S. (2009, in press) 'Towards a relational coaching', *British Gestalt Journal*.

Chidiac, M-A. and Denham-Vaughan, S. (2009) 'An organisational self', *British Gestalt Journal*, 18 (1): 42–9.

Clarkson, P. (1989) *Gestalt Counselling in Action*. London: Sage.

Clarkson, P. (1992) *Transactional Analysis – An Integrated Approach*. London: Routledge.

Claxman, G. (1990) *The Heart of Practical Buddhism*. London: Aquarian Press.

Clemmens, M. (2005) *Getting Beyond Sobriety*. London: Taylor & Francis.

Clemmens, M. (2008) Team development workshop. Metanoia Institute, UK.

Coffey, F. and Cavicchia, S. (2005) 'Gestalt in an information technology organisation: a case study', *British Gestalt Journal*, 14 (1): 15–25.

Cohn, H. (1997) *Existential Thought and Therapeutic Practice*. London: Sage.

Cooper, M. (2008a) Lecture to the 8th Person Centred and Experiential Conference. Norwich, UK.

Cooper, M. (2008b) *Essential Research Findings in Counselling and Psychotherapy: The Facts Are Friendly*. London: Sage.

Cozolino, L. (2006) *The Neuro-science of Human Relationships*. NY: W.W. Norton & Co.

Critchley, B. (1997) 'A Gestalt approach to organisational consulting', in J.E. Neumann, K. Keller and A. Dawson-Shepherd (eds), *Developing Organisational Consultancy*. London: Routledge.

Critchley, B. (2006) 'A commentary on "organisational leadership theory has arrived: Gestalt theory never left"', *Gestalt Review*, 10 (2):140–3.

Critchley, B., King, K. and Higgins, J. (2007) *Organisational Consulting: A Relational Perspective*. London: Middlesex University Press.

Crocker, S.F. (1999) *A Well Lived Life: Essays in Gestalt Therapy*. Cleveland, OH: Gestalt Institute of Cleveland Press.

d'Ardenne, P. and Mahtani, A. (1989) *Transcultural Counselling in Action*. London: Sage.

Delisle, G. (1999) *Personality Disorders: A Gestalt Therapy Perspective*. Cleveland, OH: Gestalt Institute of Cleveland Press.

Denham-Vaughan, S. (2005) 'Will and Grace', *British Gestalt Journal,* 14 (1): 5–14.

Denham-Vaughan, S. (2009) 'Re-enchantment of psychological therapies: organisational strategy, leadership & implementation as informed by a Gestalt perspective', Doctoral Thesis, Metanoia Institute UK.

Duncan, B. and Miller, S. (2000) *The Heroic Client*. San Francisco, CA: Jossey-Bass.

Eliot, T.S. (1942) *The Complete Poems and Plays of T.S. Eliot*. London: Faber & Faber.

Elliott, R. (2002) 'The effectiveness of humanistic therapies: a meta-analysis', in D. Cain and J. Seeman (eds), *Humanistic Psychotherapies: Handbook of Research and Practice*. Washington, DC: American Psychological Association. pp. 57–81.

Elton Wilson, J. (1993a) 'Towards a personal model of counselling', in W. Dryden (ed.), *Questions and Answers in Counselling in Action*. London: Sage. pp. 95–102.

Elton Wilson, J. (1993b) *Ethics in Psychotherapy*. Training Workshop. London: Metanoia.

English, F. (1975) 'The three cornered contract', *Transactional Analysis Journal*, 5 (4): 383–4.

Erskine, R.G. (1999) *Beyond Empathy*. Philadelphia, PA: Brunner-Mazel.

Erskine, R.G. and Trautmann, R. (1996) 'Methods of an integrative psychotherapy', *Transactional Analysis Journal*, 26 (4): 316–28.

Erskine, R.G., Moursund, J. and Trautmann, R.L. (1999) *Beyond Empathy*. New York: Brunner-Mazel.

Etherington, K. (2004) *Becoming a Reflexive Researcher – Using Our Selves in Research*. London: Jessica Kingsley.

Frank, R. (2001) *Body of Awareness*. Cambridge: Gestalt Press.

Frank, R. (2003) 'Embodying creativity', in M. Spagnuolo Lobb and N. Amendt-Lyon (eds), *Creative Licence – the Art of Gestalt Therapy*. Vienna: Springer-Verlag.

Frew, J.E. (2006) 'Organisational leadership theory has arrived: Gestalt theory never left', *Gestalt Review*, 10 (2): 123–40.

Gaffney, S. (2009) 'The cycle of experience re-cycled: then, now ... next', *Gestalt Review*, 13 (1): 7–23.

Gladwell, M. (2006) *Blink: The Power of Thinking Without Thinking.* London: Penguin.

Goulding, R. (1992) 'Transactional analysis and Gestalt therapy', in E.C. Nevis (ed.), *Gestalt Therapy.* New York: Gardner Press. pp. 129–46.

Greenberg, E. (1989) 'Healing the borderline', *Gestalt Journal*, 12 (2): 11–56.

Greenberg, L.S. and Malcolm, W. (2002) 'Resolving unfinished business: relating process to outcome', *Journal of Consulting and Clinical Psychology*, 70 (2): 406–16.

Greenberg, L.S. and Watson, J. (2006) *Emotion-Focussed Therapy for Depression.* Washington, DC: American Psychiatric Association.

Hargaden, H. and Sills, C. (2002) *Transactional Analysis – a Relational Perspective.* London: Routledge.

Harris, C. (1992) 'Gestalt work with psychotics', in E.C. Nevis (ed.), *Gestalt Therapy.* New York: Gardner Press. pp. 239–62.

Harris, E.S. (2000) 'God, Buber and the practice of Gestalt therapy', *The Gestalt Journal,* 22 (1): 39–62.

Harris, E.S. (2007) 'Working with forgiveness in Gestalt therapy', *Gestalt Review*, 11 (1): 108–19.

Hawkins, P. (1991) 'Approaches to the supervision of counsellors', in W. Dryden and B. Thorne (eds), *Training and Supervision for Counsellors in Action.* London: Sage.

Hayes, S., Follette, V. and Linehan, M. (2004) *Mindfulness and Acceptance: Expanding the Cognitive-Behavioral Tradition.* New York: Guilford Press.

Hooker, K.E. and Fodor, I.E. (2008) 'Teaching mindfulness to children', *Gestalt Review*, 12 (1): 75–91.

Horowitz, M.J. (1982) 'Strategic dilemmas and the socialisation of psychotherapy researchers', *British Journal of Clinical Psychology*, 21: 119–27.

Houston, G. (2003) *Brief Gestalt Therapy.* London: Sage.

Howdin, J. and Reeves, A. (2009) 'Working with suicide', *British Gestalt Journal,* 18 (1):10–17.

Hunter, M. and Struve, J. (1998) *The Ethical Use of Touch in Psychotherapy.* London: Sage.

Husserl, E. (1931) *Ideas: General Introduction to Pure Phenomenology*, vol. 1. New York: Macmillan.

Hycner, R.A. (1991) *Between Person and Person.* Highland, NY: Gestalt Journal Press.

Hycner, R.A. and Jacobs, L. (1995) *The Healing Relationship in Gestalt Therapy.* Highland, NY: Gestalt Journal Press.

Ingersoll, R.E. (2005) 'Gestalt therapy and spirituality', in A.L. Woldt and S.M. Toman (eds), *Gestalt Therapy, History, Theory and Practice.* Thousand Oaks, CA: Sage.

Jacobs, L. (1989) 'Dialogue in Gestalt theory and therapy', *Gestalt Journal*, 12 (1): 25–68.

Jacobs, L. (1996) 'Shame in the therapeutic dialogue', in R.G. Lee and G. Wheeler (eds), *The Voice of Shame.* San Francisco, CA: Jossey-Bass. pp. 297–315.

Jacobs, L. (2002) 'It's not easy to be a field theorist: commentary on "cartesian and post-cartesian trends in relational psychoanalysis"', *Gestalt!* 6 (2).

Jacobs, L. (2004) 'Ethics of context and field: the practices of care, inclusion and openness to dialogue', in R. Lee (ed.), *The Values of Connection.* Cambridge, MA: Gestalt Press.

Jacobs, L. (2006) 'That which enables – support as complex and contextually emergent', *British Gestalt Journal*, 15 (2): 10–19.

Kabat-Zinn, J. (2003) 'Mindfulness-based interventions: past, present and future', *Clinical Psychology: Science and Practice,* 10 (2): 144–56.

Kagan, N. (1980) 'Influencing human interaction – eighteen years with IPR', in A.K. Hess (ed.), *Psychotherapy Supervision: Theory, Research, and Practice.* New York: Wiley. pp. 262–83.

Kaufman, G. (1989) *The Psychology of Shame: Theory and Treatment of Shame.* New York: Springer Publishing.

Kelly, C. (1998) Body Process workshop Metanoia Institute, London.

Kennedy, D.J. (1994) 'Transcendence, truth and spirituality in the Gestalt way', *British Gestalt Journal,* 3 (1): 4–10.

Kepner, J. (1987) *Body Process: A Gestalt Approach to Working with the Body in Gestalt Therapy.* New York: Gardner.

Kepner, J. (1995) *Healing Tasks in Psychotherapy.* San Francisco, CA: Jossey-Bass, for the Gestalt Institute of Cleveland Publications.

Kepner, J. (2003) 'The embodied field', *British Gestalt Journal,* 12 (1): 6–14.

Kim, J. and Daniels, D. (2008) 'Experimental freedom', in P. Brownell (ed.), *Handbook for Theory, Research and Practice in Gestalt Therapy.* Newcastle: Cambridge Scholars Publishing.

Kohut, H. (1971) *The Analysis of the Self.* New York: International Universities Press.

Kohut, H. (1977) *The Restoration of the Self.* New York: International Universities Press.

Kopta, S.M., Howard, K.I., Lowry, J.L. and Beutler, L.E. (1994) 'Patterns of symptomatic recovery in psychotherapy', *Journal of Consulting and Clinical Psychology,* 62 (5): 1009–16.

Lambert, M. (2003) *Bergen & Garfield's Handbook of Psychotherapy and Behaviour Change,* 5th edn. New York: John Wiley.

Leader, D. (2008) *The New Black.* London: Penguin.

Lee, R.G. (ed.) (2004) *The Values of Connection – a Relational Approach to Ethics.* Cambridge, MA: Gestalt Press.

Lee, R.G. (2007) 'Shame and belonging in childhood: the interaction between relationship and neurobiological development in the early years of life', *British Gestalt Journal,* 16 (2): 57–83.

Lee, R.G. and Wheeler, G. (eds) (1996) *The Voice of Shame.* San Francisco, CA: Jossey-Bass, for the Gestalt Institute of Cleveland.

Levine, P. (1997) *Waking the Tiger. Healing Trauma.* Berkeley, CA: North Atlantic Books.

Lewin, K. (1951) *Field Theory in Social Science.* New York: Harper & Brothers.

Luborsky, L., Singer, B. and Luborsky, L. (1975) 'Comparative studies of psychotherapies: is it true that "everyone has won and all must have prizes"?', *Archives of General Psychiatry,* 32: 995–108.

Mackewn, J. (1997) *Developing Gestalt Counselling.* London: Sage.

Maurer, R. (2005) 'Gestalt approaches with organisations and large systems', in A.L. Woldt and S.M. Toman (eds), *Gestalt Therapy – History, Theory and Practice.* Thousand Oaks, CA: Sage.

Melnick, J. and Nevis, S. (1997) 'Gestalt diagnosis and DSM–IV', *British Gestalt Journal,* 6 (2): 97–106.

Melnick, J. and Nevis, S. (2005) 'The willing suspension of disbelief: optimism', *Gestalt Review,* 9 (1): 10–26.

Melnick, J. and Roos, S. (2007) 'The myth of closure', *Gestalt Review,* 11 (2): 90–107.

Menninger, K. (1958) *The Theory of Psychoanalytic Technique.* New York: Basic Books.

Micholt, N. (1992) 'Psychological distance and group interventions', *Transactional Analysis Journal,* 2 (3): 228–33.

Miller, S.D., Hubble, M. and Duncan, B. (2008) 'Supershrinks', *Therapy Today,* 19 (3): 4–9.

Mothersole, G. (2006) 'Contracts and harmful behaviour', in C. Sills (ed.), *Contracts in Counselling*. London: Sage. pp. 87–97.

Mullen, P. (1990) 'Gestalt therapy and constructive developmental psychology', *Gestalt Journal*, 13 (1): 69–90.

Muller, B. (1996) 'Isadore From's contribution', *Gestalt Journal*, 19 (1): 57–82.

Naranjo, C. (1981) 'Gestalt conference talk', *Gestalt Review*, 5 (1): 3–19.

Nevis, E. (2003) 'Blocks to creativity in organisations', in M. Spagnuolo Lobb and N. Amendt-Lyon (eds), *Creative Licence – the Art of Gestalt Therapy*. Vienna: Springer-Verlag.

Ogden, P., Minton, K. and Pain, C. (2006) *Trauma and the Body: A Sensorimotor Approach to Psychotherapy*. New York: Norton.

Ogden, T. (1982) *Projective Identification and Psychotherapeutic Technique*. New York: Jason Aronson.

Orlinsky, D.E., Grawe, K. and Parks, B.K. (1994) 'Process and outcome in psychotherapy', in A.E. Bergin and S.L. Garfield (eds), *Handbook of Psychotherapy and Behavior Change*, 4th edn. New York: Wiley.

Parlett, M. (1991) 'Reflections on field theory', *British Gestalt Journal*, 1 (2): 76.

Parlett, M. (1993) 'Towards a more Lewinian gestalt therapy', *British Gestalt Journal*, 2 (2):115–20.

Parlett, M. (2007) 'Introduction', in G. Wollants (ed.), *Gestalt Therapy: Therapy of the Situation*. Turnhout, Belgium: Faculteit boor Mens en Samenleveing.

Perls, F.S. (1947) *Ego, Hunger and Aggression*. New York: Vintage Books.

Perls, F.S. (1969) *Gestalt Therapy Verbatim*. Moab, UT: Real People Press.

Perls, F.S. (1970) 'Four lectures', in J. Fagan and I. Shepherd (eds), *Gestalt Therapy Now*. Palo Alto, CA: Science and Behavior. pp. 14–38.

Perls, F. (1979) 'Planned psychotherapy', *Gestalt Journal*, 2 (2): 5–23.

Perls, F., Hefferline, R. and Goodman, P. (1989 [1951]) *Gestalt Therapy: Excitement and Growth in the Human Personality*. London: Pelican Books.

Perls, L. (1970) 'One Gestalt therapist's approach', in J. Fagan and I. Shepherd (eds), *Gestalt Therapy Now*. Palo Alto, CA: Science and Behavior. pp. 125–9.

Perry, A. (2008) *Claustrophobia. Finding Your Way Out.* London: Worth Publishing.

Philippson, P. (2004) 'The experience of shame', *International Gestalt Journal*, 27 (2): 85–96.

Philippson, P. (2009) *The Emergent Self. An Existential-Gestalt Approach*. London: Karnac.

Polster, E. (1985) 'Imprisoned in the present', *Gestalt Journal*, 8 (1): 5–22.

Polster, E. (1991) 'Tight therapeutic sequences', *British Gestalt Journal*, 1 (2): 63–8.

Polster, E. (1995) *A Population of Selves*. San Francisco, CA: Jossey-Bass.

Polster, E. (1998) 'Martin Heidegger and Gestalt therapy', *Gestalt Review*, 2 (3): 253–68.

Polster, E. (1999) *From the Radical Centre*. Cambridge, MA: Gestalt Institute of Cleveland Press.

Polster, E. and Polster, M. (1973) *Gestalt Therapy Integrated*. New York: Vintage Books.

Proctor, B. (2007) *Group Supervision*. London: Sage.

Proctor, B. and Sills, C. (2005) 'Personal therapy for trainees – a three-cornered conundrum', *Counselling and Psychotherapy Journal*, 16 (5): 38–42.

Racker, H. (1982 [1968]) *Transference and Countertransference*. London: Karnac.

Reason, P. and Bradbury, H. (2001) 'Inquiry and participation in search of a world worthy of human aspiration', in P. Reason and H. Bradbury (eds), *Handbook of Action Research: Participative Inquiry and Practice*. London: Sage.

Resnick, R. (1990) 'Gestalt therapy with couples', *Workshop*. London: Metanoia Institute.

Rizzolatti, G., Fadiga, L., Gallese, V. and Fogassi, L. (1996) 'Premotor cortex and the recognition of motor actions', *Cognitive Brain Research*, 3: 131–41.

Robine, J-M. (ed.) (2001) *Contact and Relationship in a Field Perspective*. Bordeaux: L' Exprimerie.

Ronall, R. (2008) 'Intensive Gestalt workshops: experiences in community', *British Gestalt Journal*, 17 (2): 39–50.

Roubal, J. (2007) 'Depression – a Gestalt theoretical perspective', *British Gestalt Journal*, 16 (1): 35–43.

Scheinberg, S., Johannson, A., Stevens, C. and Conway-Hicks, S. (2008) 'Research communities in action: three examples', in P. Brownell (ed.), *Handbook for Theory, Research and Practice in Gestalt Therapy*. Newcastle: Cambridge Scholars Publishing.

Schore, A. (2000) 'Minds in the making', Seventh Annual John Bowlby Memorial Award Conference. London: Centre for Attachment-based Psychoanalytic Psychotherapy.

Schore, A. (2003) *Affect Regulation and the Repair of the Self*. NY: W.W. Norton & Co.

Seligman, M.E.P. (2002) *Authentic Happiness: Using the New Positive Psychology to Realize Your Potential for Lasting Fulfillment*. New York: Free Press/Simon & Schuster.

Shapiro, F. (2001) *Eye Movement Desensitising and Reprocessing*. New York: Guilford Press.

Shub, N. (1992) 'Gestalt therapy over time: integrating difficulty and diagnosis', in E.C. Nevis (ed.), *Gestalt Therapy*. New York: Gardner Press.

Sichera, A. (2003) 'Therapy as an aesthetic issue', in M. Spagnuolo Lobb and N. Amendt-Lyon (eds), *Creative Licence: the Art of Gestalt Therapy*. New York/Vienna: Springer. pp. 93–9.

Sills, C. (2006) 'Contracts and contract making', in C. Sills (ed.), *Contracts in Counselling*, 2nd edn. London: Sage. pp. 9–26.

Stacey, R. (2001) *Complex Responsive Processes in Organisations*. London: Routledge.

Stacey, R. (2005) *A Complexity Perspective on Researching Organisations: Taking Experience Seriously*. London: Routledge.

Staemmler, F.-M. (1993) 'Projective identification in Gestalt therapy with severely impaired clients', *British Gestalt Journal*, 2 (2): 104–10.

Staemmler, F.-M. (1997) 'Towards a theory of regressive process in Gestalt therapy', *Gestalt Journal*, 20 (1): 49–120.

Staemmler, F-M. (1997) 'Cultivating uncertainty: an attitude for Gestalt therapists', *British Gestalt Journal*, 6 (1): 40–8.

Staemmler, F.-M. (2007) 'On Macaque monkeys, players, and clairvoyants: some new ideas for a Gestalt therapeutic concept of empathy', *Studies in Gestalt Therapy – Dialogical Bridges*, 1 (2): 43–64.

Staemmler, F-M. (2009) *Aggression, Time, and Understanding*. New York: Routledge.

Stern, D.N. (1985) *The Interpersonal World of the Infant*. New York: Basic Books.

Storr, A. (1979) *The Art of Psychotherapy*. London: Heinemann.

Stratford, C.D. and Brallier, L.W. (1979) 'Gestalt therapy with profoundly disturbed persons', *Gestalt Journal*, 2 (1): 90–104.

Strumpfel, U. (2004) 'Research on Gestalt therapy', *International Gestalt Journal*, 12 (1): 9–54.

Swanson, J. (1988) 'Boundary processes and boundary states', *Gestalt Journal*, 11 (2): 5–24.

Tobin, S. (1982) 'Self-disorders, Gestalt therapy and self-psychology', *Gestalt Journal*, 5 (2): 3–44.

Tudor, K. (1997) 'A complexity of contracts', in C. Sills (ed.), *Contracts in Counselling*. London: Sage. pp. 157–72.

Tudor, K. (2006) 'Contracts, complexity and challenge', in C. Sills (ed.), *Contracts in Counselling and Psychotherapy*. London: Sage. pp. 128–30.

van Deurzen, E. (2005) 'Philosophical background', in E. Van Deurzen and C. Arnold-Baker (eds), *Existential Perspectives on Human Issues: A Handbook for Therapeutic Practice*. Basingstoke: Palgrave Macmillan.

van Rijn, B., Sills, C., Hunt, J., Shivanath, S., Gildebrand, K. and Fowlie, H. (2008) 'Developing clinical effectiveness in psychotherapy training: action research', *Counselling and Psychotherapy Research*, 8 (4): 261–8.

Verhaeghe, P. (2004) *On Being Normal and Other Disorders*. New York: Other Press.

Verhaeghe, P. (2007) 'Chronicle of a death foretold'. Keynote address at the Health4Life Conference, Dublin City University. http://www.dcu.ie/health4life/conferences/2007/.

Wampold, B.E. (2001) *The Great Psychotherapy Debate*. Mahwah, NJ: Lawrence Erlbaum Associates.

Watson, J.C., Gordon, L.B., Stermac, L., Kalogerakos, F. and Steckley, P. (2003) 'Comparing the effectiveness of process experiential with cognitive behavioural psychotherapy in the treatment of depression', *Journal of Consulting and Clinical Psychology*, 71: 773–81.

Wheeler, G. (1991) *Gestalt Reconsidered*. New York: Gardner Press.

Whines, J. (1999) 'The "symptom-figure"', *British Gestalt Journal*, 8 (1): 9–14.

Wilber, K. (2000) *Sex, Ecology, Spirituality*. Boston, MA: Shambhala Publications, Inc.

Williams, L. (2006) 'Spirituality and Gestalt: a Gestalt-transpersonal perspective', *Gestalt Review*, 10 (1): 6–21.

Williams, M., Teasdale, J., Segal, Z. and Kabat-Zinn, J. (2007) *The Mindful Way Through Depression*. New York: Guilford Press.

Woldt, A.L. and Toman, S.M. (eds) (2005) *Gestalt Therapy – History, Theory and Practice*. Thousand Oaks, CA: Sage.

Wollants, G. (2007a) 'Therapy of the situation', *British Gestalt Journal*, 14 (2): 91–102.

Wollants, G. (ed.) (2007b) *Gestalt Therapy: Therapy of the Situation*. Turnhout, Belgium: Faculteit boor Mens en Samenleveing.

Worden, W. (1991) *Grief Counselling and Grief Therapy: A Handbook for the Mental Health Practitioner*. London: Routledge.

Yontef, G. (1991) 'Recent trends in Gestalt therapy', *British Gestalt Journal*, 1 (1): 5–20.

Yontef, G. (1993) *Awareness, Dialogue and Process: Essays on Gestalt Therapy*. Highland, NY: Gestalt Journal Press.

Yontef, G. (2005) 'Gestalt therapy theory of change', in A.L. Woldt and S.M. Toman (eds), *Gestalt Therapy – History, Theory and Practice*. Thousand Oaks, CA: Sage.

Yontef, G. and Fuhr, R. (2005) 'Gestalt therapy theory of change', in A.L. Woldt and S.M. Toman (eds), *Gestalt Therapy – History, Theory and Practice*. Thousand Oaks, CA: Sage. pp. 81–100.

Yontef. G. and Jacobs, L. (2007) 'Introduction to Gestalt therapy', in R. Corsini and D. Wedding (eds), *Current Psychotherapies*. Belmont, CA: Brooks-Cole. (For free downloadable PDF of this chapter go to the PGI website: http://www.gestalttherapy.org/faculty-publications.asp)

Yontef, G. and Philippson, P. (2008) 'A unified practice', in P. Brownell (ed.), *Handbook for Theory, Research and Practice in Gestalt Therapy*. Newcastle: Cambridge Scholars Publishing.

Zinker, J. (1975) 'On loving encounters: a phenomenological view', in F. Stephenson (ed.), *Gestalt Therapy Primer*. Chicago, IL: Charles Thomas.

Zinker, J. (1977) *The Creative Process in Gestalt Therapy*. New York: Random House.

INDEX

active curiosity 23
anxiety 218
  avoidance 221
  body process 223
  cognitions 222
  existential issues 224
  managing symptoms 219
  mindfulness 220
anxiety and depression 212–14
assessment 53–67
  assessment sheet 65
  cultural factors 62
  of risk 201
  of suitability 57
awareness 31–42
  relational awareness 36
  zones of 34–6

beliefs 60, 222
body process 145–52
bracketing 18
brief therapy 229–37
  agency considerations 223
  in primary care 235

catharsis 148
client progress checklist 182
coaching 254–66
  breaches of contract 263
  contracting 257–64
  contracting matrix 262
  skills 256, 264, 265
co-creation 43, 86, 130
confirmation 46
confluence – differentiating 112
contact functions 59
contracts 10, 257
  administrative 10
  breaches of 263
  contracting matrix 262
  in coaching 257–64
core beliefs 217
countertransference 139
creative indifference 40
culture 62
curiosity 17, 18, 23, 33
cycle of experience 37

deflecting – accepting 109
depression 214
  body process and breathing 217
depression and anxiety 213–26
  hope 213
  labels 213
  secondary gain 214
description 21
desensitizing – oversensitizing 110
diagnosis 56, 58
dialogic relationship 45–52
diversity 237–41
dreamwork 154–9
DSM IV 56

eastern spirituality 247
egotism *see* self-monitoring
embodied process 59
empathy 47, 49, 152
empty chair 98
enactment 50, 94, 101, 139,
    176, 209, 264
endings 187–98
  patterns of 187
  tasks of 192
  unexpected 190
environmental support 74, 114, 188
equalization *see* horizontalism
erotic transference 141
ethical dilemmas 242–6
  polarities 243
  working through 245
existential dimensions 9, 18, 40,
    224, 248, 250
existential encounter 75
experimenting 94–104
  sequences of 94
  see also dreamwork
explaining gestalt counselling 8–9

fees 12
field conditions 62
field theory 27–9
figure and ground 26
first meetings 5
fixed gestalts 105
fragile self-process 51, 71, 73, 210

grading 96
grounding exercises 4, 148, 222, 251
groups 161, 254

holidays 82
horizontalism 22

inclusion 47–9
    communicating inclusion 48
    willingness for 49
identifying with your own experience 81
imagination 124
impasse 123
information sheet for clients 11
intake sheets 5–7
interruptions to contact 106
introjecting – rejecting 117
introjects 124
IPR 168
I–Thou, I–It attitude 50–2
I–Thou moment 51

language of self-responsibility 79

missed appointments 7, 15
modifications to contact 105–18
multi-cultural counselling 237–41
mystery 251

open communication 49

paradoxical theory of change 39
personal questions 50
personal style 168
phases of counselling and therapy 73–6
phenomenology 17–27
    clinical application 25
    phenomenological method 17–24
polarities 126
preparing for the session 4
presence 45
progress checklist 182
projecting – owning 115
projective identification 138
psychosis 13, 110, 201, 248
PTSD 119

racial identity 237
record keeping 14–15
refusing clients 13
regressive processes 201
relational gestalt 43
relational patterns 61
research 172–86
    action research 177
    effectiveness debate 173

research cont.
    evaluating research literature 184
    importance of 172
    methods 177
    personal reflective inquiry 178
    philosophy of 175
    reflexivity 180
    researching your own practice 180
retroflecting – impulsivity 108
reviews 71, 168
risk assessment and management 201–11
    rating the risk 204
    self care and support 209
risk history 204

safe emergency 95, 96, 123, 219
self-disclosure 50
self-monitoring – spontaneity 113
self-responsibility 79
self-supervision 166
sexuality 142
shame 86–93
    origins 87
    shame binds 87
    working with, 88–93
spirituality 247–53
    awareness 251
    inquiry 249
suicide risk 205
suitability 13
supervision 160–71
    choosing a supervisor 160
    making the most of 161
    self-supervision 166
    transcripts 164
support 78–85
    counsellor support 84
    evoked companion 82
    relational support 82–4
    self dialogue 81
    self process 79
support systems 59

therapeutic relationship 43–52
time limited counselling 229
top-dog/underdog 98
touch 150
transference 130–44
    enactments 139
    erotic 141
    introjective 137
    projective 134
    recognizing 133
    transformative 138
treatment considerations 68–77
    assessing suitability 57

treatment considerations *cont.*
   deciding priorities 72
   implications of diagnosis 69
   involving the client 70
   phases of treatment 73–6
   usefulness of concept 68
trial interventions 8

unfinished business 119–29, 216

working alliance 43, 56

Zen Buddhism 247
zones of awareness 34–6